Grenville C. Mackenzie

THE PURITAN

AS A

COLONIST AND REFORMER

BY

EZRA HOYT BYINGTON

AUTHOR OF "THE PURITAN IN ENGLAND AND NEW ENGLAND"
AND "THE CHRIST OF YESTERDAY, TO-DAY,
AND FOREVER"

BOSTON
LITTLE, BROWN, AND COMPANY
1899

𝔘𝔫𝔦𝔳𝔢𝔯𝔰𝔦𝔱𝔶 𝔓𝔯𝔢𝔰𝔰
JOHN WILSON AND SON, CAMBRIDGE, U.S.A.

TO MY SISTER

𝔈𝔩𝔩𝔢𝔫,

WHOSE THOUGHTFUL AND EARNEST LIFE
AS TEACHER, WIFE, AND MOTHER
ILLUSTRATES THE STRENGTH AND BEAUTY OF THE PURITAN
DISCIPLINE OF OUR EARLY HOME,

I DEDICATE THIS BOOK.

Preface

THIS book is a companion volume to "The Puritan in England and New England," which was published three years ago. The favorable reception of the earlier volume has encouraged the author to present a fuller and more connected account of the Pilgrims and Puritans as Colonists, and as Missionaries and Reformers in New England. The other book contains an account of the origin and growth of Puritanism in England, and of the religious opinions, the family and social life, and the personal traits of the Pilgrims and Puritans in this country. The two volumes are quite distinct, and yet each supplements the other.

We shall do well to observe the increasing interest in the Puritans in our time. This interest has been recently illustrated in the celebration of the three hundredth anniversary of the birth of Oliver Cromwell, who was in some respects the most notable representative of the Puritan party. It would not have been possible, a generation ago, to unite the English-speaking people of England and America and Australia in paying honor to his name, and to the principles which he defended. The number of Englishmen who have been remembered so long is very small. The fact is, there is a higher appreciation of the Puritan spirit, and of the results of Puritanism, than ever before. The political and social reforms which they secured are quite as noteworthy as the religious reforms. The world appreciates them now, because the spirit of this age is so free and progressive. We have been moving forward to the position which they occupied, and beyond it.

It is true, the Puritans were not in all respects consistent with their own principles. They were not as tolerant as they should have been. Yet they were the leaders, in the seventeenth century, in securing freedom for the people, in the Church and in the State. We owe much of the progressive spirit of our time to their foresight, and to their strenuous endeavors.

It is very doubtful whether the Puritans could have secured the triumph of their principles if they had not planted colonies on this side of the Atlantic. The conservative spirit in England was very strong in their time, as it was in France and Spain. Hampden, and Eliot, and Pym, and Coke, and the other champions of freedom against the arbitrary claims of the Stuarts, were not certain of final victory. The Restoration of Charles the Second came too soon, and it seemed to have blotted out from the English Constitution the new sections which had been written into it by Cromwell and the Long Parliament.   There was a time when the Church of England itself seemed to be going back from the principles of the Reformation.   Charles seems to have imagined that he could even extinguish the light that had been kindled in New England.   But the sea was too broad.   The new ideas of the right of the people to make their own laws, and to elect their own rulers, and to worship according to their own consciences, had a fair field in the New World.

The time came when the influence of America began to be felt in the Mother Country.   One reform bill has succeeded another in the English Parliament, until the people have gained the rights for which the Puritans struggled.   The Free Churches have been multiplied in the Home Land.   The Established Church has gained quite as much as the churches of the Dissenters.   So that it has come to pass that the Anglo-Saxon people in all parts of the world now stand for the principles of the Puritans.   It is no wonder that the political tracts of John Milton are appreciated as never before.   Shakespeare has a much higher place than he had before the Revolution of 1688, yet we miss in his dramas the democratic spirit which we find in Spenser and in Milton.   We are reading English literature in the new light that is shining all about us.

It is a good time to make a fresh study of the Puritans. We have still much to learn from them in respect to the social and political and religious questions of our time. In many ways we are following their example. The Constitution of the Republic is only a development of the teachings of Thomas Hooker in Connecticut. Our Home and Foreign missions are the expansion of the missions of Eliot and the Mayhews. Our schools and colleges for the people follow Puritan examples. Tennyson has told us that

> " thro' the ages one increasing purpose runs,
> And the thoughts of men are widen'd with the
> process of the suns."

Much of what has been the best in the nineteenth century has come from our New England ancestors, and the twentieth century is likely to follow the same line of development.

EZRA HOYT BYINGTON.

FRANKLIN STREET, NEWTON, MASS.
September 1, 1899.

Contents

I

THE PILGRIM AS A COLONIST.

II

THE PURITAN AS A COLONIST.

III

JOHN ELIOT, THE APOSTLE TO THE INDIANS.

IV

JONATHAN EDWARDS, AND THE GREAT AWAKENING

V

SHAKESPEARE AND THE PURITANS

List of Authorities Referred To

[See "The Puritan in England and New-England" xxv–xxix.]

Among My Books.   James Russell Lowell.

Bancroft's History of the United States, Centenary Edition.   6 vols.
Bibliotheca Sacra.   1855.   1897.
Bradford's (Governor) History of Plymouth Plantation.   Legislative Edition.
Brigham's Compact, with the Charter.
Bryce's American Commonwealths.
Burke's Works.   Vol. II.

Cambridge Platform of Church Discipline.
Campbell's Lives of the Chief Justices.
Campbell's Puritan in Holland, England, and America.   2 vols.
Centenary of American Methodism.   Stevens.
Chalmer's History of the Revolt of the American Colonies.
Christian History, Boston.
Clap's Memoirs.
Cockenöe.   Elliot's First Indian Teacher.   1896.   Harpers.
Colonial Records of Connecticut.
Colonial Records of Massachusetts.
Colonial Records of New Hampshire.
Colonial Records of New Haven.
Colonial Records of Rhode Island.
Congregational Quarterly.   Vol. I.–V.
Congregationalism as seen in its Literature.   Dr. Dexter.
Contemporary Review.   January, 1895.
Craik's English of Shakespeare.
Creeds and Platforms of Congregationalism.   Prof. Williston Walker.
Critical Study of Shakespeare.   George Brandes.   2 vols.

Davis History of Plymouth.
Dowden's Shakespeare, — His Mind and Art.

Early Constitutional History of Connecticut.   Dr. L. Bacon.
Election Sermons of Massachusetts.   1666–1714.
Eliot's Communion of Churches.
Eliot Genealogy.
Eliot's Indian Bible.
Eliot's Indian Grammar.
Eliot's Life, by Dr. Nehemiah Adams.
Eliot's Life by C. Francis.   Spark's American Biography.
Ellis' History of the First Church in Boston.
Elton's Life of Roger Williams.
Encyclopedia Britannica.   Art. Witchcraft.   Vol. XXIV.

Felt's Ecclesiastical History of New England.
Fiske's Beginnings of New England.

Goodwin's Pilgrim Republic.   1888.
Green's History of the English People : 4 volumes.
Green's Making of England.

Hazard's Papers.
Higginson's New England Plantation.
Historical Discourses.   Dr. Bacon.
History of Connecticut.   Alexander Johnson.
History of Congregationalism.   Professor Walker.
History of Doctrines.   Professor Fisher.
History of New England.   1630–1649.   John Winthrop.   Edition
    of 1858.
Hubbard's History.
Hume's History of England.
Hutchinson's Collections.

Johnson, Edward.   Wonder-Working Providence.
Journal of the Privy Council.

Keys of the Kingdom of Heaven.   John Cotton.

Life of Jonathan Edwards.   Prof. A. V. G. Allen.

Macaulay's History of England.

Ms. Journal of E. Parkman. Library American Antiquarian Society.

Massachusetts Historical Society's Collections. 1st, 3rd, and 4th Series.

Mather's Magnalia. 1702.

Memorials of the Pilgrim Fathers. W. Winters.

Milton's L'Allegro.

Morton's Memorial.

Mourt's Relation. Dr. Dexter's Edition. 1865.

Natick. Bigelow's History of.

Neal's History of the Puritans. 4 vols. 1732.

New England Historical and Genealogical Register. Vol. 14, Vol. 48, 1894.

New England Prospect. Wood.

Northend's The Bay Colony.

Palfrey's History of New England. 5 volumes.

Parliamentary History. Vol. I.

Prince's Annals of New England. 1736.

Protestant Missions. Dr. A. C. Thompson.

Puritan in England and New England.

Records Colony of Massachusetts Bay.

Rhode Island Historical Collections.

Schlegel's Dramatic Literature. Bohn's Edition.

Sewall's Diary. 1674-1729.

Shakespeare's Dramatic Works. White's Edition.

Shakespeare's Knowledge and Use of the Bible. Bishop Wordsworth.

Shakespeare's Life, Art, and Character. Hudson.

Shephard's Sincere Convert. 1648.

Some Aspects of the Religious Life in New England. Dr. George L. Walker.

The Great Awakening. Joseph Tracy.

The New World. December, 1896.

The Pilgrim Fathers. Rev. John Brown. 1895.

The Simple Cobbler of Agawam.   Nathaniel Ward.
Three Episodes of Massachusetts History. Charles Francis Adams.
Trumbull's History of Connecticut.

Vattel.   Law of Nations.

Way of the Churches Cleared.   John Cotton.
Willard's Body of Divinity.
Winslow's Brief Narration.
Works of Jonathan Edwards.   Worcester Edition.

Young's Chronicles of Massachusetts.
Young's Chronicles of the Pilgrim Fathers.

List of Illustrations

I

The Pilgrim as a Colonist

The Pilgrim as a Colonist

NORTH AMERICA had been known to Europeans more than a hundred years before the earliest permanent settlements were made in New England. The coasts and bays and harbors had been explored by enterprising navigators of various nations, and the narratives which they had published had awakened an interest in the country among many people. As early as 1575 from thirty to fifty English ships came every year to the Banks of Newfoundland to fish. Fifty years before the settlement of Plymouth, attempts more or less successful had been made to plant colonies within the present limits of the United States. The first permanent Colony in Virginia had been planted thirteen years earlier than the first Colony in New England. Every year the country was becoming better known. In 1607 a small Colony was planted within the present limits of Maine, but it was soon abandoned. Other attempts to establish settlements had been made, having for their leading purpose the prosecution of the cod fisheries, and the extension of the trade in furs with the Indians.

I

THE earliest permanent settlements in New England were made by the Pilgrims and the Puritans, who had been crowded out of England by religious persecution. These settlements were among the results of the Reformation in the sixteenth century.

Earliest Settlements in New England.

The Pilgrims had been driven from their native land in 1608, by the stress of persecution. They had found a hospitable refuge in Holland, where they dwelt in peace and security for twelve years. But they had learned that it was not possible for them to secure the results which they had most at heart so long as they dwelt in Holland. They could not be content with peace and security for themselves alone, because they believed they had an important mission to fulfil for the extension of the kingdom of God among their own countrymen. "A man must not respect only to live," they said, "and doe good to himselfe, but he should see where he can live to do most good to others." [1] In Holland they were likely to lose their own language, and their connection with the English people. They were not able to induce the Dutch people to keep the Sabbath according to their own convictions of duty. They could not give their

[1] Mourt's Relation, Dr. Dexter's edition, 146 R. C.

children such an education as they had received.[1]
If they should continue in Holland they would
be likely to lose their influence with the English
people, and to become incorporated with the
people of Holland. They had also, as Governor
Bradford tells us, a great hope of laying some
good foundation "for ye propagating and advancing ye gospel of ye kingdom of Christ in
those remote parts of the world." [2] "Seeing we
daily pray for the conversion of the heathens,
we must consider whether there be not some
ordinary means and course for us to take to
convert them, or whether praier for them be only
referred to God's extraordanaire work from
heaven. . . . To us they cannot come, for our
land is full; to them we may goe, their land is
emptie." [3]

The experiences of twelve years of "peace
and security" in Holland had taught these
stanch Englishmen of the Protestant faith that
the only way by which they could fulfil the
mission which God had given them was to
establish colonies in the new lands beyond the
sea. They could support themselves where they
were, but they could not transmit to other generations the liberty which they had gained.

[1] Young's Chronicles, Edward Winslow, 380.
[2] Bradford's History, 24 (edition of Mass. Historical Society).
[3] Robert Cushman in Mourt's Relation, 147, 148.

Therefore they determined to go, in spite of
their weakness and poverty. The congregation
at Leyden can hardly have numbered more than
two or three hundred.[1] Only the younger and
more vigorous members of the community could
go in the beginning. They were too poor to
provide a ship and the necessary supplies for a
colony. So they entered into an agreement
with a company of business men in London.
The company was to furnish the capital necessary to carry forward the enterprise. This was
purely a business arrangement, and the terms
were not very liberal. Those who were transported to the Colony and those who provided
the capital were to be in partnership for seven
years. The Colonists were to work for the Company, and they were to have " their meate, drink,
apparell, and all provisions out of the common
stock and goods of ye colonie." It was stipulated that they were not only to build houses,
and plant and cultivate the fields, but also to
engage in the fisheries, and that all the profits
obtained either by tilling the land, or by trading
with the Indians, or by the fisheries, should remain in the common stock until the seven years
had expired. At that time, " the houses, lands,
goods and chattels were to be divided among

[1] Young's Chronicles, chapter xxvi. pp. 455, 456. Winslow's
Brief Narration, 90. Bradford's History, 42.

those who had shares in the common stock, whether as capitalists or as colonists."[1]   It was expected that by the expiration of that period the profits of the trade with the Indians, and of the fisheries, and of agricultural industry, would have amounted to enough to repay the capital that had been invested, and to pay a profit to those who had shares in the Colony.

These terms were accepted by the Pilgrims because they were the best they could obtain, and because they were convinced that their success as a religious body depended entirely upon planting colonies in America. It was agreed that every one who joined the Colony should become a shareholder. Those who had any property put it into the common stock. Every person above sixteen years of age was considered as the owner of one share of stock, of the value of ten pounds.

The Colonists had asked the King for a definite promise that they should enjoy religious liberty in their new homes, but he had refused to make such a promise. They had attempted to secure from the Virginia Company a patent with a grant of land for their settlement. But at the time of their departure no patent had been secured. A number of persons from London and other places in England joined the Colony, and after many delays they sailed from Plymouth

[1] Bradford's History, 45, 46.

in the Mayflower, a ship of a hundred and eighty tons, September 6th, 1620, with one hundred and two persons on board.

What prospect was there that this small colony would succeed, where so many earlier colonies had failed? Their pastor, John Robinson, had set forth the reasons in a letter to Sir Edwin Sandys, three years before. He said: —

" 1st. We verily believe and trust yᵉ Lord is with us, unto whom and whose service we have given ourselves in many trialls.

" 2ly. We are well weaned from yᵉ delicate milke of our Mother countrie, and enured to yᵉ difficulties of a strange and hard land.

" 3ly. The people are, for the body of them, industrious, & frugall, as any company of people in the world.

" 4ly. We are knite together as a body in a most stricte & sacred bond and covenante of the Lord, of the violation whereof we make great conscience, and by vertue whereof we doe hould our selves straitly tied to all care of each others good, and of ye whole by each one and so mutually.

" 5. Lastly, it is not with us as with other men whom small things can discourage, or small discontentments cause to wish themselves home againe." [1]

Mr. Robinson knew his people well when he wrote these remarkable words. And the people showed, in the experiences of the next twenty years, that he had not overrated the faith, and

[1] Bradford's History, 32, 33.

patience, and energy of these Anglo-Saxon Christians.

The Mayflower had a stormy passage across the Atlantic. On the 9th of November, more than nine weeks after they had left England, they came in sight of land, which proved to be Cape Cod, "at which they were not a little joyfull." They made some efforts to sail to the south until they should reach the mouth of the Hudson River, but they were turned back by the dangers of the passage, and the " next day they gott into yᵉ Cape-harbor where they ride in saftie. . . . Being thus arrived in a good harbor and brought safe to land, they fell upon their knees & blessed yᵉ God of heaven, who had brought them over yᵉ vast & furious Ocean, and delivered them from all ye perils & miseries thereof, againe to set their feete on yᵉ firme and stable earth, their proper elemente." [1]

Before they landed they made preparations for the beginning of a settled government. We learn from a letter of Mr. Robinson, that they had determined before they set out from Leyden " to become a body politike using civil governmente amongst themselves." [2] They had also discovered during the long voyage across the sea that they had some disorderly persons in their company, who would need to be restrained by the authority

[1] Bradford, 77, 78.   [2] Bradford, 66.

of a settled government. Governor Bradford tells us that the strangers amongst them had been saying that "as soon as they should come on shore they should do as they pleased, for no one had power to command them."[1] So they entered into a mutual compact, which was the foundation of their government for many years. In this compact they say: —

"We whose names are underwritten, the loyall subjects of our dread soveraigne Lord, King James, by the grace of God, of Great Britaine, France, & Ireland King, defender of ye faith, &c., haveing undertaken, for ye glorie of God, and advancemente of ye Christian faith, and honor of our King & Countrie, a voyage to plant ye first Colonie in ye Northerne parts of Virginia; doe by these presents, solemnly & mutually in ye presence of God, and one of another, covenant and combine ourselves together into a civill body politicke, for our better ordering & preservation & furtherance of ye ends aforesaid; and by virtue hearof to enacte, constitute, and frame such just & equall lawes, ordinances, acts, constitutions, & offices, from time to time, as shall be thought most meete & convenient for ye general good of ye Colonie, unto which we promise all due submission and obedience. In witness whereof we have hereunder subscribed our names at Cape

[1] Bradford, 89.

Codd, ye 11 of November, in ye year of ye raigne of our soveraigne lord, King James, of England, France, & Ireland ye eighteenth, and of Scotland ye Fiftie fourth. Ano – Dom. 1620."[1]

To this solemn compact were appended the signatures of the adult males of the Company,[2] as representing not only themselves but the members of their families. The other English Colonies had suffered from the lack of regular authority. The idle and the dissipated had weakened the sober and industrious Colonists, and in a number of instances had ruined the Colony. Such authority as existed in those Colonies had been derived from England, either by the appointment of the Company on whose lands the settlement had been made, or by that of the King. Here, for the first time, was a provision for self-government, under the sovereignty of the King of England. At this initial point in the history of the Colony, the Pilgrims showed their skill and wisdom as Colonists. They knew how to plant a settlement for freemen. In this compact it is taken for granted that " rulers derive their just powers from the consent of the governed." The signers of this compact, and such others as they should select, were to have a voice in the election of officers, and in the enactment

[1] Bradford, 89, 90.
[2] See Morton's Memorial, 26.   Prince's Annals, 172.

and execution of laws.   " Here," said John Quincy
Adams, "was a unanimous and personal assent,
by all the individuals of the community, to the
association, by which they become a nation."
To the same effect, Mr. Bancroft said, "Here
was the birth of popular constitutional liberty.
In the cabin of the Mayflower, humanity recovered its rights, and instituted government on the
basis of equal laws enacted by the people for the
general good." [1]

After this excellent beginning, these practical
social philosophers proceeded to organize the
Colony according to this compact, as loyal subjects of the King of England.   In the first place,
they elected Mr. John Carver (a man, as they
said, "godly and well approved amongst them")
their Governor for the remainder of that year.
The same day they sent out the first party to
explore the country, and find a place for a settlement.   Fifteen or sixteen men, well armed, were
sent ashore at what is now Provincetown, to see
what the land was and what inhabitants they
could meet with.   The next month was devoted
to these explorations.   They went sometimes in
boats, and sometimes on foot.   The weather was
cold, and the severe storms of the late autumn
and of the early winter were upon them.   The

[1] Bancroft's History of the United States, Centenary Edition,
i. 244.

party went armed, so as to defend themselves
against attacks of the Indians, who were sometimes friendly and sometimes hostile. At length,
on Saturday, the 9th of December (O. S.), Captain Myles Standish and his party landed on
Clark's Island, at the entrance to the harbor
of Plymouth. Here they rested on the Sabbath
day, according to the commandment. On Mon-
day, the 11th of December (O. S.), they landed
on Plymouth rock, not "on a stern and rock-
bound coast," as Mrs. Hemans says, but "in a
goodly land with a very good harbor for their
ship," a place "very good for situation, . . . with
divers corn fields, and little running brooks, of
very sweet fresh water, . . . the best water that
ever we drunke." The brooks were full of fish.
There was an abundance of wild fowl. There
was a great variety of timber growing. "So,"
they tell us, "we returned to our Ship againe
with good newes to the rest of our people, which
did much comfort their hearts."[1]

On the 15th of December (O. S.) the Mayflower was turned toward the newly found harbor, and the next day she was anchored at the
entrance to the bay, whose shores were said to
be "like a Cycle, or Fish Hooke." On the 18th
and 19th, they were making careful examination of the various favorable points about the

[1] Mourt's Relation, 57–61.

bay. On Wednesday, the 20th (O. S.), after they had called upon the Lord to direct them, they decided upon the place for their first settlement. They were prevented from landing the two days following by a severe storm, but on Saturday, December 23 (O. S.), which was January 2 (N. S.), they made their final landing.

It was now almost midwinter. But they began at once cutting and carrying timber, for building their houses. They rested on the 24th, which was the Sabbath; but no man rested, we are told, on the 25th, which was Christmas. All who were able to work went on shore. Some were cutting timber, some were carrying logs to the place selected for building, some were sawing, and some were splitting. On Thursday they measured the ground for the house lots of the nineteen families into which they had divided their company. They were to have two rows of houses for the sake of compactness, and greater safety against the attacks of Indians. It was agreed that every man should build his own house, thinking "men would make more hast than working in common." The common house, which was designed as the place for storing the goods of the whole Colony, was the first to be completed. It was a building twenty feet square. They gathered grass from the open fields to thatch the roof. It took them about three weeks to complete it. From that time until the other houses were ready for use, those of the Colony who were on shore used the common house as a lodging place; for when the thatched roof took fire, a few days later, there were two men who were sick in bed in this house, and "the house was as full of beds as they could lie one by another." Before the end of January, they completed another building for storing their common provisions. By the 20th of February they had completed a house for their sick people, for the unusual experiences and fatigues to which these people, so recently from the city of Leyden, were entirely unaccustomed had caused a general sickness, so that at the time of greatest distress there were but six or seven well persons to care for the sick, and to bury the dead. But the true spirit of the Pilgrims was manifested in a wonderful manner during this time of general distress. Those who were well, we are told, "spared no pains, night nor day, but with abundance of toyle and hazard of their own health, fetched them wood from a distance, made their fires, and nursed them as tenderly as if they had been of their own families."[1] But the mortality was very great. Six of the small company died in December, eight in January, seventeen in February, and thirteen in March. Before the

[1] Bradford's History, 91, also foot note.

year was over, one half the whole number had died.

The work of building houses was going on through the winter. The timber was brought from the forest by the men of the Colony, for they had neither horses nor cattle, neither cows nor milk. It is not certain how many houses were completed the first winter. Until the 5th of April, when the Mayflower sailed for England, some of them were permitted to find a refuge, such as it was, on the ship.

The Indians were never far away. Now and then they showed themselves to the Colonists, but they were treated with so much kindness, and with so much fearlessness, that there was, for the most part, peace between the English and the savages. It was some months before they were able to have any communication with them. About the 26th of March, of the first winter, Samoset, an Indian who had learned a little English, came alone into the village, and bade them welcome. He told them of the various tribes of Indians, of their chiefs, and the number of their warriors. They gave him presents, and sent him away in peace. A little later he came back with five other Indians, who were also treated in a kind and friendly manner. The 1st of April Samoset returned with an Indian who was able to speak a little English, whose

name was Tisquantum. These two friendly
Indians were of very great advantage to the
settlers. They brought Massasoit, the chief of
the Wampanoags to Plymouth, and prepared
the way for a treaty of peace. The Governor
kissed the hand of the chief, and the chief kissed
the Governor. They drank strong water together, and, by the help of the interpreters, they
entered into an alliance of peace and friendship,
which was never broken so long as the chief
lived.

The extreme severity of the winter had gone
by in the latter part of January, when they had
a few " very faire Sunshinie days." On Sunday,
January 31st, they had their first service of
worship in the common house on shore. The
next day they carried their barrels of meal to
the storehouse. The latter part of March they
appointed Captain Myles Standish the com-
mander of their little army. Their cannon were
landed on the 3d of March, and were drawn up
the hill and mounted in a position to sweep
the approaches to the village in case of hostile
attack. It was on the 13th of March when
they heard " the birds singing in the woods
most pleasantly," and the same day they had
their first thunderstorm. On the 29th of March
they prepared the ground and sowed their garden seeds. About the same time the men of

2

the Colony held a public meeting, and adopted
the first laws.   The 1st of April was another
warm day, and they held another public meeting
to adopt regulations for the Colony.

The year began the last of March, according
to the old style, and on the last day of the old
year they elected the excellent Governor Carver
their Governor for another year.   About this
time they learned, from one of the friendly
Indians, that four years before the Colony was
planted, there had been a plague in those parts,
of which nearly all the inhabitants had died, so
that "there was neither man, woman, nor childe
remaining, to hinder our possession, or to lay
claim unto it."[1]   This was regarded by the Pilgrims as very remarkable, for it left the way
open for them to make a peaceable settlement.
It was also one of the indications that the
Indians of those parts were a decaying race.   It
is probable that they were becoming fewer before the settlements of Europeans were begun.
At the same time it is certainly true that the
Pilgrims treated the aborigines with great kindness, and that they never, in any instance, resorted to hostile measures, excepting when there
was decisive evidence that the Indians were preparing for hostilities.

[1] Mourt's Relation, 85.

II

GOVERNOR BRADFORD in his History begins the year 1621 the latter part of March, according to the reckoning of that time. It was the spring-time, and the affairs of the Colony were begin-ning to wear a more cheerful aspect. Several of the houses had been so far completed that the families could occupy them with a The First Spring degree of comfort. The severe sick- at Plymouth. ness was abating, and those of the Colonists who had survived the winter were regaining strength and courage. About the middle of April (N. S.), the Mayflower, which had been retained through the winter on account of the distress of the Colony, sailed for England. But no one of the Pilgrims went back in the vessel.

The people now began to plant their corn, under the instruction of Tisquantum, the friendly Indian. They had no means of ploughing the fields, so that they were obliged to prepare the ground with hoes, in the manner of the Indians. They used for seed some corn which they had found stored in the ground, where the Indians had placed it for safety. This corn they afterwards paid for at its full value. Tisquan-tum taught them how to enrich the ground which they had planted by burying in the soil the large fish which were abundant on that shore. He told them that the crop would come to nothing unless they put in an abundance of these alewives. They also sowed some wheat and pease which they had brought from England. All the work, except that in the small gardens which belonged with the houses, was done in common. This method was not adopted by the Pilgrims from choice, but because it was required by the agreement into which they had entered with those who had provided the capital for the Colony. There were only twenty-one men and six boys left to do the work. But this small company planted and cultivated twenty acres of Indian corn, and six acres of wheat and pease, or barley, besides carrying forward their building operations. A little later we find that they had eleven buildings, seven of which were dwellings, and the others houses for the general use of the plantation.

While they were busy with their planting, Governor Carver died, after an illness of a very few days. He was greatly lamented, and was buried with military honors. A few days later William Bradford was chosen Governor by the suffrages of the men of the Colony, and Isaac Allerton was chosen his Assistant.

On the 27th of May the first marriage in the Colony took place. Edward Winslow, whose wife had died during the terrible winter,

married Mrs. Susanna White, the mother of
Peregrine, the first child born after their arrival.
Her husband also had died during the winter.
There was no minister amongst them, and the
ceremony was performed by a magistrate, and
probably by Governor Bradford.

As the urgent business of the springtime was
finished, the enterprising Colony determined to
send an expedition into the wilderness to explore
the country, and to cultivate peaceful relations with
their new friend Massasoit. Edward Winslow and
Stephen Hopkins were sent by the Governor, on
the 12th of July, with their friend Tisquantum,
who was both interpreter and guide. They took
with them presents, with a message of peace, and
also an invitation to the chief to open a trade
with them in furs, which the Indians desired to
sell, as much as the English desired to buy.
They were instructed to offer to pay the full
value for the corn which they had dug out from
the Indian place of storage on their first landing.
The business was all skilfully and successfully
done. They were two days on the journey out,
and had abundant opportunities to study the
people and the country, and to make friends
among them. Massasoit was not at home when
they arrived, but he came at the call of their
messenger. They discharged their guns, and
saluted him. They then delivered their messages,

and their presents to the chief. He made them a great speech, after the Indian manner, renewed his assurances of peace and friendship, and invited them to smoke the pipe of peace. On Friday morning they set out for home, and arrived safely before the Sabbath. The result of this friendly visit was to strengthen the ties of friendship, and to prepare the way for a profitable trade with the Indians.

On the 14th of August Captain Standish was sent with his small army of fourteen well armed men into the Indian country, to rescue one of the friendly Indians, who was supposed to be detained by an unfriendly chief. This expedition pushing boldly into the wilderness impressed the Indians with the courage and strength of the Colonists. They brought back the friendly Indian in safety, and increased the influence of the English. A little later they received peaceful messages from a number of chieftains, and they had a number of opportunities to trade with the natives.

Late in September another expedition was sent to explore the country north of the settlement, to make treaties with the Indians, and to open trade with them. The party went in the shallop as far as what is now Boston harbor, some forty-four miles. There were ten men, with Tisquantum as an interpreter, and two other Indians. They made the acquaintance of the Massachusetts tribe of Indians. They were received in a friendly way, and had opportunities to extend the sphere of influence of the Colony, and to learn many things in regard to the habits of the natives. They won their confidence by their "gentle carriage towards them," and found them eager to trade their furs for such goods as the English had to sell. Some of them even sold the fur robes from their backs, and tied branches of trees about themselves, after the manner of the dwellers in Eden. The shallop was anchored in Boston Bay. The party went fearlessly into the country, and were so much pleased with what they saw that they wished they had settled there instead of at Plymouth. They came home in safety, and brought a quantity of beaver skins. They had a fair wind on the return voyage, which began at evening and ended before noon of the next day.[1]

One cannot but admire the energy and enterprise of this little Colony during this first year, which had brought them so many bereavements. There were no losses from dissipation or from idleness. They were an industrious and thrifty community. They made their own laws, and executed them. They had their military organization for defence against all enemies.

The harvest which they gathered in October

[1] Mourt's Relation, 124–130.

was abundant. "We had a good increase of Indian-Corne," they said, "and our barley indifferent good, but our pease not worth the gathering. . . . We are so farre from want, that we often wish you were partakers of our plentie." "I never in my life remember a more seasonable year," said Mr. Winslow, "than we have here *Results of the* enjoyed, and if we have once but *First Harvest.* Kine, Horses, and Sheepe, I make no question but men might live as contented here as in any part of the world."[1]   The grain was all stored in the common house, and there was found to be enough to provide a peck of meal a week for each person.   Game was abundant at that season.   Wild turkeys were numerous, and water fowl of various kinds.   They had a good supply of fish, and of lobsters, and they obtained oysters from the Indians.   They also found excellent fruits growing in the open spaces, such as grapes, and plums, and various sorts of berries.   So that Governor Bradford says: "All yᵉ somer there was no wante."[2]   Their relations with the Indians had become so friendly that Winslow tells us they went about in the woods as safely "as in the hieways in England."

So they appointed their first Thanksgiving. The Governor sent four men to shoot such game as the woods afforded, and these in one day se-

---

[1] Mourt's Relation, 133–135.   [2] History, 105.

cured "as much fowl as, with a little help beside, served the Company almost a week." They had games, and military exercises, and feasts. The Indians came in to enjoy the festival with them. This Thanksgiving lasted a number of days, and was probably accompanied by religious services, though these are not mentioned in the earlier records.[1]

The Colony consisted at this time of about fifty persons. So far as we know, there were seven dwellings. An equal division of the people would give about seven persons to a dwelling. These were built of squared timbers. The spaces between the timbers were filled in with clay, which was sometimes destroyed by the wind and rain. The roofs were thatched. The fireplaces were probably of stones, laid in clay. The chimneys, standing outside the walls, were of wood, plastered inside with clay.[2] They had oiled paper, instead of glass, for their windows.[3]

On the 21st of November, they discovered a ship making for their harbor. It proved to be the Fortune, of fifty-five tons, Arrival of the sent out by their friends in England Fortune. with a reinforcement for the Colony. There were thirty-five in this party, most of them young

---

[1] Mourt's Relation, 133.
[2] Goodwin's Pilgrim Republic 582, 583.
[3] Mourt's Relation, 142.

men. Among them were John Winslow, a
brother of Edward, and Jonathan Brewster, eldest son of Elder Brewster; Thomas Cushman,
son of Robert Cushman, afterwards Elder of the
Church in Plymouth; Thomas Prence, who married a daughter of Elder Brewster; and others
from Leyden, who became valuable citizens.
Bradford says that many of those who came were
wild young men, who little considered whither
they went. "The plantation," he says, "was glad
of this addition to its strength, but could have
wished that many of them had been of better
condition, and all of them better furnished with
provisions, but y^t could not be helpt." These
new comers were without provisions when they
landed, and were scantily furnished with cloth-
ing. The ship brought a Charter, granted by
the President and Council of New England to
John Pierce and his associates, for the benefit of
the Colony. This is now preserved at Plymouth, and is said to be the oldest document
in Massachusetts connected with her history.

The Fortune sailed for England at the end
of fourteen days, taking back the first cargo from
the Colony, which was valued at about £500.
It consisted of beaver skins and lumber, with
some sassafras. Unfortunately this precious
cargo never reached the Company in England,
for the ship was captured by a French armed

vessel, and taken to a French port. After a few days the master and his company were permitted to return to England with the ship, but the cargo was confiscated.

III.

AFTER the sailing of the Fortune the officers of the Colony began to make preparations for the winter. The number to be fed and sheltered was now increased to eighty-six. The new comers were disposed among the several families, increasing the average number to ten or twelve persons. An exact account was taken of the provisions in store, and it was found that, in consequence of the increase in their numbers, it was necessary to put them all upon a half allowance of food. "So they were presently put on half allowance, one as well as another, which begane to be hard, but they bore it patiently under hope of supply." The dwellings were made as comfortable as possible, and the scanty supplies of food were supplemented by hunting and fishing.

The Second Winter.

Soon after the Fortune had sailed, the chief sachem of the Narragansett tribe of Indians, which then possessed nearly all the territory now included in the State of Rhode Island, sent a messenger to Governor Bradford with a bundle of arrows wrapped in the skin of a rattlesnake.

This was interpreted by the friendly Indians as a hostile challenge. The Governor, with the advice of Captain Standish, stuffed the rattle-snake skin with powder and shot, and sent it back to the chief with a message that, if " they had rather have warre than peace, they might begin when they would : they had done them no wrong, neither did y^{ey} fear them, or should they find them unprepared." This bold defiance of a chieftain, who is said to have been able to lead into the field some thousands of savage warriors, seems to have prevented a hostile attack. The snake skin was sent from one chief to another, and, when no one would receive it, was re-turned to Plymouth. The Colonists, however, lost no time in enclosing their village with a strong line of palisades, extending half a mile. This task was accomplished in five weeks. In the line of palisades were bastions, from which the whole outside could be raked with musketry. Captain Standish divided his small army into four squadrons, and gave the men frequent opportunities for military discipline, and yet the Pilgrims were never attacked. The wall, which was guarded at night by vigilant sentries, sufficed to prevent the hostilities which it was built to resist.

The regular work of the Colony went on dur-ing the winter. One incident has been preserved.

On Christmas day the Governor called the men as usual to work. But some of the new comers excused themselves, and said it was against their consciences to work on that day. So the Governor told them that, if they made it a matter of conscience, he would excuse them till they were better informed. So he led away the rest and left them. But when they returned from their work at noon, he found them playing games in the street. He told them that it was against his conscience that they should play and others work. So he took away their implements, and said that, if they made the keeping of Christmas a matter of devotion, they should keep their houses, but there should be no gambling or revelling in the streets.

IV

THE foundations of the Pilgrim Republic were laid during those earliest months of its history. The people showed the same heroic spirit, with the same fortitude and patience, as the Colony grew older. Governor Bradford was re-elected in 1622, and from year to year as long as he lived, except that in 1633 he got off " by importunity," and on four or five other occasions he secured a respite for a year. The community was well regulated and orderly, mak-

The Pilgrim Republic.

ing its own laws, in subordination to the laws
of England, electing its own officers, and adapt-
ing its habits to the conditions of a new country.
The first of the laws entered in the record book of
the Colony provided for trial by a jury of twelve
honest men, to be impanelled by authority, upon
their oath. This was enacted December 27, 1623.

The Indian policy of the Colony was from the
beginning one of kindness and good faith blended

The Indian Policy. with firmness. When the Pilgrims
heard that the Indians in Virginia
had massacred some hundreds of the English settlers, they redoubled their vigilance, and
kept themselves well informed of what was going
on among their dusky neighbors. When there
seemed to be occasion for a more elaborate forti-
fication, they built their fort on the hill, and
mounted their six cannon, and kept sentinels on
duty day and night to guard against a surprise.
Yet they continued to go without fear among
those bands of Indians on whose fidelity they
had learned to rely. In the spring of 1623 they
were told that their friend Massasoit was very
sick, and likely to die. The Governor immediately sent Mr. Winslow and Mr. Hampden, with

Visit to Massasoit. an interpreter and a message of sympathy, and with some simple medi-
cines. It was more than a day's journey through
the wilderness. They found the chief at the

point of death, but succeeded in checking his
disease, and restoring him to health. Massasoit
revealed to Mr. Winslow a plot, which some of
the more distant Indians had formed, to massacre
the entire Colony, together with another English
Colony that had been planted in the vicinity.[1]
On their way homeward one of the chiefs inquired of Mr. Winslow how he dared come so
far into the Indian country. He replied that,
when there was true love, there was no fear, and
that his heart was so upright towards them that
he was fearless to come amongst them. The
Indians observed that they craved a blessing
before their meals, and returned thanks afterwards, and they inquired the meaning of this
custom. This gave Mr. Winslow an opportunity to talk with them about God's providence,
and His commandments, and the ways in which
they could secure His good will. This is a
specimen of the ways in which the Pilgrims
taught the principles of the Christian religion
to the natives.[2]

On reaching Plymouth Mr. Winslow made
known the warning he had received from Massasoit that the hostile bands of Indians were preparing to attack the Colony. The Indians had
become incensed against Mr. Weston's English

[1] Young's Chronicles, 315, 325.
[2] Young's Chronicles, 243, 257, 271.

Colony at Weymouth, because they had at various times treated them with injustice and cruelty, and they had combined to destroy not only that Colony, but the Colony at Plymouth also. Massasoit himself had been urged to join the conspiracy, but had refused.

This matter was laid before the people of the Colony at their Annual Court, April 2d, 1623, and it was voted to leave it in the hands of the Governor, his Assistant, and Captain Standish. They acted with promptness and energy, though it grieved them to shed the blood of those whose good they had been seeking. Captain Standish took eight men, with the shallop to Weymouth, where he found out who were the hostile chiefs, and what their plans were. A severe conflict followed, in which seven of the Indian leaders were slain. This broke up the conspiracy, and Captain Standish returned in a few days to Plymouth with all his party. Their pastor, John Robinson, who was still in Leyden, blamed them for shedding the blood of the savages, saying, " O how happy a thing had it been if you had converted some, before you had killed any!" But the Pilgrims had ample proof of the plot to massacre themselves, their wives and their children, as well as the people of the other Colony. They believed it was right for them to make the conflict short, sharp, and decisive. It is pleasant to know that this was the only serious trouble they ever had with the Indians of their vicinity, during the entire history of the Colony. They always treated them justly and kindly, purchasing the land they occupied at a price that was satisfactory to those who had a claim upon it.[1] So unjust is the witticism, which is sometimes repeated even now, which asserts that our forefathers, when they landed on these shores,

> " First fell on their knees,
> Then on the Aborigines."

V

IN respect to the growth of the Colony, there was a slow but real improvement from year to year. In 1622 we are told that by the end of May their scanty store of provisions was exhausted. They secured a small supply from the fishing vessels on the coast of Maine, which enabled them to give a quarter of a pound of bread a day to each person. They lived through the summer for the most part on shellfish, which they could take with the hand. The bay was full of fish, but they had no fish-hooks or seines. It was not the season for game. In May of that year they sent the shallop with ten men on a second trading voyage to Bos-

Famine in 1622.

---

[1] Young's Chronicles, 259; Congregational Quarterly, i. 129–135.

ton Bay, which secured for them a good supply of beaver skins in exchange for articles which the Indians wanted.

They planted their fields as they had done the year before, but their agricultural labor was interrupted by the necessity of building the fort on the hill, and of keeping guard against an attack by the Indians. Some of the growing corn was stolen by people who sought a refuge in their harbor while on their way to Weymouth. The harvest, when it was gathered, proved quite insufficient for their wants. Early in September, however, the ship Discovery came into the harbor, and sold them a quantity of knives and beads, such as they needed in their trade with the Indians. They also supplied themselves at that time with fishing tackle. As the fall came on, they were able to increase their stores of food by game and fish. They also bought a quantity of corn and beans from the Indians who lived about the Cape. So that they were able to live through the second winter with comfort.

As the spring of 1623 came on, it was decided to abandon, so far as practicable, the communistic methods which they had followed since the beginning of the settlement. A portion of land was assigned to each family, to cultivate for a year on its own account. This gave a new spirit to the Colony. The incentives to industry were increased, so that, we are told, much more corn was planted than in the earlier years, and even the women went into the fields to plant corn, taking their little ones with them. Still they were required to set apart a regular portion of their gains to meet the general obligations of the Colony, and to support the government. A severe drought followed in the early summer, and there was danger that they would fail to reap a harvest. A day of special prayer for rain was appointed. In the morning of the day, when they came together, "the heavens were as clear, and the drought as like to continue as ever it was," yet, "(our exercise continuing some eight or nine hours), before our departure The Great the weather was overcast, the clouds Drought. gathered together on all sides, and on the next morning distilled such soft, sweet, and moderate showers of rain, continuing some fourteen days, and mixed with such seasonable weather, as it was hard to say whether our withered corn or our drooping affections were most quickened." [1] The pagan Indians, we are told, took notice of these wonderful answers to their prayers, and were impressed with the goodness of the God of the English. The Pilgrims soon kept a day of public thanksgiving on account of the abundant rain.

Until the time of harvest there was great

[1] Young's Chronicles, 349–351.

scarcity of food. The people lived on ground
nuts, clams, and fish. There was neither bread
nor corn for months together. Sometimes at
night they did not know where to have a bit in
the morning. Yet the people were orderly and
hopeful, and continued their regular work. Six
or seven fishing companies were formed, and as
they had but a single boat, the companies took
turns in going out for fish. No sooner had one
company returned than the next went out in
the boat. Neither did they return till they had
caught something, though it was five or six days,
for there was nothing at home, and "to goe
home emptie would be a great discouragement
to y⁰ reste."[1]

In August they were encouraged by the arrival
of two ships from England, the Anne, and the
Little James, bringing ninety-six passengers for
the Colony. Many of these were from the old
Church in Leyden, and several were wives, children, and kindred of the early settlers. There
were many pleasant reunions. Yet the new
comers were disappointed at what they found in
the Colony. Their friends were greatly changed
by the hardships of two years. The best dish
they could present their friends was a lobster, or
a piece of fish, without bread, or any thing else
but a cup of spring water. Some of them were

[1] Bradford, 137.

ragged, and they had lost the freshness of their complexion.

The ninety-six passengers who came in these ships, together with thirty-five in the Fortune, and a hundred and two in the Mayflower, — two hundred and thirty-three in all, — make up the number of those who are known as the Pilgrims, or the First Comers, or the Forefathers. The passengers who came this year were all in good health excepting one, and they found that those who came in the Mayflower had enjoyed good health since the time of the great mortality of the first winter.

The new comers had brought a supply of provisions sufficient to last them until they could raise a crop the next summer, and it was agreed that the growing crops should belong to those who had planted them, while those just arrived should depend upon their own provisions. But when the time of harvest came, all such matters were forgotten. In place of famine there was an abundance of food for all, and under the new arrangement of personal property in crops the face of things was soon entirely changed. All had enough, and some of the more industrious had to spare, so that from that time there was no season of famine or of want.

The village had grown by the addition of a number of dwellings. The lower story of the fort had been finished, so that it was used for religious services on the Lord's day, as well as for general meetings of the Colony. It was a great gratification to the people that they were able to load with furs and with lumber the ship Anne, which sailed for England late in September, and thus to make a good beginning in paying the debt which the Colony owed to those who had furnished their supplies. In November, however, there was a serious fire at Plymouth, which consumed three or four dwellings. It began next the general storehouse, in which was the stock of trading goods for the Colony, and the provisions for the coming year. Governor Bradford states that if this storehouse had been destroyed, the plantation must have been abandoned. So critical were the hours when they were trying to extinguish the flames.

VI

THE year 1624 was one of prosperity for Plymouth. The success of the experiment of giving to each family a portion of land to cultivate led to the abandonment of the communistic plans which they had followed, not from choice, but because they seemed to be required by the terms of their agreement with the capitalists in England. In certain matters the business of the Colony was still carried on as that of one company, which was accumulating funds to pay a large debt which rested upon the entire Colony. But besides that, it was now provided that a portion of land should be divided amongst the inhabitants, giving one acre to each person as his own. Ninety-seven small lots were assigned at this time, including about two hundred acres, and all the lots were as near the settlement as possible. No larger sections were assigned until the end of the seven years during which they were bound to carry on the business of the Colony as a common interest.[1] There were at this time thirty-two dwelling-houses in Plymouth, besides the buildings erected for public uses. This spring the first cattle were brought into the Colony from England: "three heifers and a bull, the first beginning of that kind of cattle in the land."[2]

Plentiful harvests followed from year to year, under the new method. The people not only raised corn enough for their own wants, but had a surplus, which they were able to sell at six shillings a bushel. They extended their trade in furs, and lessened from year to year the old debt in England. Their stock of cattle increased so that there were twelve cows in 1627. In 1626 a number of goats were brought into the Colony. We have an interesting account of the condition

[1] Bradford, 167.   [2] Bradford, 158.

of the settlement in 1627 by Isaac de Rasieres,
secretary of the Dutch Colony at Manhattan.
He says:—

"New Plymouth lies on the slope of a hill, with one
broad street. The houses are constructed of hewn
planks, with gardens also enclosed behind and at the
sides, so that their houses and courtyards are arranged
in very good order, with a stockade against a sudden
attack. At the ends of the streets there are three
wooden gates. In the centre, on the cross street,
stands the Governor's house, before which is a square
enclosure upon which four cannon are mounted. Up
the hill they have a large square house with a flat roof,
made of thick sawn planks, stayed with oak beams, upon
the top of which they have six cannon which shoot iron
balls of four or five pounds, and command the surround-
ing country. The lower part they use for their church,
where they preach on Sundays and the usual holidays.
They assemble by beat of drum, each with his musket
or firelock, in front of the captain's door. They have
their cloaks on, and place themselves in order, and are
led by a sergeant without beat of drum. Behind comes
the Governor in a long robe: beside him, on the right
hand comes the preacher with his cloak on, and on the
left the captain with his side arms and cloak."

It is probable that there was more of martial
array on this particular Sunday than usual, on
account of the presence of the Dutch secretary.
But the Pilgrims were on guard night and day,
Sundays as well as week days, and they were
never taken by surprise.

The end of the first seven years was a marked period in the history of the Colony. A settlement was made with the capitalists in England who had provided the funds for the Colony; and it was found that the balance of debt was £1,800. Security for the payment of this sum was given by eight enterprising men of the Colony. Among them were William Bradford, Myles Standish, Edward Winslow, William Brewster, and John Alden, who bound themselves to pay £200 a year until the whole sum was paid.[1] This settlement left the Colony entirely free from the restrictions which had hindered its growth, and opened the way for a more rapid development.

First of all, they made a new division of land. The good land nearest the settlement was laid out into shares of twenty acres each. One share was assigned by lot to each man in the Colony, another to his wife, and one to each of their children. This was in addition to the land they already had. There were one hundred and fifty-six shares of land assigned at this time. The records of the Colony show that, besides the one hundred and fifty-six who received lots of land, there had been one hundred and eleven other members of the Colony, fifty-three of whom had removed to other places before that time, and fifty-eight had died, making two hundred and

[1] Bradford, 212–214.

sixty-seven in all.   There had been only seven
deaths since the great mortality of the first year.

In order to provide for the debts of the Colony
those who had given bonds to the English capitalists formed themselves into a company, which
is known in this history as "The Undertakers."
It was agreed that the Undertakers should have
control of the trade of the Colony for the term of
six years.   The profits of this trade would go far
towards paying the debts.   They also engaged to
import such goods as the Colonists needed, which
were to be sold to them in exchange for corn at
six shillings a bushel.   Each holder of a share of
land was to pay to the Undertakers three bushels
of corn or six pounds of tobacco each year for
six years.   All the shares of land were to be
holden for the payment of the debts.   Thus the
Undertakers acted as the agents of the Colonists,
and each Colonist agreed to contribute a small
sum each year towards the payment of the debt.
In the end the debt was honestly paid in full, and
the encumbrances upon the lands of the Colonists
were removed.

VII

THE Plymouth Colony was a Democracy.   The
Compact signed in the cabin of the Mayflower
assumed that those who signed it were freemen,
and voters in the new commonwealth.   The

common law of England was always recognized as in full force in the Colony, and from time to time they insisted that they had all the rights and privileges of Englishmen. In subsequent years men were admitted   Institutions of the Pilgrims. to the rights of freemen in the Colony by vote of the citizens. There was never a religious test of citizenship. Some of the men of greatest influence, such as Myles Standish, were never members of the church at Plymouth. The people were very tolerant of those who differed with them. Yet they had a high ideal of the responsibilities of citizenship. In 1671 it was provided that one to be eligible to citizenship should be of " sober and peaceable conversation, and orthodox in the fundamentals of religion."

Their manner of life was very simple. The houses contained not more than two or three rooms. The floors were of hewn planks or of earth, sprinkled with sand or rushes. Some of the rooms contained furniture brought from England or from Holland. But the most of the furniture was very simple and rude. There was now and then a silver spoon, but there were more pewter spoons and platters. Most of the table furniture was of wood. There were a few books. Governor Bradford left a library of two hundred and seventy-five volumes. Brewster had four hundred volumes at the time of his

death. Myles Standish had Homer's Iliad,
Cæsar's Commentaries, Bariffe's Artillery, His-
tories of Queen Elizabeth, of England, of Germany, and of Turkey, Calvin's Institutes, Wilson's
Dictionary, a number of Commentaries on the
Scriptures, and other books appraised at £11 9s.
In the other Pilgrim homes we may be sure
there were copies of the Geneva Bible, with
some books of history and of devotion.

Most of the Pilgrims were able to read and
write. They had lived twelve years in Holland,
when "every child went to school." [1] At Plymouth they taught their children themselves so
long as they were unable to maintain a public
school. As soon as practicable they passed
laws for the maintenance of public schools for
all the children. There are constant references
to schools and schoolmasters in their earlier history. They planted the church and the school
side by side in their settlements.[2]

Their dress was like that which was then common in England. One can see illustrations of
it in old English portraits of that period. They
wore loose cloaks, and felt hats with broad brims
and high crowns, — short coats commonly belted
at the waist, broad linen collars and cuffs turned
back, knee breeches, long stockings, and low shoes

[1] Campbell's Puritan in Holland, i. 161.
[2] Bradford, 161, 162. Pilgrim Republic, 494, 495.

with silver buckles over the instep. There was more color in the dress of the men than is common in our time. The dress of the women was much more like that which is now worn than that of the men. It was not of costly materials, and the styles did not change from year to year.[1]

Their life was simple and frugal and industrious. The men put up the buildings, tilled the fields, without the help of horses or oxen in the earlier years, hunted the wild game, or took the fish from the brooks or the sea. The women cared for their homes, prepared the food, took care of their children (which were numerous in the new settlement), and nursed the sick. There were times when the women and children went into the fields to assist in planting, and in caring for the growing crops.

They were a thoughtful people, and were prone to free discussion. They managed their democratic government intelligently and wisely. They were a very patient people. In some instances they were greatly wronged by those who had been appointed to do their business in England. There was no need that the debts of the Colony should have hung over it so many years. They did use such means as they could to obtain their rights. But their poverty, and the smallness of their numbers, and the distance of the English

[1] The Simple Cobbler of Agawam, 25, 26.

markets made it very difficult for them to enforce
the contracts which they had made with their
agents. The gentleness and patience of the
people, as they continued their toil year after
year, were sublime.

It was a great sorrow to them that their pastor,
John Robinson, was never able to come to Plymouth from Holland. He died in Leyden in
1625, and was buried in St. Peter's Church. So
long as he lived they regarded themselves as still
under his ministry. He sent them frequent letters, which were read by them instead of his discourses. But their Elder, William Brewster, who
had been an officer of the church while they were
in Leyden, preached " twice every Sabbath, both
powerfully and profitably to y⁰ great contentment
of y⁰ hearers. Many were brought to God by his
ministrie." In 1624 Mr. John Lyford, an edu-
The Pilgrim   cated clergyman of the Church of
Church.   England, was sent to Plymouth by
the capitalists in England, through whom the
Pilgrims did their business. He was kindly received, and for a time he alternated with Elder
Brewster in preaching. But Mr. Lyford did not
easily fall in with the methods of these Separatists,
and after a few months he began to hold services
in a private house, using the Book of Common
Prayer. The community was too small to maintain two congregations, and, after much discussion,

Mr. Lyford was sent out of the Colony.[1] He went first to Salem, and later to Virginia.

In 1629, Mr. Ralph Smith, who is said to have been a university man, came to Plymouth. He had been ordained in the Church of England, but had become a Separatist. He was chosen the pastor of the Pilgrim Church, and continued in that office five or six years. He had as an associate in the ministry for about two years the celebrated Roger Williams, who left Plymouth in 1633. In those years the Pilgrims had for the first time a minister who was authorized to administer the sacraments, which they prized very highly. Mr. John Norton came in 1636, and remained one year. After him came Mr. John Reynor, "an able and a godly man," who ministered to them most acceptably seventeen years as teacher of the church. There are very slight references to the salaries of these ministers, but we find that in 1642 the Plymouth Church bought the house and barns and gardens of Mr. Smith, with six acres of land, and presented the estate to Mr. Reynor. In 1638 the learned and brilliant Charles Chauncy came to Plymouth, having been obliged to flee from England by the stress of persecution. He was made the pastor of the Church in connection with Mr. Reynor, and continued there until 1641.

[1] See a full account of the troubles with Mr. Lyford in Bradford, 171–196.

In the service of song the Pilgrims used Ains-
worth's metrical version of the Psalms, with
tunes printed in only one part. The singing
was congregational. They used the Geneva
Bible in their services. Two or three chapters

Services of Wor- were read, and a full exposition was
ship in the Pil- given. A prayer was offered at the
grim Churches. beginning, and another at the end of
each service. Two Psalms were usually sung in
unison at the beginning and at the end of the
service. The sermon had a prominent place
always. The sacraments were administered at
stated times, and there was a collection for the
support of the minister of the Church, and for
the poor.

Among the most useful men in the Colony
was Samuel Fuller, the first deacon of the
Church, and the beloved physician. He was
also for some years an officer in the Colony.
We read of him as prescribing not only for his
own people, but also for the friendly Indians.
More than once he was called to the Massachusetts Colony in times of special suffering from
the diseases incident to a new settlement. He
seems to have been loved and trusted by all, and
to have exerted an influence in both Colonies,
which was in some respects greater than that of
any other of the Pilgrims. He died in 1633.

VIII

In 1630, the Council for New England sent over from London a new and more liberal and definite patent of the territory of Plymouth. It included what is at present the three counties of Plymouth, Bristol, and Barnstable, excepting the towns of Hingham and Hull. The title ran to William Bradford and his Extension of the Colony. heirs. At a later time he transferred his rights to the Colony. This patent gave to him and his associates the power to establish a government, and to make and execute laws. Still the Colony always recognized the Mayflower compact as the fundamental law.

The population of the Colony increased but slowly. In 1627 it numbered a hundred and eighty. In 1630, it numbered three hundred. In 1643, it had increased to about three thousand. In 1690, there were eight thousand.

As the danger of attacks from the Indians became less, there was a strong tendency to scatter the settlements over the whole territory covered by their patent. The settlement in Duxbury was begun in 1632; that at Scituate in 1636. Mansfield was incorporated in 1640. A few years later the towns of Yarmouth, Sandwich, Barnstable, and Taunton were settled.

4

These towns were represented by their deputies in the General Court.

By the year 1632, there had been a great increase in the number of domestic animals, and the work on the farms was carried on by the use of oxen, and in some instances of horses. In 1637, apple orchards had become common in Duxbury.

In the earlier years, the corn was pounded in hand mortars. In 1633, the first rude mill was built. In 1636, there was a grist mill near Plymouth, where the corn was ground.

The legislation of the Colony was such as was required from time to time, under the limitations of the laws of England. It was ordered in 1628 that thatched roofs should be changed for roofs of boards or paling. The earliest liquor law was passed in 1633. It provided that not more than two pence worth of liquor should be sold to any **Laws of the Colony.** person except to strangers. In 1636, there was a careful revision of the laws, and from that time we have a regular record of the Acts of the General Court. This body consisted at first of all the freemen. As the settlements extended, it was enacted that every town within the Colony should make choice of two of its freemen, and the town of Plymouth of four, to serve as deputies; and these deputies, in connection with the officers of the Colony,

were to constitute the General Court. There
was a second revision of the laws in 1658, and a
third in 1671, when the laws were printed for the
first time. In 1685, the fourth and last revision
of the laws was made. The General Court used
to meet at 7 A. M. in summer, and at 8 A. M. in
winter.

The legislation of the Colony provided for the
annual election of the Governor and his Assistants, and of the Deputies. The rights of conscience were carefully guarded in the legislation.
The laws were such as were needed in a new
country, where the permanent settlers were liable
to annoyances from the lawless and irresponsible
people who came in the ships that resorted to the
harbor. There were little settlements, at that
time, all along the coast, made up of very different people from the Pilgrims. Some of these settlements were so lawless that they existed only a
short time. The people of Plymouth were constantly troubled by these unwelcome strangers.
As the population increased, there were laws to
regulate the taking and sale of fish, the burning
of forests, and trading with Indians. There were
laws respecting roads, ferries, bridges, fairs, ale-
houses, military service, marriage, and the collection of taxes. Profane swearing was forbidden.
In the later years of the Colony persons were
fined for desecration of the Lord's day, for ab-

sence from public worship, and for reviling the ministers. In 1658, a law was passed for supporting the ministers by a tax levied upon all citizens.

The Pilgrims shared the common opinions of their time in respect to witchcraft. The later laws of Plymouth required that a witch should be put to death. There were two trials for witchcraft, one in 1661, the other in 1677. In both cases the verdict of not guilty was rendered by the jury. There were also laws against the Quakers, which seem very severe to the people of our time. They were executed with more or less severity, but they were not in accordance with the gentle and charitable spirit of the Pilgrims.

IX

ONLY a part of those who settled within the limits of Plymouth Colony were Pilgrims. We have seen in the earlier pages that the two hundred and thirty-three who landed at Plymouth before 1624 were called the Forefathers, or the Pilgrims. The next party that came from Leyden in 1629 was made up of thirty-five. A smaller party came from Leyden the next year. These two parties, in addition to those who were here before, make less than three hundred. These were, for the most part,

Not all were Pilgrims.

good representatives of that rare body of men from whom the plan for emigration to America had its spring. They were gentle, charitable, and tolerant. That which we call the Pilgrim spirit came from these men and women.

After the larger Colony of Massachusetts was planted, in 1628 there were influences exerted upon the Old Colony to modify its ruling tendencies. There was a constant and friendly intercourse between the people of the two Colonies; and this made the Puritan somewhat like the Pilgrim, and the Pilgrim more or less like the Puritan. A good many of those who landed at Plymouth removed after a time to Massachusetts. A large number from Massachusetts settled within the bounds of the Old Colony. Judge Davis of Plymouth has stated that "the old Pilgrim Colony was inundated and overwhelmed by migrations from her sister Colony. Taunton, Rehoboth, Barnstable, Sandwich, and Yarmouth had all been settled by emigrants having little or no affiliations with the Colony into which they had come."[1] A more recent writer has stated " that the territory of the Plymouth Colony was settled by people from Massachusetts Bay, with the exception of Plymouth, Duxbury, Marshfield, and Eastham."[2]

[1] History of the Town of Plymouth, William T. Davis, 65, 66.
[2] The Bay Colony, William D. Northend, LL. D., 16.

In 1643, the four Colonies of Plymouth, Massachusetts, Connecticut, and New Haven were
The Confederation. united in a Confederation called The United Colonies of New England.
This Confederation brought the Colony of Plymouth into constant communication with the Puritan Colonies, and it led to some modifications of the earlier methods. Plymouth lost something of its independence of thought and action, and it adopted some of the laws of the Bay Colony. The most severe laws of the Plymouth Colony, such as those for the punishment of Quakers and for the punishment of witchcraft, were enacted after the time of the Confederation, and after the people of the Bay Colony had come in great numbers into the territory of Plymouth.

These tendencies toward the lessening of the differences between the Pilgrims and the Puritans were strengthened by the act of the English government in 1692, which united the two Colonies of Plymouth and Massachusetts Bay under the name of the Province of Massachusetts. And yet it is an open question which section was most influenced by the other. Very much of the spirit of the Pilgrim fathers remains to this day in the great State of Massachusetts. Many of the best elements in New England character are our inheritance from them.

X

IT is not the purpose of this narrative to give a complete history of the Pilgrims, but simply to show some of the qualities of that people as Colonists.   Conclusion.

It must be admitted that the Anglo-Saxons, among the people of modern times, have been most successful in planting vigorous colonies in the outlying parts of the world. They have had the freedom, and the enterprise, and the faith from which successful colonies could be developed. The English Pilgrims had the instinct of colonization. They were so few, and their resources were so slender, that the plan to cross the Atlantic and plant settlements in New England seemed quite impracticable. We are reminded again of the memorable words of their pastor, John Robinson, who was perfectly sure they would succeed, because they were *industrious, and frugal, and temperate,* and *accustomed to overcome difficulties,* and because they *looked for direction in all their ways to the Ruler of the world,* and because *they were bound together in Christian bonds.* It was because they were such a people that they secured the confidence and good will of the people of Holland, and were able to charter ships for the voyage across the Atlantic, and to secure capital with which to procure supplies for their settlement, and were able to put up dwellings at Plymouth in the depth of winter; to organize and govern their little commonwealth without the aid of a royal charter; to win the confidence of the savages by their gentleness and good faith, and to control them by their steady courage. Other English settlements on the coast were failing because of the lack of stamina among their people, but the Pilgrim settlement held on its way, with singular patience and wisdom, until, in its third year, it reached the point where the harvest was not only sufficient for its wants, but where it had food to sell to its neighbors. The Pilgrims were always kind and gentle in their dealings with the Indians, but they were also vigilant and courageous. If the savages would make war upon them, they were always ready to accept the challenge. They were safe because they were soldiers, well armed and disciplined, and always on the alert against the attacks of a crafty enemy.

They were enterprising as well as industrious. They never forgot the obligation to repay the money which had been advanced to them. They carried on a profitable trade with the Indians all along the eastern coast. They planted trading stations on the Kennebec and the Connecticut. They were among the most successful fishermen and fur-traders. In some instances they were obliged to pay thirty and even fifty per cent for the use of money. They were grievously wronged by some of the agents whom they had employed. But in the end every shilling which they owed was paid. They had the respect of the Indians and of their Dutch neighbors, and of the great Colony which the Puritans planted to the north of them. There was nothing weak or slippery about those gentle Christians. If they sung psalms they took their muskets with them to the place of prayer, and they were always ready, not only to defend their own homes, but to send help to their neighbors in times of danger. Their gentleness had made them great. They had the faith that rises above adversity. If they had no meat or bread, they could live on fish. If they had no fish, they could live on shell-fish, and thank God that they had still "the abundance of the sea, and treasures hid in the sand."

They had learned in Holland how to order a free state. They never forgot that "all religions were free" in that land. They respected the rights of conscience at a time when other English Christians denied those rights. They regarded the individual as the unit of the state, and they made all citizens equal before the law. They planted the school by the side of the church in all their settlements, and kept alive even in the hardest years the love of knowledge.

With a great price they obtained their freedom, and they spared no pains to preserve it. They honored the Lord's day and His word. They sought out men of learning and piety as their religious teachers, and they went constantly to the place of worship.

So the Colony grew and prospered. There were great men among them, — men of learning and of statesmanship as well as of piety. Some of those men had stood before kings. Some of them wrote books the world will not willingly let die. One of these books has just been brought back to Massachusetts, and deposited in the archives of the State, two hundred and fifty years after it was written, a treasure which the Mother Country yielded gracefully to the keeping of the great nation which had embodied in its constitution the principles which Governor Bradford and his associates had so clearly stated in the "Compact" written in the cabin of the Mayflower.

It is to the credit of the Pilgrims that they lived in good fellowship with the larger Colony at the Bay. They learned some things from them, while they gave them some of their own principles. The New England spirit did not come altogether from the Pilgrims, nor altogether from the Puritans. They both came from different sections of the great English

people. They both came here on account of
persecution for their religious views and practices. They were both the champions of civil
and religious liberty. They were both very far
in advance of their age. It was well that they
both came to the New World, because they were
able here to work out their principles more freely,
and with a stronger hold upon the future, than
they could have secured in the Old World.

II

The Puritan as a Colonist

The Puritan as a Colonist

THE Pilgrim Colony at Plymouth prepared the way for the larger Puritan Colony of Massachusetts Bay. From the time when the Pilgrims settled at Plymouth, the eyes of the English Puritans were directed towards them. They studied their progress with increasing interest, as it became more probable from year to year that the only way by which they could provide for the exercise of their religion, and secure their liberties as Englishmen, was by planting colonies in America. We have the well known message of one of their leaders: " Let it not be grievous unto you that you have been instrumental to break the ice for others. The honor shall be yours to the world's end."

There had been Puritans in England for two or three generations before they began to plant colonies. They were increasing in numbers and in influence through the reigns of Elizabeth and of James the First. They had a controlling influence among the English people during the first half of the seventeenth century. In 1604, the French ambassa-

The English Puritans.

dor wrote to the French Court that the English Parliament was "composed mostly of Puritans." They included a large part of the intelligent and prosperous middle classes of the English people, —the country gentlemen and the commercial classes,—with a fair proportion of the professional men. The merchants and traders of England had been rising rapidly in wealth and in social position and influence. The common people of that age were becoming more intelligent. Hume tells us that the aggregate property of the Puritan House of Commons of 1629 was computed to be three times as great as that of the Lords.[1]

The Puritans were the advanced Protestants of their time. In respect to the methods of Church government they were in closer sympathy with the Reformed Churches on the Continent of Europe, and with the Church of Scotland, than with the Church of England. And yet they were not Separatists. They were disposed to maintain their rights and liberties inside the National Church, and inside the kingdom. As a party, they used all constitutional methods to secure a reform both in the Church and in the State. They sent their sons to the English Universities, where they were prepared to become leaders in the struggle for civil and religious liberty. They elected a majority of the

[1] Hume, chap. i. Greene, iii. 6–8.

House of Commons a number of times, and they were able to limit very much the arbitrary plans of the King, and to compel him to recognize the rights of the people. They were constantly insisting in Parliament upon the principle that "governments derive their just powers from the consent of the governed." It was not stated in those terms precisely in those days, but that was the substance of the contention of the statesmen of that period. King James told his Parliament that their "privileges were derived from the gracious concessions of their monarchs," and that it was "treason for them to question his royal prerogative." But the Commons informed the King, through Sir Edward Coke, that he "possessed no prerogative whatever except by the law of the land."[1] King James said, "The properties and causes of calling a Parliament are to confer with the King and give him their advice in matters of greatest weight and importance." "I am your kindly King," he said, "therefore do what you ought. Show a trust in me, and go on honestly as ye ought to do, like good and faithful subjects, and what you have warrant for, go on with, and I will not be curious unless you give me too much cause."[2]

But the Commons refused to vote money un-

[1] Lord Campbell, Lives of the Chief Justices, chap. viii.
[2] Parliamentary History, i. 1373–1376.

5

less the King would respect the laws of the land,
and when they did vote money they appointed
a committee to attend to the disbursement of
the revenues. It was their policy to keep the
national treasury under their own control, as
the most effective means of limiting the arbitrary power of the King. James claimed more
power than any English sovereign had ever
claimed before; and the people insisted more
resolutely than ever before upon their rights
and liberties.

The crisis, which was inevitable, came in the
early years of Charles the First. He insisted
upon the royal prerogative as strenuously as his
father had done. The House of Commons drew
up the famous Petition of Right, in behalf of the
laws and the ancient liberties of the English people, to which the King gave a reluctant assent.
But he continued to levy taxes without authority
of law, and to make arbitrary arrests, and he instructed his officers who had the prisoners in
charge not to recognize the writ of Habeas Cor-
pus. He dissolved three Parliaments in succession, and for eleven years he governed England without the authority of Parliament, collecting revenues in such ways as he found most
convenient.

In the mean time some of the leading clergymen in the Established Church were preaching

the doctrine of passive obedience, and, as a recent writer has said, they were turning religion into a systematic attack upon English lib- *The Church of* erty. Laud was now Bishop of Lon- *England.* don, and he already had a leading part in the administration of ecclesiastical affairs. Many of the Non-Conforming ministers were driven from their parishes by the Court of High Commission. Some of them were imprisoned. Others were compelled to flee from the country. At the same time some of the conforming clergymen were introducing the doctrines and ceremonies of the Church of Rome. It seemed to the Puritans that their Mother Church was likely to discard the Protestant faith.

The Puritans were not agreed as to the best course to pursue. Some of them were inclined to remain in their native land and defend their rights in the Church and in the kingdom. The great majority of them were of this opinion, and a few years later they took up arms against the King, and established the Commonwealth. A smaller number of the Puritans believed that it was necessary to plant colonies beyond the sea, and establish free Christian states there, which would be places of refuge in future years, not only for themselves, but for their Protestant fellow countrymen.

The outlook for freedom in Europe was not

promising. The earlier hopes of the growth of Protestantism had been grievously disappointed. In France, the Huguenots were already at the mercy of their enemies. In Germany the Thirty Years' War had reached the darkest period for the cause of Protestantism. In England there seemed to be very little promise of security for civil or religious liberty. Several of the leading members of Parliament had been arrested and committed to the Tower. They were held at the King's pleasure, and were required to make their submission to the King as the condition of their release. The most eminent of them all, Sir John Eliot, was kept in prison until he died. Charles proclaimed his purpose to govern without a Parliament until the people should cease their opposition to his policy.

I

It was at that time that a large and influential portion of the English Puritans began to prepare to transport themselves and their families to America. Their plans were formed with great care and deliberation. It was two or three years before they were matured.

Among those who had a leading part in preparing the way for the first Colony was the excellent John White, who had been the Puritan

rector of Trinity Church in Dorchester   Rev. John
for more than twenty years.   The Pu-   White.
ritans were numerous in that part of England.
A number of the merchants of Dorchester were
engaged in the business of fishing on the coast
of New England.   A number of vessels went out
every year from Dorchester for the fishing grounds.
By the influence of Mr. White an association was
formed with the name of "The Dorchester Ad-
venturers," and with a capital of three thousand
pounds, to form a settlement on Cape Ann, where
the fishermen could be employed in agricultural
pursuits when not employed in taking fish, and
where a minister could be supported, to impart religious instruction to the fishermen who resorted
there, and to teach the Indians the Christian faith.

The Dorchester Company sent a small party
to begin the settlement in 1624.   In 1625 they
appointed Mr. Roger Conant Governor at Cape
Ann, and invited Mr. John Lyford to become
the minister of the plantation.   Both these men
had removed from Plymouth because they did
not accept the principles of the Separatists.   Mr.
Lyford probably conducted religious services after the Episcopal forms.   In the fall of 1626 the
settlement was removed to Naumkeag, where a
number of houses were erected, and where the
settlers planted corn, and prepared to make their
permanent home.

The fact that a settlement had been commenced at that point led a number of men of
Settlement
at Salem.   wealth and influence in England to
                        make plans for sending a colony of
Puritans to that place.   In 1628 a grant of
land was secured from " The Council for New
England," including a large part of what is now
Massachusetts.   A new company was formed,
which purchased from " The Dorchester Adven-
turers " all their property at Cape Ann and
Naumkeag.   Mr. John Endicott, one of the most
virile of the Puritan leaders, was appointed to
conduct the Colony.   He sailed from Weymouth
in the ship Abigail, June 20th, 1628, with a small
company of men and a few cattle, and landed at
Naumkeag on the 6th of September.   He found a
small company of the old settlers on the ground.
The whole number, including the new comers,
was between fifty and sixty.   There was some
difficulty between the old settlers and the new
Colonists, which was amicably adjusted, and on
that account the name of the plantation was
changed to Salem, which means peace.   Endicott
at once made preparations, in accordance with
his instructions, to begin another plantation at
the place that is now known as Charlestown.[1]
The Colony at that time was without a minister,

[1] Young's Chronicles of Massachusetts, 5-16.   Northend's Bay
Colony.   Palfrey, i. 284-296.

as Mr. Lyford had departed for Virginia, but religious services were probably held under the forms of the Church of England.

In the mean time the friends of the enterprise were taking measures to obtain a new charter from the King, which would strengthen The New their title to the territory, and give Charter. them power to make laws for their people and administer government in the Colony. They had a number of influential friends at Court, among whom were Earl Warwick and Lord Dorchester. They succeeded in obtaining from Charles a charter, which constituted them a body politic and corporate, under the title of " The Governor and Company of the Massachusetts Bay in New England." It is dated March 4th, 1629. One of those who were active in securing it wrote, a little later, concerning the charter, that it " was obtained from his Majesty's especial grace, with great cost, favor of personages of note, and much labor." [1] It was granted at the very time when Charles was beginning the experiment of governing without a Parliament.

This charter, which is very long, filling some twenty-five closely printed pages, was the fundamental law of the Colony of Massachusetts for

[1] It is stated by some authorities that the charter cost the Company two thousand pounds. Charles was in great need of money at that time.

fifty-five years. It conveyed to the Company of Massachusetts Bay all the land between Charles River and the Merrimac, and three miles north of the Merrimac, and three miles south of the Charles, from the Atlantic on the east to the South Sea on the west, with the havens, ports, and rivers, and all the islands on the eastern or western coasts of America lying within these limits.[1] It gave to the Company power to elect its own officers, and to make laws for the good of the Company, and for the government of the people dwelling on its territory, provided the laws were not contrary to the laws of England.

The fact that the Company had planted a settlement in New England, and that this charter had been secured from the King, attested by the Great Seal of England, gave a new impetus to the great Puritan exodus. Descriptions of the new country were circulated among the people, and the question of emigration was discussed in every Puritan household. Ships were chartered by the Company to transport a large number of emigrants in the spring.

The earliest records of the Massachusetts Bay Company are dated February 23d, 1629. The ship George Bonaventure, of three hundred tons, armed with twenty cannon, sailed in April with fifty-two planters, provisions, and cattle for the

---

[1] For the original charter, see Hazard, i. 239, or The Bay Colony, Northend, Appendix.

settlement, and arrived at Salem June 22d. A little later the ship Talbot, of three hundred tons, sailed with above one hundred planters, some goats, and provisions for the Colony for twelve months ; and the Lion's Whelp of one hundred and twenty tons, carrying fifty planters with provisions. These reached Salem June 29th. Later still, three other ships, the Four Sisters, the Mayflower, which had carried the Pilgrims nine years before, and the Pilgrim, sailed, carrying planters and provisions. The records indicate that during that year the Company sent over three hundred men, eighty women, and twenty-six children, with a hundred and forty head of cattle, forty goats, and with necessary apparel, provisions, tools, and arms, including a number of pieces of ordnance. The Company had been careful "to make plentiful provision of godly ministers" for the Colony. Mr. Skelton, Mr. Higginson, Mr. Bright, and Mr. Smith went in the first three vessels.

They found "about half a score of houses, and a fair house newly built for the Governor." There were fields of corn that gave promise of a good harvest. They lost no time in dividing their company between Salem and Mishawam (now Charlestown). Two thirds remained at Salem, and the remainder went to Mishawam to prepare the way for the larger number expected the next year.

Important letters were sent to Endicott, the Governor of the Colony, notifying him that

Government of the Colony. they had confirmed him as Governor of the plantation; that they had joined with him as a Council seven persons, who might select three others from the men on the plantation, or from the new comers, and that the old planters might choose two. They enjoined him to treat the Indians justly and courteously, and to educate their children; and reminded him that the main end of the plantation was to bring the Indians to the better knowledge of the Gospel. They also gave instructions that if any of the Indians claimed title to any of the lands covered by the patent, they should endeavor to purchase their title, so as to avoid the least appearance of intrusion. In order that the Sabbath might be celebrated in a religious manner, they directed that all who inhabit the plantation be permitted to cease labor at three o'clock Saturday afternoon, and that they spend the rest of that day in catechising, and in preparation for the Sabbath, as the ministers shall direct.

It was provided in the instructions to Endicott that each person who transported himself and his family to the plantation should have fifty acres of land, — and more if the Governor and Council should deem it necessary in any case, — conveyed to him in the name of the Company, to which the Seal of the Company should be affixed; fifty acres to each person who was sent over by any adventurer in the common stock at his own charge, servants as well as others; and two hundred acres to each adventurer who had contributed £50 to the common stock, and at the same rate for additional contributions.[1]

This was the beginning of the earliest Puritan Colony. There was no trace of communism in it. Nor was there any considerable democratic element. It was at that date a Colony governed by a foreign corporation, under a charter from the King of England, which corporation had power to make laws for the government of the Colony without the consent of the inhabitants. The Company had been fortunate in securing a good title to a territory large enough to furnish homes for the great body of English Puritans. Each planter had the opportunity to secure a generous portion of land, to which he could secure a legal title. The people were expected to gain a livelihood by agricultural pursuits; but they had an opportunity to supplement their incomes by fishing and by trading with the Indians. This was the beginning. The State of the democratic elements were to come Colony. into the government of the Colony at a later time. The religious spirit of the Colony was

[1] Mass. Colonial Records, i. 398.

excellent. Mr. Higginson wrote home: " That
which is our greatest comfort and means of defence above all other is that we have here the
true religion and holy ordinances of Almighty
God taught among us. Thanks be to God, we
have here plenty of preaching and diligent catechising, with strict and careful exercise, and
good and commendable orders to bring our people into a Christian conversation, with whom we
have to do withal. And thus we doubt not but
God will be with us, and if God be with us who
can be against us ? " [1]

II

THE Governor of the Company in England
wrote in his first letter to Endicott, that "for the
The First Church propagating of the Gospel, — our aim
at Salem.   above all things in settling the plantation, — we have been careful to make plentiful
provision of godly ministers for those of our
nation, and for the Indians." He also informs
him that they had joined three ministers with
him as members of his Council, namely, Mr.
Francis Higginson, Mr. Samuel Skelton, and Mr.
Francis Bright.[2] These were all clergymen who
had been ordained in the Church of England,

[1] Higginson, New England Plantation, 123.
[2] Mass. Colonial Records, i. 37.   March 23, 1628.

and who had been for years in charge of parishes. Mr. Bright soon returned to England, but the two others had a very important part in organizing the churches of New England.

Mr. Higginson was born in 1588, graduated at Jesus College, Cambridge, in 1609 or 1610, received the degree of A. M. in 1613, and was minister of a parish in Leicester for a number of years. He was a man of unusual gifts, and was much beloved by his parishioners. He became a Non-Conformist, and was deprived of his parish by the Bishop. At the time when he was invited by the Company to join the new Colony he was expecting to be arrested and sent to London for his Non-Conformity. Although he could not conform to all the requirements of the Established Church, he was far from being a Separatist. His memorable words, spoken, according to Cotton Mather, when the ship was passing out of sight of Land's End, show that he regarded the Church of England as a true church. "We do not go to New England," he said, "to separate from the Church, but only to separate from the corruptions of it, and to practise the positive part of church reformation, and to propagate the Gospel in America." [1]

Mr. Skelton was graduated at Clare Hall, Cambridge in 1611, and received the degree of

[1] Mather's Magnalia, i. 362.

A. M. in 1615. He was minister of a parish in Dorsetshire; became a Non-Conformist and was deprived of his parish. Endicott had known him in England, and had "profited by his ministry."

We cannot be quite sure what were the plans of these clergymen in respect to the beginning of a church in the new Colony. The letter of Governor Cradock to Endicott states that they had left to the ministers whom they had sent over the decision as to " *the manner of the exercising their ministry.*" We do not know what plans had been formed by the Puritans before the Colony was sent over, in respect to a church organization. There is reason to believe that the matter had been very carefully considered for a long time. They were quite familiar with the methods of the Reformed Churches in France and Switzerland and Scotland. Hutchinson tells us they "consulted about settling a Reformed Congregation according to the rule of the Gospel, as they apprehended, and the pattern of the best Reformed Churches." [1] Their contention had been, for a long time, that some things in the Church of England were not according to the New Testament, and not favorable to the growth of true religion. It would have been very inconsistent if the Puritans had organized prelatical churches in the new country. They must have

[1] See in Mass. Hist. Collections, Series ii., v. 117.

come to the Colony prepared to begin the church
after a pattern such as the larger number of the
Protestants of Europe had approved.

The ministers found on their arrival that the
Governor of the Colony, Mr. Endicott, was already prepared for such an organization. The
little Colony had suffered much from sickness
during the winter, and they had sent to Plymouth and secured the services of the excellent
physician, Deacon Samuel Fuller of the Pilgrim
Church. His skill and his knowledge of the
diseases of the coast had been of great service
to the suffering Colonists. He had also given
Mr. Endicott an account of the organization of
the Pilgrim Church, and of its forms of worship.
Mr. Endicott accepted these as in accordance
with the teachings of the New Testament. He
tells us that they were the same which he had
" preferred and maintained ever since the Lord
had revealed himself to him." [1]   In fact, if they
were to discard the " Historic Episcopate," the
question of organizing a church was comparatively simple.

There must have been earnest consultations at
Salem between the ministers and the Colonists.
Morton tells us that Mr. Higginson and Mr.
Skelton consulted with Mr. Endicott, and the
rest of the godly people whom they found in-

[1] Bradford's History, Legislative Ed., 316.

habitants of the place, and the chief of the passengers who came over with them, "*about settling a Reformed Congregation*." [1]

The result was that, about four weeks after the arrival of the new Colonists, Governor Endicott appointed the 20th of July as "a solemne day of humiliation for ye choyce of a pastor and teacher." The people came together at that time, and after fasting, prayer, and a sermon, they cast their ballots and chose Mr. Skelton to be pastor and Mr. Higginson to be teacher. Then Mr. Skelton was solemnly set apart for his office. Mr. Higginson and three or four of the gravest members of the church laid their hands on Mr. Skelton, and Mr. Higginson prayed. Then the same service was repeated for Mr. Higginson, with prayer by Mr. Skelton. These things are stated in a letter by Mr. Charles Gott, who was present, and who was afterwards deacon of the church in Salem. [2]

A little later the Governor appointed August 6th as another day of fasting and prayer, for the election and setting apart of elders and deacons. Mr. Higginson had been requested to draw up a covenant for the members of the church. At the appointed time he read the covenant which he had prepared, and it was solemnly assented to by thirty members, and a copy was given to each.

[1] Morton's Memorial, 97.   [2] Bradford's History, 316.

This covenant was included in a single sentence, as follows : —

"We covenant with the Lord, and one with another, and doe bynd our selves in the presence of God, to walk together in all his waies, according as he is pleased to reveale himself unto us in his Blessed word of truth."

After the acceptance of this covenant, the two ministers were again ordained in the same manner as they had been on the 20th of July, as was also Mr. Houghton, who had been chosen ruling elder.[1] Some of the old writers state that Governor Bradford, coming by sea as a representative of the church in Plymouth, "gave them the right hand of fellowship, wishing all prosperity, and a blessed success unto such good beginnings."[2]

The real meaning of this action of the Puritans at Salem was made plain by a discussion which began immediately. Two of the lead- Significance of ing men, who had just come into the their Action. Colony from England, took exception to the course that had been followed by the ministers, and by the great majority of the people of the Colony. Mr. Samuel Brown and his brother John were both original members of the Massa-

[1] The literature relating to their transactions is very extensive. See Prof. Walker's Creeds and Platforms of Congregationalism, 93–116. Northend's Bay Colony, 50–52.

[2] Morton's Memorial, 99. Goodwin's Pilgrim Republic, 325.

chusetts Company, and also members of the
Governor's Council. One was a lawyer and the
other a merchant. They were men of wealth and
of influence, and were disposed to push their own
opinions in the plantation. They refused to have
anything to do with the organization of the new
church, which they regarded as a secession from
the National Church, and, gathering a company
of people who were of the same mind, they set
up a separate congregation where worship was
conducted according to the Book of Common
Prayer. They were themselves Non-Conformists,
but they were not prepared to break entirely with
the Church of England. When they were brought
before the Governor to explain their proceedings,
they said that the ministers were leading the people into extremes, — that they had already become
"Separatists and would be Anabaptists." To this
the ministers replied very plainly, that they were
"neither Separatists nor Anabaptists; that they
did not separate from the Church of England nor
from the ordinances of God there, but only from
the corruptions and disorders there; that they
came away from the Common Prayer and ceremonies, and had suffered much for their Non-
Conformity in their native land, and therefore,
being in a place where they might have their
liberty, they neither could nor would use them,
because they judged the imposition of these

things to be sinful corruptions of the worship of God." [1]

This disagreement was a serious matter for the infant Colony. Endicott had written instructions from the Company that persons not "conformable to their government be not permitted to remain within the limits of their grant." He called the Browns to account for what he termed their "seditious" proceedings, and, finding that they were likely to cause serious trouble in the Colony, he told them that " New England was no place for such as they," and sent them back to England. This seems to have been done on the principle that the corporate body owned the territory, and that as the owners they had a right to send out of their bounds all such persons as were likely to cause them trouble or loss.

The new churches that were planted in the Puritan Colonies followed the same principles that had guided the church in Salem. They were free churches. In respect to their organization and the methods of administration, they were like the Pilgrim Church at Plymouth. They emphasized the local church as a body made up of believers, bound together by a covenant for Christian worship and service. But these churches claimed very positively that they were not "Separatist" churches. This statement was

[1] Morton's Memorial, 100, 101.

made not only at the time, but by their leading
men in subsequent years. When Roger Williams
came into the Colony, he objected to the churches
because they were not Separatist churches. He
would not commune with them because they recognized the Church of England as a true church.
John Cotton, in his work entitled " The Way
of the Churches Cleared," published in 1648,
states explicitly, that we do not deny " that the
parochial Congregations in England are true
churches. Our separation from them is not a
separation from them as no churches, but rather
a separation from the corruptions found among
them."[1]

The action of the people of the Colony in
establishing churches that were not under the
control of the Church of England was in accordance with the understanding at the time they
received their charter. It was well known that
those who were seeking to establish a settlement
in New England were Non-Conformists, and that
it was their purpose to establish a colony where
they could worship God in accordance with the

[1] See Cotton's Way of the Churches Cleared, chap. iii. sect. 3.
Also pp. 14–16. He denies that Independency is a fit name for our
churches. " Sure I am," he says, " that Mr. Skelton, their pastor,
was studious of that way before he left Holland in Lincolnshire.
. . . He is much mistaken who saith the Congregation of Plymouth
did leaven all the vicinity. . . . Those who came over were not such
as would be leavened by vicinity of neighbors."

dictates of their own consciences. Governor Winthrop states that, at a hearing before the King and his Council in 1633, the agents of the Council were told that " His Majesty did not intend to impose the ceremonies of the Church of England upon us, for that it was considered that it was the freedom from such things that made people come over to us."[1] In all the complaints that were afterward made against the Colony, it was never alleged that the establishing of churches without Episcopal supervision was inconsistent with the understanding on which the charter was given.

III

In the summer of 1629 the General Court of the Company was considering a proposition to transfer the government of the Colony to New England. The plan was brought forward by Governor Cradock at a meeting on the 13th of May, and it was further discussed at meetings held in August and September. A committee was chosen to take the advice of counsel as to the right of the Company to transfer its charter to New England. In the charters of all similar companies prior to

Transfer of the Company to New England.

[1] Winthrop, i. 103. Young's Chronicles of Massachusetts, 295 Northend's Bay Colony, 53–55.

that of Massachusetts, it had been stipulated that the chief government should remain in England. But in the charter of the Massachusetts Colony there was no such stipulation. Those who held the charter found that some of the leading men among the Puritans were not willing to enter a Colony that was to be under the government of a corporation beyond the sea. They claimed that the Puritan Colony should be self-governing. The future growth and prosperity of the Colony were believed to depend upon the decision of the question concerning the removal of the government to the Colony itself.

On the 26th of August, a memorable meeting was held at Cambridge by a number of leading Puritans who were considering the question of a removal to New England. Among them were Sir Richard Saltonstall, John Winthrop, Isaac Johnson, Thomas Dudley, John Humphrey, William Pynchon, Increase Nowell, Thomas Sharp, **The Meeting at Cambridge.** and William Vassall. The result of this meeting was that twelve gentlemen, including all those named above, signed an agreement to embark with their families for the plantation in New England by the first of March next, provided " that before the last of September next, the whole Government, together with the patent for the said Plantation, be first, by an order of Court, legally transferred and established to remain with us, and others which shall inhabit upon the said plantation."

The General Court finally decided to transfer the government to New England. At a meeting held October 20th, 1629, Governor Cradock having resigned his office, John Winthrop was elected Governor, and thereupon he accepted and took the oath to that place appertaining. John Humphrey was chosen Deputy Governor, and Sir Richard Saltonstall, Isaac Johnson, Thomas Dudley, John Endicott, Increase Nowell, William Vassall, William Pynchon, Samuel Sharp, Edward Rossiter, Thomas Sharp, John Revell, Matthew Cradock, Thomas Goffe, Samuel Aldersey, John Venn, Nathaniel Wright, Theophilus Eaton, and Thomas Adams were chosen Assistants. It was agreed that the members of the Company who were to remain in England should have a share in the profits of the trading stock for the term of seven years, and the management of the stock was intrusted to ten gentlemen, five of whom were to remain in England, and five to go to New England.[1]

These events gave a great impulse to the plans for a removal to New England. The far-reaching plans of the leaders of the enterprise had been successful, and a large number of the best

[1] Colonial Records, i. 49.   Hubbard, chap. xviii.   Hutchinson's Collections, 25, 26.

people of England were ready to avail themselves of the advantages of the liberal charter, and to follow the well known leaders to the Bay Colony. The emigration was on a scale beyond any similar movement in England before. " The principal planters of Massachusetts," according to the testimony of one of their opponents, " were English country gentlemen of no inconsiderable fortunes, of enlarged understandings, improved by liberal education."[1] They came from every part of England, but a large majority were from the eastern counties. " It was not by accident," says Mr. John Fiske, "that the earliest counties of Massachusetts were called Norfolk, Suffolk, and Essex, or that Boston in Lincolnshire gave its name to the capital."

John Winthrop, the Governor, was born in Groton, Suffolk, in 1587, was a student for two years at Trinity College, Cambridge, and was bred to the law. His father and grandfather were lawyers. He was a man of great ability, and of wide influence in England, and had an income of six or seven hundred pounds a year, equal to two thousand pounds at this time. John Humphrey, the Deputy Governor, was a man of learning, activity, and piety, and had been the familiar companion of the patriotic noblemen of the time. Thomas Dudley, who

[1] Chalmers's History of the Revolt of the American Colonies, i. 58.

was of a very different type from the suave and
charitable Winthrop, came of an ancient family,
and brought to the service of the Colony a mind
trained in active life, full of energy and courage.
Sir Richard Saltonstall of Yorkshire was a generous contributor to the Colony. Isaac Johnson,
a son in law of Lord Lincoln, was an extensive
landowner, and was esteemed the richest of the
emigrants. Theophilus Eaton was a merchant
in London, and had been Minister of Charles
the First to Denmark. Simon Bradstreet, the son
of a clergyman, had studied at Cambridge, and
inherited a fine estate in Suffolkshire. These
men represented that which was the best and
most progressive in England at that time. And
those were the times of Lord Bacon, and Sidney,
and Shakespeare, and Milton. The mind of the
nation had been awakened from its lethargy, and
it was evident that a new era of progress was at
hand.

Governor Winthrop, Mr. Johnson, Mr. Saltonstall, Mr. Dudley, Mr. Phillips, and Mr. Codding-
ton sailed on the 8th of April from Yarmouth on
the Arabella, and arrived at Salem on the 12th
of June, having in their possession the charter of
the Company. On leaving England they issued
a printed address to " their Brethren of the
Church of England," which they speak of as their
dear mother. They express much affection for

their native land which they are leaving, and ask their brethren to pray for them without ceasing, " making continual requests for us to God in all your prayers."

Sixteen other vessels went with them to Massachusetts during the year, carrying not less than one thousand persons, with sixty horses, two hundred and forty cows, a large supply of provisions, stores, and goods of various kinds for trading with the Indians. Some of the ships landed at Salem, some at Charlestown.

The condition of the Colony on their arrival was discouraging. More than a quarter of those who had come over a year before had died, and many of the survivors were sick. The supply of provisions was small. They had not enough corn to last a fortnight when the fleet arrived. A portion of the provisions of the new comers had spoiled on the passage. By mistake, some provisions designed for the Colony had not been shipped. The supplies were so limited that they were obliged to discharge from their indentures a large number of servants who had been sent over during the two years preceding.

Governor Winthrop lost no time in making arrangements for distributing among the different plantations the large number of Colonists who had just arrived. He went to Charlestown, where was already a considerable settlement, and to Medford and Boston. A good many of the new comers were soon settled at Charlestown. The Governor with some of the Assistants took possession of the "great house" which had already been erected for them. In August, Mr. Johnson, one of the Assistants, settled in Boston, where he found a good supply of wholesome water. On that account Governor Winthrop, took over the frame of a house which he had constructed at Charlestown, and late in the autumn Winthrop, Dudley, and some other leaders of the Colony erected cottages there. Sir Richard Saltonstall with a company of his friends settled at Watertown, with Mr. George Phillips as their minister. Mr. Pynchon with a party of his friends settled in Roxbury, and another party settled at Matapan, now Dorchester. Mr. Cradock began a plantation at Medford, and a few families settled at Saugus. Before the winter eight plantations had been commenced, namely, Salem, Charlestown, Boston, Matapan, Watertown, Roxbury, Medford, and Saugus.

The rude habitations which the Colonists were able to erect were a poor substitute for the comfortable homes they had left in England. "They lived many of them in tents and wigwams at Charlestown," says one of the old writers; "their meeting place being abroad, under a tree, where I have heard Mr. Wilson and Mr. Phillips preach

many a good sermon."[1] Deputy Governor Dudley
wrote, " I have no table, or other room to write
in than by the fireside upon my knee in this
sharp winter; to which my family must have
leave to resort, though they break good manners,
and make me many times forget what I would
say, and say what I would not."[2]

Many of the Colonists were sick of scurvy and
of fever contracted on the voyage. Many died
soon after their arrival. There was great suffering from exposure to the weather, and before
December two hundred of the new comers had
died. Among the first of these were Mr. Isaac
Johnson, one of the Assistants, and his wife, the
Lady Arabella. In November they succeeded
in buying a hundred bushels of corn from the
Indians on Cape Cod. In August, Governor
Winthrop had sent the ship Lion to the nearest
port in Ireland or England for provisions. This
ship returned the 5th of February loaded with
provisions, at a time when the inhabitants were
subsisting on clams and mussels, and on bread
made from ground nuts and acorns. When the
ship arrived, the day of fasting and prayer which
had been appointed for the 6th of February was
changed to a day of Thanksgiving, and this day
was observed the 22d of February.

[1] Clap's Memoirs.   Young's Chronicles of Massachusetts, 351.
[2] Young's Chronicles of Massachusetts, 303.

The great suffering of that first winter, and the large number of deaths, caused some of the Colonists to lose hope. When the vessels went back to England about one hundred of the people went back. Mr. Bright, the minister at Charlestown, and Mr. Vassall, one of the Assistants, were among those who returned. But the great body of the people remained, and bore with wonderful fortitude the hard experiences of the earlier years, determined to work out the difficult problems connected with the new Colony.

IV

AMONG the first things which the Puritan leaders provided for was the support of ministers for the people, and the gathering of The Early churches. At the first meeting of Churches. the Court of Assistants, held at Charlestown, it was voted that houses be built for Mr. Wilson and Mr. Phillips, at the public charge, with convenient speed. It was also voted that Mr. Phillips "should have, for his maintenance, three hogsheads of meal, one of malt, four bushels of Indian corn, one of oatmeal, one half a hundred pounds of salt fish; and for apparel and other provisions, twenty pounds: or if he preferred to be paid in money, he should have forty pounds per annum, and find his own provisions." It

was also ordered that " Mr. Wilson should have
twenty pounds per annum till his wife came
over." All these were to be a common charge
upon the Colony, those at Salem and Matapan
excepted, because they had their own ministers
to support. Provision was also made at that
time for Mr. Gager, a physician, at the public
charge, and for James Penn, beadle, who was to
wait upon the Governor, and to execute his
commands.[1]

The first Puritan church to be formed after
the one at Salem was organized in England.
The method of organization is full of historical
significance. It was made up from a company
gathered by that energetic Non-Conformist minister, the excellent John White of Dorchester, England. The people came from the counties of
Devon, Dorset, and Somerset, in 1629 and 1630.
They assembled at the New Hospital at Plymouth, England, just as they were ready to sail.
An old writer tells us : —

" These godly people resolved to live together; and
therefore, as they had made choice of those reverend
Servants of God, Mr. John Wareham and Mr. John
Maverick, to be their ministers, so they kept a solemn
Day of fasting in the New Hospital in Plymouth, in
England, spending it in Preaching and in Praying:
where that worthy man of God, Mr. John White of
Dorchester in Dorset was present, and Preached unto

[1] Massachusetts Colonial Records, i. 73, 74.

us the Word of God in the forepart of the Day; and in the latter part of the Day, as the people did solemnly make Choice of, and call these godly Ministers to be their Officers, so also the Revd. Mr. Wareham and Mr. Maverick did accept thereof, and expressed the same." [1]

It is uncertain whether there was a formal ordination, by the laying on of hands, of these ministers. We do not certainly know whether the members of the church gave their assent to a covenant at that time. There is a conflict in the testimony that has come down to us. Roger Clap, who has given the most definite account of what was done, was admitted into fellowship with this church on their arrival in New England. This implies that their organization was already a complete one.

This whole transaction shows what views the Puritan Non-Conformists in England had adopted in respect to the essentials of a Christian church. John White was a fair representative of them. Evidently they were not in favor of the transfer to New England of the Episcopal Church. In the Mother Country they remained in that church, but they did not regard prelacy as essential to a true church. On the other hand, they were not Separatists, as the people at Plymouth were. And yet, when they came into the new

[1] Roger Clap's Memoirs, 39. Young's Chronicles of Mass., 346-367. See also Prof. Walker's Creeds and Platforms, 149, 150.

Colonies, they organized their churches in much the same way as the Pilgrims had done. The Dorchester church, which was formed at the New Hospital in Plymouth, England, was very much like the church that had been formed at Salem the year before.

The third and fourth Puritan churches were organized in Charlestown and Watertown on the 30th of July, 1630.[1] Only four persons united to form the church in Charlestown; namely, Governor Winthrop, Isaac Johnson, Thomas Dudley, and John Wilson. Five others were admitted to fellowship a few days later, and others in rapid succession. This process indicates the care that was taken to make up the church of those who were esteemed fit for membership. It was almost a month later when the church observed another day of fasting and prayer, and at that time selected John Wilson, teacher, Increase Nowell, ruling elder, and William Gager and William Aspinwall, deacons. These officers were then installed by the laying on of hands. It was expressly stated in the case of Mr. Wilson, that the act of ordination was to be understood only as his consecration to the service to which he was now called, and not as a denial of the validity of his Episcopal ordination in England.[2] In forming this church the advice

Churches at Charlestown and Watertown.

---

[1] Mather's Magnalia, i. 377.   [2] Winthrop, i. 32, 33.

and counsel of the Pilgrim Church at Plymouth was sought, and was freely given.

The Covenant of the Church in Charlestown was as follows: —

"In the name of our Lord Jesus Christ, & in obedience to His holy will & Divine Ordinance:

" Wee whose names are hereunder written, being by His most wise & good Providence brought together into this part of America in the Bay of Massachusetts, and desirous to unite our selves into one Congregation or Church, Vnder the Lord Jesus Christ our Head, in such sort as becometh all those whom He hath Redeemed, & Sanctified to Himselfe, do hereby Solemnly and religiously (as in His most holy Presence), Promise & bind ourselves to walk in all our wayes according to the Rule of the Gospell, & in all sincere conformity to His holy Ordinances, & in mutual love, & respect each for other, so neere as God shall give vs grace." [1]

Not long after the organization of this church Mr. Wilson and a number of the prominent members removed to Boston, and the church became the First Church of Boston. At a later time the people of Charlestown formed themselves into a church by a mutual covenant. On the 30th of July the good people of Watertown also entered into a covenant, which is preserved in the pages of Cotton Mather.[2] It is longer than the covenant of the churches of Salem, or Dorches-

[1] History of the First Church in Boston, A. B. Ellis, 3.
[2] Magnalia, i. 377.

7

ter, or Charlestown, but is made up of the same elements.

This is sufficient to show how the Puritan Churches in New England were formed. Their members had been members of the Episcopal Church in England. Their ministers, almost without exception, had been educated in the English Universities, and had been ordained by the Bishops and Presbyters of that Church. They had the learning and the manners of English clergymen. They did not believe, however, that the orders or the services of that Church were the only ones that had any validity. The essential thing in a church, in their opinion, was a company of believers, associated together by a mutual covenant, living in Christian love and fellowship with each other, and with all other Christians, and observing the ordinances which are set forth in the New Testament. The Puritans formed free churches in their Colonies, according to a very simple pattern, and these free churches, after an experience of more than two hundred and fifty years, are still lights in the world, sending out Christian influences in all the earth, working zealously, in connection with Christians in other communions, in the service of the Master, for the redemption of all the nations of men.

V

WE are next to trace the plans of the Puritan Colonists in providing for the social, and economic, and political life of the people. The large number of Englishmen who came into the Colony of Massachusetts Bay in the earlier years were from different callings and occupations in life. There was an unusually large proportion of University men. Governor Winthrop and some of his associates in the General Court were lawyers. William Gager was not the only physician among them. By the end of 1630 there were seven or eight clergymen in the Colony. There were a number of merchants who brought into the new country considerable wealth. These men were able, in the course of a few years, to develop profitable business enterprises, by the fisheries and the fur trade with the Indians, and by trade with their own people. The largest number of the pioneers were farmers, who availed themselves of the proposals of the Company and became the owners of land in the different plantations. These men were able within a few years to erect comfortable dwellings in the midst of fruitful fields and orchards, that brought them an ample support. Many of the Colonists brought with them servants whose passage they had paid, and for whose support they were

Variety among the Colonists.

responsible. These servants bound themselves
to repay them by their labor. The first Colonists
also brought with them horses and cattle of various kinds, and goats and sheep, and such tools as
were needed for building and fishing and farming.
The Colonists were characterized from the first
by habits of industry and frugality, as well as by
energy and thrift.

We have already seen that it was the policy
of the Massachusetts Company to encourage the
Owners of the   settlers to gain a title to the land
Soil.   which they cultivated.[1]   There was
at one time a probability that some families of
the English nobility would come to New England, and would become owners of large tracts
of land, and lay the foundation for a land system
like that of Great Britain. Formal inquiries
were made as to whether they could have certain hereditary rights, which would secure to
them a share in the government similar to that
of the English peers.[2]   All such proposals were
declined in courteous though decided terms, because they were not in harmony with the best
aspirations of the people who had crossed the
sea to lay the foundations for a *new* England.
The free democratic principle was continually

---

[1] Colonial Records of Massachusetts, i. 398.

[2] Winthrop, i. 135–137.   Hutchinson's History, i. 433, 490.
Palfrey, i. 390.   Edmund Burke, ii. 145.

asserting itself. No hereditary privileges could be conceded even to such generous friends and patrons as Lord Say and Sele, Lord Brook, and the other "persons of quality" who united with them in their proposals. The right to own the land which they cultivated was secured to the Colonists in the early years.

The Colonial government at first had few of the elements of a democracy. In the beginning the Corporation, which owned the territory, and which had the right to make laws for the people, was a foreign body, holding its meetings in England. The transfer of the charter to New England prepared the way for the people to gain a share in the government. *The Colonial Government.*

The first session in New England of the "General Court of the Company of Massachusetts Bay" was held in Boston, October 19th, 1630. This General Court consisted of the Governor, Deputy Governor, and eighteen Assistants, and of such freemen as they had chosen. There was at that time no representation from the people of the Colony, and yet the General Court had power to enact such laws as they should think proper for the people inhabiting the Colony, provided the laws were not contrary to the laws of England. At this first meeting of the General *First Meeting of the General Court in New England.*

Court, one hundred and nine persons applied for admission as freemen. This admission would make them members of the Company, and entitle them to vote at all elections of officers, and on all proposals for the enactment of laws. This number must have included a large proportion of the adult males of the Colony. Had this application been granted, it would have brought the government of the Colony under the control of those who desired to become freemen. But the officials had too little confidence in the people to grant the application. They did not think it would be for the interest of the Colony that the election of officers and the enactment of laws should be confided to inexperienced men. And yet they could not well refuse to admit the people to some share in the government. The General Court decided, on this account, to lessen the power of those who should be admitted as freemen. They voted that the election of Governor and Deputy Governor should be by the Assistants, and not by the freemen; that the power of making laws and choosing officers to execute the same should be limited to the Governor and Deputy Governor with the Assistants. They granted to the freemen the power of electing Assistants whenever there should be a vacancy in the board. At the annual meeting of the General Court, held at Boston, the 18th of May,

1631, one hundred and sixteen persons, including most of those who had applied in October, were admitted as freemen in the Company, on taking the prescribed oath. It was ordered at that time by the General Court, that once a year at least there should be a session of the General Court for the election of officers and for other purposes. At this annual session "the commons" (that is, the freemen) could nominate any person or persons whom they should choose for the office of Assistant, provided there were any vacancies in that body. The Commons could also express their desire for the removal of one or more of the Assistants, "for any defect or misbehaviour."

These orders were designed to make the office of Assistant a permanent office, unless the occupant should be removed by the freemen for defect or misbehavior. It was also ordered by the General Court at that time, that for the time to come no man should be admitted to be a freeman but such as are members of some of the churches within the limits of the Colony. At that session of the General Court, Winthrop was re-elected to the office of Governor, and Dudley to that of Deputy Governor.[1]

But the action which had been taken by the General Court restricting the rights of the free-

1 See Massachusetts Records, i. 79–87.

men in the election of Governor and Assistants
was looked upon by the people as an assumption
of power. It was plainly in conflict with the
charter, and public opinion in the Colony was
decidedly favorable to the right of the people to
a generous share in the government. At the session of the General Court in May, 1632, it was
ordered that the election of Governor, Deputy
Governor, and Assistants shall be by the whole
court, consisting of all the freemen, as well as of
the Governor, Deputy Governor, and Assistants,
and that the Governor shall always be chosen out
of the Assistants.[1] This was a very large concession to the people. From that time they had a
large and increasing share in the government of
the Colony.

It was provided in the charter that the Court
of Assistants, with the Governor, may hold meetings once a month for such business relating to
the Colony as may require to be done. This provision resulted in a great increase in the power
of the Assistants. Most of the judicial functions
rested in them, and they were called " the magistrates." They appointed justices of the peace
with powers like those of such officers in England. They levied taxes, appropriated money,
tried suits, punished offenders, and framed laws
for the Colony. They assumed to be an es-

[1] Massachusetts Records, i. 95.

tate above the freemen, who were called the Commons.

The question of the right of the Court of Assistants to levy taxes without the consent of the people was raised in the early years of the Colony. In consequence of the representations of the freemen, it was voted by the Court of Assistants that every plantation within the Colony should have the right to appoint two deputies to confer with the Court in regard to the assessment of taxes. This also was a concession to the democratic tendencies in the Colony.

VI

One of the objects of those who went to the Colony of Massachusetts Bay was to teach the Indians the Christian religion. It was stated in the charter of the Colony that it was " the principal end of the plantation to winn and incite the natives of the country to the knowledge and obedience of the only true God and Saviour of mankind, and the Christian faith." [1] Governor Cradock, in his letter to Endicott in February, 1629, enjoined him to treat the Indians justly and courteously, and to educate their children. At a meeting of the

Dealings with the Indians.

---

[1] Bay Colony Charter, Northend, 526.

Court held in 1631, it was ordered that satisfaction should be made to the Indians for a
canoe which Thomas Morton had unjustly taken
from them, and that his house be burned in
sight of the Indians for their satisfaction for
the wrongs he had done them. " It is the
earnest desire of our whole company," wrote
Governor Cradock, "that you have a diligent and
watchful eye over our own people, that they de-
mean themselves justly and courteously towards
the Indians." At one time it was agreed that
" Sir Richard Saltonstall shall give Sagamore
John a hogshead of corn for the hurt his cattle
did him in his corn"; and also that " Nicholas
Frost, for theft committed by him upon the
Indians shall be severely whipped, and banished
out of this patent."[1]   These are specimens of the
action that was taken for the protection of the
Indians against dishonest white men.

There were few Indians in the vicinity of Massachusetts Bay at the time of the settlement by
the English. That region had been almost de-
populated by an epidemic which had prevailed
before the arrival of the English, and was for the
most part open for the settlers without interference with the rights of the aborigines. Not a
foot of land previously in their occupation was
appropriated except by purchase. Vattel, in his

[1] Massachusetts Colonial Records, i. 102, and 100, 121, 133.

Law of Nations, says: "We cannot fail to applaud the moderation of the English Puritans who first established themselves in New England, who bought from the savages the land which they wished to occupy."[1] There were occasional acts of injustice towards the red men by individuals who belonged in the Colony, and sometimes a white man was robbed or murdered by the Indians; but these occurrences were rare and exceptional. The relations between the Colonists and the Indians were friendly up to the time of the Pequot war, and the legislation relating to the Indians was just and humane through the whole period of Colonial history. When the Indians were sick, and their own people were afraid to take care of them on account of the danger of infection, their white neighbors came to their help. The Indians were much affected by the kindness of their English friends, who came to them daily to minister to their wants. They also buried their dead, and gave homes to their orphan children.[2] The relation of the Indian chiefs to Governor Winthrop was very friendly. They were desirous to put on English garments, and the Governor encouraged them to do so. He was careful to redress any

[1] Vattel, Law of Nations, book i. chap. xviii.   Palfrey, i. 362. Winthrop, i. 89, 116, 119.
[2] Winthrop, i. 119.

wrongs they had suffered from white men, and
on a number of occasions he invited them to
dine with him at his house, and treated his dusky
guests with especial respect and courtesy.

VII

THE general history of the Colony during the
early years was much like that of other English
The Colony in   Colonies.   The settlement at Boston
1630 to 1633.   grew rapidly.   A new plantation was
begun at Newtown, now Cambridge, in 1631,
and it was proposed to make it a fortified town,
and to remove the cannon and the stores of
ammunition to that place.   There was a plan
to make Newtown the capital, and to induce
the Governor and Deputy Governor and most
of the Assistants to build houses there.   But the
influence of the people in Boston induced Winthrop to remain there, and the majority of the
officials remained with him.

In 1631, only a few joined the Colony from
England.   Among those who came were the
wife and some of the children of Governor Winthrop, and John Eliot, who was known in later
years as the Apostle to the Indians.

It was ordered in April that every captain
shall train his company on Saturday of each
week; and later, that there should be a general

training once a month. It was the policy of the Colony to accustom the settlers to the use of arms, so as to be ready to resist attacks from the Indians or from other enemies.

Two hundred and fifty came from England to the Colony in 1632. Among them was Mr. Wilson, pastor of the church in Boston, who had gone to England for his family; Thomas Welde, who was soon after ordained minister at Roxbury; and Thomas James, who was afterwards minister at Charlestown. Mr. Eliot, who had come the year before, was ordained at Roxbury. Thus the churches which had been formed in the new settlements were provided with ministers.

It was "thought by general consent that Boston was the fittest place for public meetings of any place in the Bay." [1] It was ordered that a market should be kept there every Thursday. A house of correction was also erected. A meeting-house was built in Boston, and a house for the pastor, by a voluntary contribution of about one hundred and twenty pounds. It is said to have had mud walls and a thatched roof, and to have stood on the south side of what is now State Street, near the corner of Devonshire Street. The settlement at that time consisted of only a few dwellings.

In 1633, seven hundred persons came to Mas-

[1] Colonial Records, i. 101.

sachusetts from England.   Among them were
John Cotton, Thomas Hooker, and Samuel Stone,
ministers; and Mr. Haynes, Mr. Pierce, and Mr.
Goofe, who became leading men in the Colony.
Mr. Cotton was ordained by imposition of hands
as teacher of the church in Boston, of which Mr.
Wilson was pastor; Mr. Hooker was ordained as
pastor, and Mr. Stone as teacher, of the church
in Newtown.

The year 1634 was a notable one in the history of the Colony.   It now contained about
three thousand people, scattered through sixteen
plantations.[1]   When notice of the meeting of the
General Court in May was sent out, the freemen
in the different settlements elected delegates,
three from each town, who came to Boston and
desired to see the charter of the Colony.   After
the examination the deputies were sure that the
power of making laws was in the General Court,
including all the freemen.   In this opinion the
General Court, after an examination, agreed with
the deputies, and voted that the General Court
has power to make laws, elect officers, levy taxes,
dispose of lands, and to elect freemen.   These
votes gave to the freemen, who were represented
by the deputies, the control of the affairs of the
Colony, and they were determined to maintain
their rights under the charter.   The election

[1] Wood, New England Prospect, 44.

sermon was preached by Mr. Cotton, in which he stated "that a magistrate ought not to be turned into the condition of a private man without just cause." The deputies determined to effect a change in the office of Governor, not because they had less confidence in Mr. Winthrop than before, but because he stood before the people as representing the doctrine that a magistrate has a claim to be continued in his office. The vote for Governor was taken "by papers," that is by ballot, after the custom in the Dutch Republic, and Mr. Dudley was chosen Governor and Mr. Ludlow Deputy Governor.

In this way the democratic element in the Colony asserted itself, and from that time the people were recognized more and more definitely as the source of political power.

VIII

ONE of the characteristic things in the Puritan Colonies was the division of the territory into towns. Many of the ideas of the Puritans tended towards republicanism, and they naturally organized their towns as little republics in which the people should manage their local affairs in their own way. There was nothing in England at that time from which they could have borrowed the idea of the town. It was somewhat like the tun-

moot of the Anglo-Saxons.[1]   It was in accordance with the best traditions of Teutonic liberty.
There was something like it in some of the oldest Cantons in Switzerland, — and in the chartered towns of the Netherlands,[2] in which some
of the Puritans had lived.   Mr. Bryce quotes
the words of Jefferson in regard to the towns
of New England : " They are the vital principle
of their government, and have proved themselves
the wisest invention ever devised by the wit of
man for the perfect exercise of self-government,
and for its preservation."[3]

The settlers of New England had the advantage of planting in a new country, when there
were no class distinctions or vested rights to
limit the freedom of their action.   The terms
plantation and town were used indiscriminately
in the early years.   Companies of immigrants
were authorized from time to time to settle in
places that had been designated by the Court.
These settlements were recognized in the course
of time as towns or plantations.   Their boundaries were fixed by the Court, sometimes after
consultation with the inhabitants.   The General
Court exercised jurisdiction over the towns, re-

[1] The Making of England. Green, 187.

[2] The Puritan in Holland, England, and America. Douglas
Campbell, i. 143–147.

[3] The American Commonwealth, i. 567.

quiring them to provide themselves with ministers, to provide arms for the inhabitants, and
to provide a place for the safe keeping of arms;
also, to provide standard weights and measures;
and, a little later, to support schools. In 1636 the
General Court defined the powers of The Town
the towns. They were to order their System.
local affairs, dispose of their lands, and to elect
their officers. The voters in town meeting were
those who had been admitted as freemen. Some
who are now living can remember when the
annual town meeting was called the "freeman's
meeting," a reminiscence of the time when there
was a distinction between a citizen and a freeman. The town meeting was usually held in the
meeting-house.

So the New England town meeting came into
existence to meet a definite want of the people
of the town. The little republic grew up in the
plantation of pioneers, and they were trained in
the duties and responsibilities of citizenship in
a free state, while they were doing the business
that belonged to their own community. This
institution of the Puritan fathers has been planted
wherever their descendants have gone, in the
East and the West, with the possible exception
of Oregon. The town meeting had its full
share in the development of the great Republic.
Within the town were gathered the institutions

8

which were especially valued by the fathers. At a time when the means of communication were very limited, the town was the permanent home of the family. They seldom went beyond its bounds. Certain eccentricities of speech and of manner characterized the people of certain towns.

The public schools in the earlier years were supported by the towns. We find these schools in existence at a very early date.
The Public
Schools.
The people had brought their English Bibles across the sea, and they must needs teach their children to read the Bible. In the first years the parents were the teachers.[1] As the towns grew larger, other teachers were employed, and the children were sent to school. The money was sometimes raised by voluntary subscriptions. There is preserved an interesting list of such subscriptions for a school in Boston, made in 1636. Governor Henry Vane gave ten pounds; John Winthrop, ten pounds. There are forty-five names in all, and the amounts vary from three shillings to ten pounds. This paper shows in an interesting way how much those people, some of whom had not been a year within the Colony, cared for schools. As early as 1635 it was voted that Philemon Pormont " shall be intreated to become schoolmaster for the teaching and nurturing of children." We read in Win-

[1] Bradford, 161, 162. Winthrop, ii. 267.

throp's Journal of free schools in Roxbury, whereof every inhabitant bound some house or land for
a yearly payment for the support of schools. In
Boston, he tells us, an order was passed in 1645
to allow fifty pounds a year and a house to the
master, and thirty pounds to an usher. The
children were to be taught to " read and write,
and cypher, and Indians' children were to be
taught freely. . . . Other towns did the like,"
he tells us, "providing maintenance by several
means."[1] In 1647 the Colony was so far advanced that a general law was passed which
required every town of fifty families to employ
a teacher "for all such children as shall resort to
him, to write and read." Every town of one hundred families was required to set up a grammar
school, " the master thereof being able to instruct
youth so far as they may be fitted for the University." No distinction was made in any of the
early laws between boys and girls. The schools
were provided for *all children.* There was a
penalty of £5 to be collected from towns that
should fail to provide schools. It was left with
the inhabitants to determine in what way the
money for the support of schools should be
raised.[2]

Much earlier than this, in October, 1636, the

[1] Winthrop, ii. 267. Bradford, 161, 162.
[2] Massachusetts Records, ii. 203.

General Court voted to raise £400 towards a school or college, the location and character of the buildings to be determined at the next session of the Court. A year later the Court located the college at Newtown, and appointed a committee to oversee the work. A little later the name of the town was changed to Cambridge, after the town of the favorite Puritan University in England.

Harvard College. Mr. John Harvard, of Charlestown, a graduate of Cambridge University, died soon after, leaving half of his estate, worth some £700, and the whole of his library, as an endowment for the College, and in 1639 the Court gave it the name of Harvard College.[1] The first class was graduated in 1642, with nine students. No instance can be found in previous history of so wise and so generous a provision, by a new Colony, for the education of the people, as this which was made by the Puritan fathers of Massachusetts.

In the Colonial times, as we have seen, the voters in town meeting were all members of **Support of Ministers.** the church. The minister was called, and settled by vote of the freemen of the town. The early Puritans believed that ministers should be maintained by the free and voluntary offerings of the people.[2] That was

---

[1] Massachusetts Records, i. 183, 208, 217, 253.
[2] Walker's Creeds and Platforms, 71-79.

the method followed by the Pilgrims at Plymouth in the earlier years. In Boston, the money for building meeting-houses and for the support of ministers was raised by voluntary contributions through most of the Colonial period. The same method was followed in the beginning by the other churches. Winthrop says that it was offensive to some of their people in his time to raise money by taxation for the support of the Gospel.[1] The people were taught that it was the duty, not only of members of the churches, " but of all that were taught in the Word to contribute unto him that teacheth in all good things." As attendance on public worship was required by law, this principle brought all the people under this obligation.

At the same time, the Puritans, unfortunately as it seems to us at this day, brought with them from England the principle of the union of Church and State. They held, as they say in the Cambridge Platform, that "the magistrates are nursing fathers and nursing mothers " to the churches.[2] That is, they did not trust the churches to stand without external aid. There were practical difficulties in raising money to build meeting-houses, and to support ministers in some of the towns.

Union of Church and State.

---

[1] Winthrop, ii. 93.
[2] Cambridge Platform, chap. xi. 4.

The money was not always in the hands of those most willing to contribute. And yet the law required every town to have a minister, and to build a meeting-house. So that, in the course of time, the power of the government was called in to enforce the obligation to support public worship. The friends of the church paid their proportion voluntarily, but those who were indifferent or unfriendly were compelled to pay. After some years, the custom was adopted of collecting the salary of the minister by the same constables who gathered the other taxes. This method of imposing a tax upon the people for the support of the churches did not tend to increase the good will of the people towards the churches. It probably interfered with the natural influence of the ministers upon the people. There grew up in all the Puritan Colonies a class of dissenters, who claimed, and in the end secured, the right to determine for themselves how much they should pay for the support of the church, and to whom they should pay it. The most serious difficulties which the Puritan churches met, in later years, grew out of the assumption, which was unfortunately made in the earlier times, that they were the "Standing order," and as such entitled to certain exclusive rights and privileges.[1]

[1] Massachusetts Records, i. 117–120.

IX

THE year 1634 developed the spirit of the people of the Colony in a number of ways. They had already passed in safety some of the severest trials of a new settle- Growth of the Colony. ment. They had become acclimated in the new country, and had learned to adapt themselves to the necessary conditions of life in the wilderness. They were producing, from year to year, food enough for themselves and their cattle. They were now so numerous that they had ceased to apprehend an attack from the Indians. The people in the towns were learning how to secure their right to a share in the legislation of the Colony. The whole number who had been admitted as freemen was three hundred and sixty-six. This was about twelve per cent of the number of inhabitants,—a small proportion, yet large enough to secure to the people a real voice in moulding the institutions of the Colony. There was no complete code of laws, but some of the most important points had been fixed by the General Court, such as the right of trial by jury, and the equitable assessment of taxes upon property, and not upon the polls, as had been the earlier custom.

At the same time, the growth of the Colony was attracting unfavorable attention from the

English government. King Charles probably did not anticipate, when he granted the charter, that a large and prosperous Colony of English Dissenters would be formed within a few years, which would become a refuge for those who were prosecuted for their Non-Conformity by the Court of High Commission. Archbishop Abbott had died the year before, and Bishop Laud had succeeded him as Primate of all England. He was a member of the Privy Council, and he was using his great influence in the most decided way in opposition to the Dissenters, whether within or without the kingdom. Ten large ships which were ready to sail for Massachusetts were forbidden to depart. An Order in Council was issued, which set forth that "great numbers of His Majesty's subjects were being transported out of this kingdom to the plantation of New England, amongst whom divers persons known to be ill affected, discontented not only with civil but ecclesiastical government here, are observed to resort thither, whereby such confusion and distraction is already grown there, especially in point of religion, as, beside the ruin of the said plantation, cannot but highly tend to the scandal both of Church and State here." [1]

Mr. Cradock, who was regarded as the representative of the Company in England, was ordered

[1] Journal of the Privy Council, February, 1634.

to produce the charter before the Privy Council, that the proceedings of the Colony might be compared with its provisions.[1] He sent a request to Governor Dudley to send the charter to England. These proceedings caused great anxiety in the Colony, but they united the people for the defence of their rights. The Governor replied diplomatically to Mr. Cradock, that he had no authority to transmit the charter without an order from the General Court, which would meet in September. Mr. Edward Winslow of the Plymouth Colony was sent to England to mediate in behalf of the Colony, and to correct the false statements in respect to a violation of the terms of the charter.

The ships had been permitted to sail under certain conditions, and in June fourteen ships had reached Boston and Salem, bringing a large number of Colonists, with provisions and cattle, and also " ordnance, muskets, and powder bought for the public, by moneys given to that end : for godly people in England began to apprehend a special hand of God in raising this plantation and their hearts were generally stirred to come over."[2]

The complaints against the Colony were renewed before the Privy Council, and an alarming report reached Boston to the effect that the charter had been declared void, and that a gen-

[1] Winthrop, i. 135.   [2] Winthrop, i. 138.

eral governor was to be sent over by the King.[1]
This report caused the greatest alarm. It was
believed that if a general governor should be sent
over, with unrestricted powers, the ruin of the
Colony would be inevitable. The people determined at once to resist by force, if necessary, the
execution of such a plan. They were of course
aware that a large part of the people of England
were in sympathy with them, and that the King
could ill afford to add to the discontent which
had been caused by his arbitrary methods of
government. They determined to erect fortifications on Castle Island, and at Charlestown and
Dorchester, and they asked the people at Salem
to fortify their harbor. They appointed a committee, consisting of the Governor and four other
leading men, to " give command for the managing
and ordering of any war that may befall us for
the space of a year next ensuing." Orders were
given for training the companies of militia, and
providing them with efficient arms. Warrants
were sent to all the constables in all the towns
requiring the people to send money, or workmen
to labor three days apiece towards the fort at
Boston. Orders were given to impress men and
carts, to help make carriages and wheels for the
ordnance. A cannonier was appointed for the
fort at Boston. A tax of £600 was also laid

[1] Winthrop, i. 138.

upon the Colony. A beacon was set on Beacon Hill in Boston, and plans were matured for sending messengers to all the towns upon the discovery of the approach of danger.

All the ministers of the Colony, except one who had just arrived, were called together by the Governor and Assistants, and they were asked "what we ought to do if a general governor should be sent out by England." They replied, "that, if a general governor were sent, we ought not to accept him, but to defend our lawful possessions, (if we were able,) otherwise to avoid, or protract."[1] These proceedings show that the people of the Colony were prepared to defend, by force if necessary, their rights under the charter from the King. It was in reliance upon that charter that they had made their homes in the wilderness, and it would have been necessary to break the whole power of the Colony before a ship with a governor from England could have entered their harbors.

They were protected, not only by their own unity and courage, but also by the weakness of their adversaries. Matters in England were rapidly approaching a crisis. The effort of the King to govern without a Parliament was breaking down. He was not prepared at that time to enter into a contest with the Colonists, in which

[1] Winthrop, i. 154.

he would have been sure of the opposition of a large portion of the people of England. Some proceedings were held in the Privy Council. The old Council for New England, of which Gorges and Mason were the most active members, offered to surrender their charter, and requested that the charter of the Company of Massachusetts Bay be revoked, so as to leave the country open for a royal government. In September following, upon the application of the Attorney General of England, a writ of *quo warranto* was issued, and served upon the members of the Company in England. Some charges were presented, and some judgments were entered against them. Preparations were made to send an armed force to Boston. In July, 1637, Sir Ferdinando Gorges was appointed governor general of the whole country. But the governor general could not carry out the orders that had been given him among such a people as the Colonists were, without an army, and the King had no army to send.[1] In the end nothing was done to interrupt the growth of the Colony. The General Court declined to surrender the charter, and after the storm had gone by, it was found that the validity of the charter was still unimpaired, and the Colony continued the government according to its provisions.[2]

[1] Chalmers, i. 37.   [2] Chalmers, i. 55.

X

FOR a number of years after the events just narrated, the course of the Colony of Massachusetts Bay excited little attention in England, because the English people were absorbed in the great contest between the King and the Parliament. That was the opportunity for the Colony to grow, and to develop its political and religious principles. The disturbances in the mother country also tended to increase the number who came to these shores. In 1638, according to Winthrop, twenty ships and at least three thousand persons came to New England.[1] These large accessions gave new courage and enterprise to the pioneers. They began very early to look beyond the bounds of the Colony. Between 1634 and 1640, there were planted three Puritan Colonies besides Massachusetts. In each instance, the planting of a new Colony was the indirect result of a variety of views, such as is likely to show itself among people who have been trained to independent thinking. The early Puritans needed plenty of room. If they had been shut up within a single Colony, with a single type of government, they would have been uncomfortable.

Development of the Colonies.

[1] Winthrop, i. 268.

One of these newer colonies was that of Rhode
Island, under the lead of Roger Williams, who

Settlement of
Rhode Island.
arrived at Boston in February, 1631.
Winthrop notes his arrival in his
Journal, and speaks of him as a "godly minister."[1] He was probably a native of Wales, and
was not far from thirty years old, when he came

Roger Williams.
to Massachusetts. He had been a
student at Pembroke College, Cambridge, where he took the degree of Bachelor of
Arts in 1627. He was a man of unusual ability
and scholarship. He was probably ordained in
the Church of England, and afterwards became
a Non-Conformist. He said, in one of his letters,
" Truly it was bitter as death to me when Bishop
Laud pursued me out of this land, and my conscience was persuaded against the national Church,
and ceremonies, and bishops."[2]

On arriving in Massachusetts, he found himself
out of sympathy with many things in the government. It would have been better if he had gone
at once to Plymouth, for he was at that time a
rigid Separatist, and could have no communion
with the church in Boston, because its members
would not make a public declaration of their
repentance for having had communion with the
churches of England while they lived there.[3] He

[1] Winthrop, i. 41.   [3] Winthrop, i. 52.
[2] Benedict, i. 473. Elton's Life, 89.

did not approve of some of the laws of the Colony. He declared that the magistrate ought not to punish violations of the Sabbath, or any other offences "against the laws of the first table." In fact, the government of the Colony had to deal at that time with a very positive Dissenter, who took no pains to conceal his opinions. The church in Salem invited him to become their teacher. The Court of the Colony sent a letter of remonstrance to Salem against his settlement, on account of the opinions he had set forth, and this seems to have caused some delay in the proceedings.[1] After a little time we find him in Plymouth, where "he exercised his gifts," and where "he was admitted a member of the church, and his teaching was well approved."[2] He seems to have been an assistant of the pastor, Mr. Ralph Smith. A year or two later, Bradford wrote that Mr. Williams "began to fall into some strange opinions, and from opinions to practice." This caused controversy and discontent in the Pilgrim Church, on which account he left them abruptly, receiving however a letter of dismission to the church in Salem. For some time he was an assistant to the pastor, Mr. Skelton; and, after his death, he was chosen pastor

[1] Hutchinson's History of Massachusetts, i. 40. Felt's Ecclesiastical History of New England, i. 149.

[2] Bradford, 310.

in his place. He had a short and troubled ministry there, and in April, 1635, he was summoned to appear before the Court of Assistants, and was charged with certain errors in his preaching. The errors were condemned by the magistrates, and by the ministers who were called in to assist the magistrates. They related to the authority of magistrates, and to the administering of oaths to persons who were not regenerate, and to joining in worship with such persons. Time was given Mr. Williams for consideration, but, as he gave no satisfaction, at the next session of the General Court, in September, 1635, he was ordered to depart out of the jurisdiction of the Colony within six weeks next ensuing. Afterwards permission was given him to remain through the winter. He spent the time in making preparations for a new settlement, which he proposed to plant on Narragansett Bay, and in enlisting a company of adherents. He lived a part of the winter among the Indians at Sowans, now Warren, and in the spring he removed to what is now Providence,[1] where he purchased a tract of land from the Indians, which he paid for by mortgaging his house in Salem. He gave land freely to all who joined the Colony.

There are few at this day who would deny that the banishment of Roger Williams was one of the

[1] Winthrop, i. 158–176.

mistakes of the Puritans. It is not necessary to agree with all the opinions which he expressed, or to approve the methods he employed in setting them forth. But a strong Colony of intelligent Christian men, who had expatriated themselves that they might enjoy liberty of conscience, could well afford to tolerate so intelligent and conscientious a Dissenter as Roger Williams. If he had been permitted to work out freely his principles in Massachusetts, it is very likely that he would have secured the adherence of the good people of that Colony to those principles of religious liberty which have made his name illustrious.

Williams called the place where he settled Providence, from "a sense of God's merciful providence unto me in my distress." The Colony of Rhode Island. The little Puritan Colony which he founded was bound together by a simple compact. "We do promise," they said, "to subject ourselves in active and passive obedience to all such orders or agreements as shall be made for the public good of the body in an orderly way by the major consent of the present inhabitants, masters of families, incorporated together into a township, and such others as they shall admit into the same, only in civil things." [1]

Two years later a settlement was begun on the

[1] Rhode Island Colonial Records, i. 14.

island of Rhode Island.[1]   In 1642 Mr. Williams
was sent to England as the agent of the Colony,
and he secured a patent for the incorporation
of Providence Plantation.   In 1663 another and
more satisfactory charter was secured from the
King for " Rhode Island and Providence Plantations," and this charter continued to be the
fundamental law of Rhode Island till 1842.

XI

A LITTLE before the time when the settlement
of Rhode Island was begun, a request was presented to the General Court of Massachusetts, at its session in September,
1634, by Thomas Hooker and others of Newtown, for permission to remove to the Connecticut
Valley.   They gave as the reasons for this request, first, the want of accommodation for their
cattle, because the towns were set too near together; second, the fruitfulness of Connecticut,
and the liability that the Dutch would possess it;
and thirdly, "The strong bent of their spirits
to remove thither." [2]   Of these reasons, the last
was probably the most potent.   There were men
in Newtown, and in some other plantations of
the Colony, who did not favor the restriction of
the suffrage to members of the churches, or the

The Colony of
Connecticut.

---

[1] Rhode Island Colonial Records, i. 137.
[2] Winthrop, i. 140.

accumulation of power in the hands of the magistrates. Mr. Cotton had already declared that democracy was no fit government either for church or commonwealth. Governor Winthrop, in a letter to Thomas Hooker, had advocated the restriction of the suffrage, by saying that " the best part is always the least: and of that best part the wiser part is always the lesser." Hooker had replied that, " in matters which concern the common good, a general council, chosen by all, to transact businesses which concern all, I conceive most suitable to rule, and most safe for relief of the whole." Those who were the leaders in planting a new colony on the banks of the Connecticut were intent upon a truly democratic government, based upon free suffrage.

Democratic Ideas of Hooker.

The request of the people of Newtown was not granted at first. The next year, however, the Court gave leave " to the inhabitants of Watertown, Roxbury, and Dorchester to remove to any place they should desire to, provided they continue still under this government." [1] The next year commissioners were appointed by the General Court for the government of the people who should remove to Connecticut.

In the course of the summer of 1635 a small company from Dorchester found their way to

[1] Winthrop, i. 160.

Windsor, where the Plymouth Colony had already begun a settlement. They purchased the right of this company for the sum of £50, including what the Plymouth people had paid the Indians for their lands. Late in the autumn another party of sixty persons, including women and children, driving cattle before them, set out for the new Colony. They experienced great hardships on account of the severity of the weather, and a portion of the party returned. In June, 1636, a large party from Newtown, under the lead of Hooker and Stone, set out. They drove a herd of a hundred and sixty cattle, which grazed as they journeyed and supplied them with milk. Early berries, which they found growing by the way, gave variety to their diet. The journey was over in a fortnight. Mrs. Hooker, by reason of illness, was carried on a litter. Other companies came during the summer from Dorchester and Watertown. Their ministers came with them; — Mr. Henry Smith from Watertown, and Mr. Wareham from Dorchester. Within a year the population of the towns on the Connecticut was estimated at eight hundred, including two hundred and fifty adult men, distributed among the three towns of Hartford, Wethersfield, and Windsor. A little earlier in the season, William Pynchon of Roxbury, with a small company of pioneers, made his way through

Emigration to Connecticut.

the wilderness, following the Bay Path, and began a settlement which they called Agawam, afterwards changed to Springfield.[1] The four settlements were organized as independent towns in the beginning. In May, 1639, a General Court was held at Hartford, made up of fifteen members, chosen from the several towns.[2] At this meeting of the Court, Mr. Hooker preached a memorable sermon in which he said : " The foundation of authority is laid in the free consent of the people: the choice of public magistrates belongs unto the people, by God's own ordinance : they who have power to appoint officers and magistrates have the right to set the bounds and limitations of the power and place of those who are called."[3]

In January, 1639, the freemen of the different towns met at Hartford, and adopted a written constitution for the government of the Colony. It is said to be "the earliest example of a written constitution, constituting a government, and defining its powers."[4] It was an independent government, not recognizing any external human authority, on either side of the ocean. It gives the right of suffrage to all such persons as shall be adjudged to be worthy of it by the freemen of

[1] The Puritan in England and New England. Byington, 191-218.

[2] Connecticut Colonial Records, i. 9.

[3] Palfrey, i. 536, note.

[4] Dr. Bacon, Early Constitutional History of Connecticut, 5, 6.

the towns, and who take an oath of allegiance to the commonwealth. It provides for two meetings a year of the freemen of the Colony. At the meeting in April of each year they were to elect by ballot a Governor, (who must be a member of some church,) and as many magistrates and other public officers as should be found requisite. There were to be four deputies from each of the existing towns; and from towns subsequently formed as many as the General Court should determine. The General Court was to consist of the Governor and at least four magistrates, and the deputies from the towns. It should have power to make laws, to grant levies, to admit freemen, to dispose of lands, to call any officer or other person to account for any misdemeanor, and to deal with any other matter that concerns the commonwealth, except election of magistrates, which was to be done by the whole body of freemen. In the absence of special laws, "the rule of the word of God" was to be followed.[1] This constitution was that of an independent state, and it continued in force a hundred and eighty years. The Colony was, by its terms, a federation of independent towns, not only of such as existed at that time, but of all towns that should come into being on that territory. This Constitution of Connecticut, framed by a few Puritan pioneers on the borders

[1] Connecticut Colonial Records, i. 20–25

of the wilderness two hundred and sixty years ago, contains the germs of the Constitution of the United States. " The little federal republic," says Mr. John Fiske, " grew till it became the strongest political structure on the continent: . . . and, in the chief crisis of the Federal Convention of 1787, Connecticut, with her compromise, which secured equal State representation in one branch of the national government, and popular representation in the other, played the controlling part." [1]

In the early months of 1638 another Puritan Colony was founded at Quinnipiack, on Long Island Sound. The leader of the party was Theophilus Eaton, an original member and an officer of the Massachusetts Company. He was a wealthy merchant of London, a parishioner of John Davenport, who had been a Non-Conforming minister of St. Stephen's Church in London. Mr. Davenport was a man of learning and eloquence, who had been driven from his parish by Bishop Laud. Eaton had come to Settlement of Boston with a party of friends, in two New Haven. ships, prepared to begin a new settlement. His company included three ministers, — John Davenport, Samuel Eaton, and Peter Pruden. The voyage from Boston took them two weeks. They kept their first Sabbath under the shelter of an oak, where they listened to a sermon from Mr.

[1] Beginnings of New England, 128.

Davenport. A few days later, they entered into a civil compact, in which they agreed to be governed by the rules which the Scriptures hold out, not only in the gathering and ordering of a church, but also in all civil affairs. In June they adopted a form of government, which was more conservative than any other in New England. It provided that the suffrage should be limited to members of the church; and that they should be governed in all matters, civil as well as ecclesiastical, by the rules which are set forth in the Scriptures. Twelve men were chosen, who were to select seven of their own number to begin the church. The church members were constituted freemen, and they elected Mr. Eaton a magistrate for one year, and four others as deputies. A General Court of the new independent state was held in October: land which had been purchased from the Indians was divided into lots, which were distributed among the members of the Colony; and arrangements were made for building a meeting-house, for regulating the prices of commodities and of labor, for defence against hostile Indians, and for determining who should be permitted to become members of the Colony. The next year the name of the town was changed to New Haven.

A large number of Puritans of similar sentiments came into the new Colony within a few years. Milford and Guilford were settled in 1639. In 1643 these independent towns were confederated, and the General Court of the Colony of New Haven began to hold semi-annual sessions.[1] Mr. Eaton was chosen Governor, and Stephen Goodyeare was chosen Deputy Governor.

While these new Colonies were forming in the southern parts of New England, there arose in Massachusetts a controversy more The Colony of serious than the one connected with Massachusetts. Roger Williams, and one which led to a still wider extension of the Puritan settlements. It grew out of the teachings of Mrs. Anne Hutchinson, who came to Boston in September, 1634. She had known Mr. Cotton while in England, and had been an attendant at his church. One motive in coming to Massachusetts was her desire to attend his ministry. She is described by Winthrop as a "woman of ready wit, and bold spirit."[2] She must have had a good deal of ability, and an unusual power to draw others after her.

Some time after coming to Boston she commenced holding meetings for women, at her own house. These meetings were attended every week by large numbers, from Boston and the other towns in the neighborhood. She conducted them herself, and in the course of time

[1] New Haven Colonial Records, 57–116.
[2] Winthrop, i. 200.

she began to set forth religious opinions, which
were not new, but which were very different from
those which were preached by the ministers of
that Colony. She made much of a certain inner
light and assurance, which came, as she said,
from the indwelling of the Divine Spirit. Much
of what she said reminds one of the teachings
of the Quakers, and of the German Mystics of
the fourteenth century. She believed that she
had a very close and intimate relation with the
Almighty, which enabled her to speak by direct
revelation, and to prophesy future events. She
became very much opposed to Mr. Wilson, the
pastor of the church, and turned her back upon
him when he arose to preach. She criticised the
most of the ministers of the Colony, as " under
a covenant of works," while she declared that Mr.
Cotton and Mr. Wheelwright, and such others as
seemed to agree with her, were under a covenant of grace. Mr. Winthrop says that she
brought with her " two dangerous errors : the
first, that the person of the Holy Ghost dwells
in a justified person ; and the second, that no
sanctification can help to evidence to us our
justification." At one time she numbered among
her followers Governor Vane, Mr. Cotton, the
teacher of the church, and nearly all the members except Governor Winthrop and Mr. Wilson,
the pastor. The fact that so well educated a

man as John Cotton gave his approval to some of her teachings indicates that they were not quite absurd.

Things were growing worse every day. The churches of the Colony were involved in the controversy. The people were divided into hostile parties, and the powers of the government were weakened. After about two years of controversy, measures were taken, under the lead of Governor Winthrop, to bring the trouble to an end. All the ministers of the Colony came together to consider what should be done. By their advice, the General Court summoned a Synod, to be composed of all the ministers of the Puritan Colonies. This body met at Newtown, August 30, 1637, and continued in session three weeks. Thomas Hooker of Hartford was one of the Moderators. A list of eighty-two doubtful teachings was drawn up, and these were all condemned by the Synod as erroneous. These included most of the opinions which had been advocated by Mrs. Hutchinson and her followers. If this decision had been accepted by Mrs. Hutchinson, or if she had been willing to cease the agitation of these matters, there would have been an end of the troubles. But she continued to hold meetings twice a week at her house, and kept up the excitement among the people.

Synod of 1637.

In the end, the General Court determined to put an end to the contention. It brought the leading agitators to trial, as disturbers of the peace of the Colony. Some of them were disfranchised; others were sent away from the Colony. Mrs. Hutchinson was tried for continuing the meetings at her house after the decision of the Synod, and for railing at the ministers. The trial lasted two days. She defended herself with great energy, and laid claim among other things, to prophetic inspiration. At the conclusion, "the Court proceeded and banished her: but because it was winter, they committed her to a private house, where she was well provided, and her own friends and the elders were permitted to go to her, but none else."[1]

As the result of these proceedings her adherents were scattered among the Colonies. Mrs. Hutchinson, with some of her followers, joined the Colony of Rhode Island. Mr. Wheelwright went north, and began a settlement at Exeter, within what is now New Hampshire. Others settled at Dover and at Hampton.[2] And so the contention in Boston came to an end. It is fair to state that the proceedings against Mrs. Hutchinson seem to have been on account of the

[1] Winthrop, i. 146.   Massachussetts Colonial Records, i. 207.
[2] New Hampshire Historical Collections, i. 299.   Charles Francis Adams, Three Episodes of Massachusetts History.

factious and turbulent way in which she promulgated her opinions, rather than on account of the opinions themselves.

XII

FROM the time of the landing of the Pilgrims at Plymouth, there had been friendly relations, for the most part, between the white men and the Indians in both Colonies, down to the year 1636. One reason was that the number of Indians in the vicinity of Plymouth and of Boston was not large. The officers of the Colonies had always recognized the rights of the Indians, and had purchased so much of the land as they needed to occupy. Whenever white men had treated the Indians with injustice, they had been severely punished. If the settlements had not extended beyond the eastern part of the territory, where the whites were able to protect each other, it is probable that these friendly relations would have continued for many years longer.

The extension of the settlements to Narragansett Bay, and to the valley of the Connecticut, brought the Colonists into conflict with the large and powerful tribes of Indians whose country extended from Narragansett Bay to the Connecticut. That country had a large population of Indians. In 1636, some Indians of Block

Island captured a small vessel on Long Island Sound, and murdered John Oldham, whom they **The Pequot War.** found on board, and captured two boys who were with him.   Governor Vane sent a messenger to demand that the murderers should be punished.   As nothing came of it, he sent Endicott, the last of August, with ninety men, who ravaged the island, without finding the Indians, and then sailed to Fort Saybrook, a military post at the mouth of the Connecticut.   Later, he attacked the Pequots on the mainland, burned a large number of wigwams, and returned to Boston without the loss of a man.

All this served only to irritate the Indians. The Colonists in Connecticut were kept in constant alarm through the winter.   Indians hung about the settlements to capture such of the settlers as ventured to go to a distance from their dwellings.   These they tortured and murdered. In the spring of 1637, the Indians made an attack upon Wethersfield, killed nine persons, and carried away some captives.   In all some thirty of the settlers were killed during the year.

At that time there were only three hundred white men in Connecticut.   Ninety of them were enlisted for a campaign against the Indians, under Captain John Mason, a soldier of experience and of courage.   A call for aid was made upon Ply-

mouth and Massachusetts. Roger Williams used
his influence with the Narragansetts to prevent
them from joining the Pequots against the English, and by his persuasion the chiefs of the
Narragansetts made a treaty of alliance with
the Colony of Massachusetts. Only twenty Massachusetts men, under Captain Underhill, had
reached the seat of war when the active campaign was begun.

Captain Mason, with the Connecticut men,
and with a force of Indian allies, went directly
into the country of the Pequots, and attacked
one of their strongholds so early in the morning
that he took the Indians by surprise. It was a
stockade with two narrow entrances, one on the
east and the other on the west. Mason divided
his small force and attacked the Indians at both
entrances. His men forced their way into the
fort and prevented the escape of the people.
The Indians defended themselves with vigor,
but the wigwams were set on fire. The English
were well armed, and more than six hundred Indians perished by the fire and by the sword within
a few hours. A party of two hundred Pequots
from the other stockade attacked the little force
under Mason later in the day, but they were
beaten off. He soon met Captain Patrick with
forty Massachusetts men, who had been coming
with the utmost speed to his assistance. A

larger party from Massachusetts was sent later.
The war was continued through the summer.
In the end the Pequots who remained surrendered
to the English, and were distributed between
other Indian tribes, and this warlike nation ceased
to have a separate existence.

The Pequot war served to draw the Colonies
into a closer sympathy with each other. It impressed the savage tribes with a sense of the
immense superiority of the English as soldiers.
The Colonists also learned a lesson of the great
value to their own peace of a good understanding with their savage neighbors. As a result,
for more than the lifetime of a generation, until
King Philip's War, there was no serious trouble
between the white men and the Indians.[1]

XIII

THE Long Parliament met at Westminster,
November 3, 1640. This was a marked period in
the history, not only of Great Britain,
but of New England. With the call-
ing of that Parliament the friends of liberty in
the old country were assured of a fair field for the
struggle in behalf of the rights of Englishmen.
The meeting of that Parliament also marked the

*The Long Par-
liament.*

[1] History of Connecticut, by Alexander Johnston, 34–55. Sand-
ford's Connecticut, 21–28. Trumbull's Connecticut, 59–87.

end of the immigration to this country. Between 1620, when the Pilgrims landed at Plymouth, and 1640, about twenty-one thousand persons had come across the sea to New England. They had come over in two hundred and ninety-eight ships. The cost of transporting the people, and their goods, and their cattle, was not far from half a million dollars. During the next century and a quarter, very few came from the mother country. For the next twenty years a considerable number went back to England to take a part in the contest that was going on there.

"God had sifted three kingdoms," said William Stoughton, half a century later, "that he might send choice grain into the wilderness." They were of pure English blood. Mr. Savage, our highest authority on such a subject, states that ninety-eight per cent of the people in New England at that time were of strictly English descent. Now and then we come upon the name of a Welshman among the New England Puritans, but very few at that day were of Scottish or Irish descent. The immigration consisted largely of English country gentlemen. They were thrifty and prosperous people, — the friends of law and order, as well as of freedom. It is not unreasonable to suppose that one fourth of the present population of the United States is descended from the twenty-one thousand Pilgrims and Puritans who came to these shores from England and Holland.

At the close of the Pequot War, some magistrates and ministers of Connecticut held a conference with the authorities at Boston with regard to a Confederation. Later, Massachusetts proposed a plan for a Union, to which Connecticut did not agree. In 1642, Connecticut made overtures to Plymouth, New Haven, and Massachusetts, and in May, 1643, commissioners from these four Colonies met at Boston and agreed upon Articles of Confederation, which were afterwards ratified by the General Courts of the four Colonies. They took the name of the United Colonies of New England. It was a federative union, not an absorption of the separate Colonies. The preamble to the Articles of Confederation states that the people in the different Colonies had come to America for the same purpose, which was "to advance the kingdom of Christ, and to enjoy the liberties of the Gospel in purity and peace." It states the reasons for union to be the unexpected spread of the settlements over the country, the peril from the Indians, the danger from the settlements of other people of strange languages to the north and the south, and the distractions in England. Each Colony retained its power to control its internal affairs. The Articles provided for the

The Confederation.

appointment of two Commissioners from each Colony, who must be members of churches. These Commissioners were to meet annually, on the first Thursday in September, and as much oftener as should be necessary, in the different Colonies, in rotation, beginning in Boston, to provide for common interests and for common defence. Each Colony was to provide men, provisions, and other expenditures in the proportion of its male inhabitants between sixteen and sixty. The Commissioners were to have power to call upon the Colonies to furnish their respective quotas. It was provided that fugitives from one Colony might be arrested by the authorities of another Colony.[1] The Confederation was to have entire control over all dealings with the Indians, or other foreign powers.

The Colonies north of Massachusetts were not invited to become members of the Confederacy, nor the Colony of Rhode Island. This Confederacy did not exist by authority of the King or of the Parliament. The Articles of Confederation served as models for the Continental Congress when they framed the Articles of Confederation of all the Colonies in 1781. At the date of the Confederation of the four Colonies, Massachusetts had about fifteen thousand people, and the other Colonies about three thousand each.

[1] Winthrop, ii. 101-106.

The influence of the Confederation upon the Colonies of New England was very great. It promoted an exchange of opinions, which in those scattered settlements was of great importance. It tended to limit the prevalence of local peculiarities. It tended, on the whole, towards strengthening the democratic tendencies among the people, and limiting the aristocratic influences which had been imported from the old country. It increased the feeling of security, and helped the development of popular institutions. From the date of the Confederation, the difference between the Pilgrim Colony and the Colonies of the Puritans was less perceptible than in the earlier years.

At the date of the Confederation there were forty-nine towns in the four Colonies. Plymouth had eight, Massachusetts thirty, Connecticut six, and New Haven five. Each Colony was a federation of little republics, all of which were represented in the Colonial government. They appointed their selectmen and their other officers to have charge of the general business of the town. The basis of the suffrage was not uniform. In Plymouth and Connecticut the freemen conferred the franchise upon such citizens as they esteemed most worthy of it. In Massachusetts they were restricted to those who were members of the churches. Taxes

Government of the Colonies.

were assessed upon property, not upon the polls. Each Colony had a Governor, and all but Plymouth had a Deputy Governor, elected annually by the freemen. Plymouth and Massachusetts had boards of Assistants. In Connecticut and New Haven these were called Magistrates. In each Colony Deputies were elected by the freemen of the towns, who were members of the General Court of the Colony. In 1644, the Deputies in Massachusetts became a co-ordinate branch of the General Court, meeting by themselves. This change was made in Connecticut in 1645.[1]

Courts of Justice were established in each Colony in its early years. At first the Governor and the Assistants were the magistrates. A little later, there were local courts. Justices of the Peace were appointed in Massachusetts during its first year. Juries were called for the trial of cases in all the Colonies except New Haven.

Plymouth had a code of laws in 1632. Massachusetts adopted "The Body of Liberties" in 1641. It had been drawn up by Mr. Nathaniel Ward, pastor of the church at Ipswich. He had been a lawyer while in England.[2] A part of this

---

[1] Connecticut Colonial Records, i. 119.

[2] See a fuller account in The Puritan in England and New England, 255.

code was adopted by Connecticut in 1643. In New Haven, "the judicial laws of God, as they were delivered by Moses," were the rule for the guidance of the courts. In all the Colonies there were laws, such as existed in England at that time, to regulate the prices of commodities and of labor.[1] In New England, as in Virginia and in England, the support of the ministers and attendance upon public worship were required by law.[2]

The churches in all the Colonies were organized after the Congregational way. Each church was independent. The officers of a Congregational Church at that time were a pastor and a teacher, who were both preachers, of equal authority; one or more ruling elders, and one or more deacons, who had charge of financial affairs, and especially the duty of providing for the poor.[3] In 1643 there were about eighty ministers in New England.[4] The places of worship were called meeting-houses. As bells were seldom to be had, the people were called together by the beat of the drum. The men were seated on one side of the audience room, and the women on the other. The first service of public worship began

[1] Macaulay's History of England, chapter iii.
[2] Massachusetts Colonial Records, i. 140.
[3] The Puritan in England and New England, 146–162.
[4] Winthrop, i. 265, note.

at about nine o'clock in the forenoon, and the second at one or two in the afternoon. The services consisted of the singing of the Psalms from a metrical version, by the congregation, without the aid of musical instruments; unwritten prayers, the exposition of the Scriptures, and sermons. Children were baptized in the meeting-house, commonly on the Sunday following their birth. The sacraments were administered at frequent intervals. Marriages were performed by the magistrates. The dead were buried by their neighbors and friends, without any religious rites.

In the earlier years the houses of the people were built of logs, with thatched roofs. The floors were of clay or of split logs. The ground floor was divided by partitions into two or three rooms. The fireplace was of rough stones, and the chimneys were of boards, plastered inside with clay. Lumber was sawed by hand in saw-pits. Later, sawmills were constructed.

In the second period, the better class of houses were of two stories. The frame timbers were of oak and very heavy. The windows were two and a half to three feet long, and eighteen inches wide. The glass was in diamond panes of three or four inches. The windows were sometimes on hinges. The principal article of food in the early days was

Indian corn. Wild game was abundant. Bean porridge, and hasty pudding and milk, were also very common articles of food. Beer was brewed in families, and the orchards soon yielded an abundance of cider. Wine and rum were very commonly used in those days, although, if we may credit the statements of early travellers, intoxication was uncommon. The dress of the largest number of the people was plain. Economy in dress was enjoined, not only in moral teachings, but by the laws of the Colony. The General Court passed orders forbidding the "excessive wearing of lace, and other superfluities."[1]

The ministers of that time exercised a great deal of influence. They preached to the people, catechised the children, visited at the homes of the Colonists, and were constantly called upon for advice and counsel. They usually wore the gown and bands in the pulpit. It was the practice of the General Court of Massachusetts to propound important questions to the ministers, which they answered in writing. "The proceeding," says William D. Northend, LL. D., "was similar to that requiring the justices of the Supreme Judicial Court to give to either branch of the Legislature, or to the Governor and Council, upon request, opinions upon important questions of law." He adds: "The opinions given

[1] Massachusetts Colonial Records, i. 274.

by the ministers which have been preserved
are very able, and will, in logic and sound rea-
soning, bear a not unfavorable comparison with
opinions of the justices, given under this provision of our Constitution." [1]

XIV

THE first meeting of the Commissioners of the
Confederacy of New England was held in Boston,
September 7, 1643. Edward Winslow   First Meeting of
and William Collier were there from   the Confederacy.
Plymouth; John Winthrop and Thomas Dudley,
from Massachusetts; George Fenwick and Edward Hopkins, from Connecticut; and Theophilus Eaton and Thomas Gregson, from New
Haven. Winthrop was elected President. The
matters that came before the body were of great
importance. The Commissioners agreed to the
incorporation of Milford into the Colony of New
Haven, and of Southampton into the Colony of
Connecticut. The Indian question engaged much
of their attention. The Narragansetts and the
Mohegans were the most powerful tribes of southern New England. They had both been on
friendly terms with the Colonists, and were both
jealous of each other. There were strong reasons
for the opinion that the Narragansetts were plan-

[1] The Bay Colony, 204, note.

ning a general massacre of the English. Their chief, Miantonomo, was summoned to Boston, where he made promises that were for the time satisfactory. There were contentions between Samuel Gorton and some other troublesome white men, on the one hand, and the Indians, about the purchase of a section of land, which tended to make the troubles more serious.[1] These things all came before the Commissioners of the Confederacy. They were satisfied that there was a conspiracy to destroy the white men of the Colonies, and that the Narragansett chief was at the head of it. They recommended to the Colonies to make preparations for war. But in the end the two great tribes went to war with each other. Miantonomo was taken prisoner, and, after some delay, was put to death by his Indian captors, with the assent of the white men, and so for the time the danger was averted.

The Confederacy also dealt with the other European Colonies in America. The Swedish Governor in Delaware had ill treated some New Haven people who had begun business within his Colony, and New Haven made a complaint to the Commissioners. A letter from Winthrop brought a promise from the Swedes that they would not molest any visitors who should bring authority

[1] Rhode Island Historical Collections, ii. 191.   Massachusetts Historical Collections, xxi. 2.

from the Commissioners. The Dutch at New Amsterdam complained of encroachments by Connecticut upon their rights. The Commissioners succeeded in adjusting this matter without serious trouble. The French on the north were in conflict among themselves. La Tour and D'Aulnay both sought the aid of Massachusetts. The Federal Commissioners, at their second session, made a declaration of neutrality, saying "that no jurisdiction within this Confederation shall permit any voluntaries to go forth in a warlike way against any people whatsoever, without order and direction of the Commissioners of the several Colonies."

The second meeting lasted a fortnight, or longer. The Commissioners advised the General Courts of the Colonies to make permanent provision by law for the maintenance of the clergy. They recommended that every family throughout the plantations should make a contribution every year toward the maintenance of poor students in the College at Cambridge. They authorized Massachusetts to receive Martha's Vineyard into its jurisdiction. They forbade the selling of arms and ammunition to the Indians. They provided for a yearly census of all the males from sixteen years to sixty, in each Colony; and they instructed their President to engage an agent to lay out the best course for a road from Boston to the Connecticut River. They also asked the ministers to inquire what measures could be taken to provide a confession of doctrine and discipline to be used in the churches. In these very decided and well considered ways the Confederacy of the Colonies began its work.

XV

THE next important event in the Colonies was the meeting of the Synod which framed the Cambridge Platform. The general purpose of the Synod was "to consult and advise of one uniform order of discipline in the churches agreeable to the Scriptures." The form of church polity which had grown up among the Pilgrims and the Puritans was comparatively new in modern times. It was a decided departure, not only from the prelatical episcopal system, but also from Presbyterianism, and from the polity of

The Cambridge Synod. most of the other churches of the Reformation. There were some people of influence in New England who did not approve of the Independent churches that had grown up here. There was an increasing number who objected to limiting the franchise to members of the churches. A vigorous effort was in progress to induce the Parliament to impose the Presbyterian system upon these Colonies.

The Westminster Assembly was in session, with a majority of Presbyterians, and it had agreed upon a statement of church polity that was strictly Presbyterian. But in New England it was generally maintained that the members of the church should decide questions relating to the admission of members, the discipline of the churches, and the selection of ministers.[1] John Cotton had prepared his "Way of the Churches of Christ in New England," and his "Keyes of the Kingdom of Heaven," in which he had set forth the views commonly held by the churches of the Pilgrims and the Puritans. Thomas Hooker of Connecticut, who was perhaps the ablest of the ministers, had also prepared his "Survey of the Summe of Church Discipline." In this treatise Hooker brought out more plainly than the earlier writers had done the relation of the Independent churches to each other, and the need of councils to express the fellowship of the churches. In 1647, the church in Windsor, Connecticut, adopted its creed covenant, which was one of the earliest Confessions of Faith in New England.

It was fully time for setting forth the principles of church government on which the New England churches could unite. There had been some decided advance since the first churches

---

[1] Walker's Creeds and Platforms, 138, 139.

were organized. There were already treatises prepared by individual ministers. But there was need of a standard for all the churches. The preparation of such a standard would require the united wisdom of the best men in all the Colonies. So, in accordance with the custom of the time, some of the ministers asked the General Court of Massachusetts to convene a Synod. The Magistrates (or the Upper House) passed an act for that purpose. The Deputies of the towns (or the Lower House) objected, on the ground that the civil magistrates have no right to exercise authority over the churches. This act of the Deputies was very significant, as an indication that the power of the Theocracy was waning. The matter was settled by a compromise, according to which the act of the General Court took the form of an invitation, instead of a command.[1] The General Court of Massachusetts invited the several churches of the Colony to meet at Cambridge on the 1st of September next ensuing, by their Elders and Messengers, in a public Assembly, to consider "such questions of church government and discipline" as they shall think needful, so as to set forth "one forme of government and discipline," such as "they judge agreeable to the Holy Scriptures." The General Court directed that copies of this invi-

[1] Winthrop, ii. 330–332.

tation be sent to all the churches within the Confederation, and that they be desired to send their
Elders and Messengers to this Assembly, who
should have the same rights and privileges in
the body as those of Massachusetts.

All the churches of Massachusetts but four
were represented in the Assembly or Synod
when it met at Cambridge the 1st   Meeting of the
of September, 1646 (O. S.).   Two of   Synod.
the absent churches sent their representatives
a few days later,[1] so that the Synod at that
time contained representatives from twenty-eight
churches of Massachusetts, two of New Hampshire, and a few, we do not know how many,
from the other Colonies.   The Synod appointed
John Cotton and Richard Mather of Massachusetts, and Ralph Partridge of Plymouth, to prepare, each one by himself, a model of church
government for submission to the Synod at its
next session.   The body then adjourned to the
8th of June of the following year, after a session
of only fourteen days.

The Synod met again, June 8, 1647, and after
a short session adjourned to the 16th of August,
1648.   This last session did its work rapidly.
The " Platform of Church Discipline," drawn up
by Richard Mather of Dorchester, was adopted,
with some amendments.   The Synod also ac-

---

[1] Creeds and Platforms, 168.

cepted the Confession of Faith of the Westminster Assembly, "for the substance thereof," as the doctrinal standard. They had thus put the churches on a platform which was accepted as orthodox by the English Puritans, and they had set forth the Congregational method of discipline and government in a consistent and logical order, such that they could meet successfully the charges of looseness and of heresy which had been put forth as reasons for the interference of the English Parliament.

The Platform was accepted by the General Court, and commended to the churches. " It is," The Cambridge the Court said, "for the substance Platform. thereof that we have practised, and do believe." It is two hundred and fifty years since it was adopted, and for a considerable part of that time it has been the recognized standard of the Congregational Churches. It sets forth the power of each local church to control its local affairs, under the direction of the New Testament. It emphasizes the relation of the churches to each other in fellowship, and it provides for the calling of Ecclesiastical Councils, for advice on matters in which all the churches have an interest. This part of the Platform has been more fully developed in modern times, and the Mutual and Ex parte Councils have become characteristic features of the Congregational Churches.

In respect to the power of the magistrate in ecclesiastical matters, the provisions of the Platform have been essentially modified since the union of Church and State has been given up. All that part of the Congregational system which has to do with the missionary work, at home and abroad, has been developed in later periods.

About the time when the Cambridge Synod was doing its work, there was the beginning of a very important missionary enterprise among the Indians. The Pilgrims **Missions to the Indians.** and the Puritans had made the conversion of the native tribes to the Christian faith prominent among the reasons for coming to this country. They had done a good deal of work for the Indians from year to year. We should especially note that Roger Williams learned the language of the Indians, and preached to them with a good degree of success. In 1632 he published his "Key to the Languages of the Indians." In 1636 the General Court of the Plymouth Colony passed an order to encourage the preaching of the Gospel among the Indians. In 1644 Massachusetts asked the ministers to point out the best methods of teaching the truths of religion to the Indians. Two years later the Court asked the ministers to choose two of their number, every year, to preach to the Indians in their own language. About the same time, Thomas Mayhew, and his son of the same name, began to preach to the Indians on Martha's Vineyard. The work was carried on by the father, the son, and the grandson for many years, and a large number of Indians were gathered into Christian communities and churches.

In 1646, John Eliot, one of the ministers of the church in Roxbury, began to preach to the Indians at Nonantum. He translated the Bible into the language of the Massachusetts tribe, and gathered the Christian Indians into communities at Nonantum and Natick, and at other places. A large number of the natives were taught to read. They were gathered into schools and churches and congregations. There was a considerable number of well educated Indian teachers and preachers. Good people in all the Colonies were enlisted in the work, and there was a prospect at one time that the Indians of New England would accept the religion and the civilization of their white neighbors. King Philip's War, however, interrupted the missions. Many of the Indians lost their lives during the war. Those who remained had become discouraged, and to a degree demoralized. After that time, the native tribes were scattered among the more distant tribes, and the Indian never appeared again as an important factor in the population of southern New England.[1]

At that time there was a very friendly feeling between the English Puritans and the people of Massachusetts, and much of the money which was used in carrying forward missions among the Indians, and in printing Bibles for them came from England. But there were questions arising from time to time as to the authority which the English government had over the Colonies, which it was very difficult to settle. In 1643, the Commons passed an ordinance freeing New England from taxation " until the House should take further order." But in the same year Parliament appointed a Board of Commissioners to have charge of the administration of the Colonies. It was claimed by the people of Massachusetts that, under their charter, *Claims of the Colonists.* they had exclusive authority to maintain local government, so long as their laws did not contravene the laws of England. They even claimed the right to control their harbors. When the master of a vessel commissioned by Parliament threatened to capture a ship in the King's service in Boston Harbor, Winthrop ordered the master to come on shore, and forbade him to meddle with any ship in the harbor.[2] The Gen-

[1] See the chapter in this volume entitled " John Eliot, the Apostle to the Indians."
[2] Winthrop, ii. 194.   Colonial Records of Massachusetts, ii. 121.

eral Court sent a petition to the Parliament praying "that no such attempt may be made hereafter upon any ships in our harbors, or of any of our confederates in New England." These acts came very near to a claim to independence of the Mother Country. When certain parties presented to the Parliament an appeal from the action of the General Court, Mr. Edward Winslow of Plymouth, a skilful diplomatist, was sent to England as the agent of Massachusetts, to ask the Commissioners for Foreign Plantations to "confirm our liberties granted us by charter, by leaving delinquents to our just proceedings, and discountenancing our enemies, and disturbers of our peace." The request of the Colonists was granted by the Commissioners, and assurances were given that their administration under the charter should not be interfered with. During the time of the Commonwealth the spirit of the English government was on the whole friendly to New England. The Colonists on their part showed their good will to the government in the Mother Country, while maintaining very firmly their own rights.

Between the years 1651 and 1658, nearly the entire territory of Maine came under the government of Massachusetts, which had some time before acquired a title to the settlements in New Hampshire. Oliver Cromwell had a plan to transfer the people of New England to Ireland and to Jamaica, and he made them generous proposals to this end.[1] These proposals were carefully considered, but the people had already come to love their new homes, and were quite unwilling to leave them. In 1651, the General Court was informed by Winslow that the Parliament desired that the Colony should take out a new patent, in the name of the new government of England. They replied that under their present charter they had a right to live " under magistrates of their own choosing, and under laws of their own making," and they made it plain that they had no desire to change their government.[2] In 1652 the General Court established a mint, and proceeded to coin money, stamping upon one side of the coin the name Massachusetts and a tree in the centre, and upon the other side New England, and the year of the coinage. This coinage was continued for more than thirty years.

In 1660, Charles the Second became King of England. Plans were soon formed for sending a Governor General to New England, **Restoration of** with authority to govern the Colonies **Charles II.** in the name of the King. The General Court, however, sent an address to the King, praying for his gracious protection of their religion and their

[1] Massachusetts Colonial Records, iv. (1) 110.
[2] Ibid., iv. (1) 72.

liberties, according to the patent which they had received from his royal father. A loyal address was also sent to the Parliament. This was virtually a recognition of the new government as the government of England *de facto.* In 1661 the King was formally proclaimed by order of the General Court. The Plymouth Colony, the Colony of New Haven, and that of Connecticut, also acknowledged the King as " the lawful King of England, Scotland, France, and Ireland," according to the ancient form. The government of Rhode Island joined with the other Colonies in acknowledging the King, and ordered that all writs, warrants, and all other public transactions, should be issued in the name of His Majesty.

One result of the submission of the Colonies to the King was the granting of a very liberal char-**Royal Charter** ter to Connecticut, which was dated **for Connecticut.** May 10, 1662. It included the New Haven Colony within the boundaries of Connecticut, so that the more liberal policy with respect to the suffrage which had been adopted by the first settlers of Connecticut was extended over the other Colony. The charter had been secured by John Winthrop, Jr. It provided for a Governor, Deputy Governor, twelve Assistants, and a House of Deputies, to consist of two members from each town ; all to be elected annually by the freemen of the Colony. This charter was received

in Connecticut with great joy. The General
Court committed it to the custody of three leading citizens, who were sworn to keep it safely.
They declared all the laws and orders of the
Colony to stand in full force, and they proceeded
at once to assume jurisdiction over the New
Haven Colony. This called forth a vigorous
protest from New Haven. In the end, however,
the General Court of that Colony submitted, under protest, to the royal charter, and New Haven
became a part of Connecticut.[1]

On the 8th of July, 1663, a royal charter was
granted to the Colony of Rhode Island and
Providence Plantations. It was a liberal charter,
and was the foundation of the government of
Rhode Island for a hundred and eighty years.
It contained this provision, which must have been
very acceptable to Roger Williams : " No person
within the said Colony, at any time thereafter,
shall be any wise molested, punished, disquieted,
or called in question, for any differences of
opinion in matters of religion, which do not actu-
ally disturb the civil peace of the said Colony ;
but that all and every person may freely and
fully have and enjoy his and their own judgments and consciences in matters of religious
concernments." [2]

[1] Colonial Records of New Haven, ii. 551–557.
[2] Massachusetts Historical Collections, i. 281.

This charter was received with great joy in Rhode Island. The next spring the new government was inaugurated, and the officers were elected under the charter. From that time this Colony had a stable government, and enjoyed a good measure of prosperity. It had in 1663 a population of between three and four thousand people.

XVI

AMONG the weaknesses and inconsistencies of the Puritans, we must place their treatment of those who differed with them. They **The Quakers in England.** were very earnest in claiming liberty for themselves, but the majority of them were not willing to concede the same liberty to others. The people who call themselves Friends, and who are known by others as Quakers, have won for themselves in our day the confidence and good will of the world. They are quiet and useful citizens, and sincere Christians. They have been the consistent opponents of slavery and of war. The sect originated in England about the middle of the seventeenth century. George Fox was reputed to be its founder. It spread rapidly among the people. Its leaders claimed to have direct revelations from Heaven, and its members all professed to be guided by an "inner light," which directed them in all their lives. They adopted a peculiar style of dress and of speech. In the earlier years they were undoubtedly severe and denunciatory in their treatment of those who did not follow their teachings. They aroused opposition by their charges against rulers and judges. In England they were whipped, and set in the pillory, and were often mobbed. At one time as many as four thousand of them were in English jails. But the more they were persecuted, the more rapidly their numbers increased. They sent missionaries to other lands to preach their tenets, who had less success than those in England.

The authorities of Massachusetts were on the watch for them in 1654. They remembered the troubles which had come from the Antinomian debates, and they dreaded the renewal of the controversy. Before any Quakers reached the Colony, a day of fasting and prayer was appointed in view of the danger from the errors that abounded, and especially the danger from the Quakers. The day was hardly past before two Quaker women from Barbados were landed in Boston. The magistrates sent them back by the same vessel that had brought them. These had but just left Boston when Quakers in eight other Quakers arrived from Massachusetts. England. They were promptly taken to jail, and after eleven weeks of confinement they were

sent back to England in the vessel that had
brought them. While these Quakers were detained in prison, the Federal Commissioners
proposed to the General Courts of all the Colonies that all Quakers, and other notorious heretics, should be forbidden to come into any of
the Colonies, and that if any should find their
way into any Colony they should be removed
forthwith out of the jurisdiction.[1] Each of the
Confederated Colonies acted upon this recommendation. Connecticut imposed a fine of five
pounds a week upon every town that should en-
tertain Quakers, or other heretics; and directed
magistrates to commit them to prison until they
could be sent out of the jurisdiction. New
Haven and Plymouth enacted simi-
lar laws. Plymouth forbade the holding of Quaker meetings by strangers
or others.[2] Massachusetts imposed a fine of one
hundred pounds upon shipmasters who should
bring into the jurisdiction any of the heretics
commonly called Quakers, " who write blasphe-
mous opinions, despising government and the
order of God in Church and Commonwealth;
speaking evil of dignities, reviling magistrates
and ministers, seeking to turn the people from
the faith." [3] They also required such shipmas-

Action of other
Colonies.
1656-57.

[1] Records in Hazard, ii. 349.
[2] Brigham, Compact with the Charter, etc., 102-104.
[3] Massachusetts Records, iv. (1) 277.

ters to give security for returning such passengers to the port from whence they came. It was also enacted that Quakers who should find entrance to the Colony should be whipped and committed to the house of correction, and kept constantly at work, and prevented from holding communication with any person while in confinement. Heavy fines were imposed upon those who should have in their possession Quaker books, or who should defend their opinions.[1]

These enactments show the excitement and the terror of the Colonists. One can hardly comprehend why Colonies of some forty thousand intelligent Englishmen should have been thrown into a panic by the apprehension that a few Quaker missionaries would come among them. The severe laws were quite ineffectual. The Quakers came, and suffered the penalties prescribed by the laws. Several of them were women. They were fined, and imprisoned, and scourged. The laws were made more severe. The fines were increased. It was enacted that Quakers who should return after having been once punished should have their ears cut off, according to the custom in England at that time. Finally, on the recommendation of the Federal Commissioners, it was enacted in Massachusetts in 1658, that, if any Quaker should

[1] The Puritan, 174, 175.

return to the Colony after having been banished, he should be put to death. This law met with decided opposition in the House of Deputies, and was finally passed by a majority of one vote. There is good reason for the opinion that a decided majority of the people in the Colony never approved this law. A year after it was enacted, two men, William Robinson and Marmaduke Stevenson, who had come into the jurisdiction expressly to defy the law, were publicly executed on Boston Common, in accordance with its provisions. Mary Dyer, who had been condemned to death at the same time, was reprieved at the foot of the gallows, and committed to the care of her son, who took her to her home in Providence. The next year she returned to Massachusetts, and was again condemned to death. A pardon was offered her on condition that she would depart and promise to remain away from the Colony, but she refused to give the promise. "In obedience to the will of the Lord I came," she said, "and in His will I will abide faithful unto death." And so she died. A few months later, William Ledra was sentenced to death under the same law. He also was offered a pardon if he would depart from the Colony never to return, but he refused the offer, and the penalty was inflicted upon him.

The execution of these four willing victims

gave the victory to the Quakers. The reaction against the law among the people was so strong that it was soon modified. Later, this law became a dead letter, and finally it was repealed. A little earlier the magistrates of the Colonies received a message from the King requiring them to stop the punishment of the Quakers, and to send them to England for trial. They promised to obey the mandate, but no Quakers were sent to England for trial. Those who had been imprisoned were set at liberty, however, and there was less energy in the execution of the law. After that time no severe punishments were inflicted. The Quakers continued to give unreasonable provocation to their persecutors. They would sometimes hoot at the magistrates in the streets. They sometimes disturbed the congregations during the hours of public worship, in order to give their testimony against them. One of them came into the meeting-house in Boston, and broke two glass bottles which he had in his hands, exclaiming, " Thus will the Lord break you in pieces." Deborah Wilson, a "young woman of modest and quiet life," was constrained by her convictions of duty to go naked through the streets of Salem "as a sign unto the people." Another " young and chaste woman " went into the church in Newbury without any clothes, as " a sign to them."

In such ways as these the Quakers deprived themselves of much of the sympathy which they had excited by their fortitude under suffering. On the whole, they made an extremely small number of converts among the people in New England. This showed how unnecessary were the severe measures that had been adopted against them. Roger Williams, the President of Rhode Island, was far wiser, when he replied to the request of the Federal Commissioners that the Quakers should be excluded from his Colony: "We have no law amongst us whereby to punish any for only declaring by words their minds concerning the things and ways of God, as to salvation, and our eternal condition. . . . We find that where the Quakers are suffered to declare themselves freely, and only opposed by arguments, there they least of all desire to come. . . . Any breach of law shall be punished," he declared, " but the freedom of different consciences shall be respected."

There were Baptists in Massachusetts in 1644, and they seemed likely to become more numerous. A law was enacted that they should be banished.[1] At the time when the law was passed, the President of Harvard College denied the lawfulness of infant baptism, and his successor held

Persecution of the aptists.

[1] Massachusetts Records, ii. 85.

that immersion was essential to the rite.[1] For
a long time the law was a dead letter. A congregation of Baptists was organized in Charlestown. Five of them were disfranchised in 1665,
and two were sent to prison, where they remained nearly a year. They renewed their meetings after their release, and three of them were
sentenced to banishment. A petition against
this severe measure was signed by several influential citizens of the Colony, and presented
to the magistrates. After this time the Baptist
congregation held its meetings for a long time
on Noddle's Island in Boston Harbor. In 1668
there was a public debate in the meeting-house
in Boston which lasted two days, between the
Baptists on the one hand and six ministers of
the churches on the other. Two months later
three leading Baptists were banished from the
Colony, and forbidden to return. There was a
strong remonstrance presented from a number
of the most eminent men in the Colony, and
another from thirteen English ministers, against
these punishments. These things show that the
days of persecution in New England were drawing toward the end. The sentence of banishment was never executed, and the church on
Noddle's Island continued to meet for worship
on the Lord's day. Five years later they began

[1] Palfrey, ii. 349.

to hold their services in Boston. A few years afterwards the agents of the Colony in England were able to declare that "as for the Anabaptists, they are now subject to no other penal statutes than those of the Congregational way."

The belief in witchcraft was almost universal in the seventeenth century, not only in New England, but in Great Britain, and in all the countries of Europe. Many thousands in those countries had been tried for witchcraft, and put to death by drowning, or hanging, or burning. Sir Matthew Hale, Chief Justice of England, said in a charge to the jury, in the case of two persons on trial for witchcraft in 1665, " That there are such creatures of witches I make no doubt at all." [1] Other eminent men of that century expressed similar opinions with equal confidence. Governor Winthrop makes frequent references to witchcraft in his Journal, and he evidently regarded it as a reality. He mentions that in March, 1647, a person whom he does not name was executed at Hartford as a witch. The next year, he relates that Margaret Jones of Charlestown was convicted, and executed for witchcraft. A few years later, Mrs. Anne Hibbins, the widow of a leading citizen,

Witchcraft.

---

[1] State Trials, vi. 687.   Prof. Fisher's History of the Christian Church, 479–483.   Encyclopædia Britannica, Article Witchcraft. The Puritan, 176, 177, 196–234.

was convicted of witchcraft, and suffered death. There were two prosecutions for witchcraft in Plymouth, but in both instances the accused were acquitted by the jury. These prosecutions seem to have occurred in the ordinary administration of the law, without any special excitement. The people took it for granted that there were people among them who had dealings with the Evil One. They read in their English Bibles, " Thou shalt not suffer a witch to live," and they assumed that they were competent to discover the witches. And yet during the first sixty years in the history of New England, the charges of witchcraft were very few.

In the years 1691 and 1692 occurred the famous epidemic of folly and cruelty known as Salem Witchcraft. It came at a time of general depression in Massachusetts. Salem Witchcraft. The people had been through a period of great political excitement. They had lost the charter by which they had been guided and protected from the beginning. The religious spirit in the churches was much below the mark of earlier years. The age of faith seemed to have given place to an age of doubt. It was a favorable time for the revival of superstition: and it came with the power of a cyclone.

It is not necessary to dwell upon the incidents of the catastrophe. There was an astonishing number of charges of witchcraft in Salem. A hundred persons were in jail under the charge at one time. The new royal Governor convened a special Court for the trial of the accused. He exceeded his authority in so doing. The accused were all tried by juries. The evidence was of no value at all to people who were in their senses. Yet in the course of a few weeks twenty persons, some of them venerable for their years and eminent for their virtues, were adjudged guilty of witchcraft, and were put to death. The madness was over in a few months. For a time there were new charges, and new trials. But juries could not be found who would convict on such testimony as was presented. A little later the judges who had been engaged in the trials began to make confession of their folly and wickedness. The jurors also began to regain their senses, and to confess that they were guilty of the blood of their innocent neighbors. Some of the ministers who had encouraged the prosecutions came to a clear sense of the wickedness of the whole proceeding, and made public acknowledgment of their errors. After the sad experiences at Salem, there was a final end of the delusion in the Puritan Colonies, though it lingered in England many years longer.

XVII

AMONG the stirring events in the later history of the Puritan Colonies was King Philip's War. The events in this war will be nar- King Philip's rated in the section relating to the War. work of the Apostle Eliot. One of the results of the war was the crippling of the missions which that devoted man had planted.

For thirty-eight years there had been no war between the Colonists and the red men. One reason was the terrible punishment which the white men had inflicted upon the Pequots when they entered the war path. But a stronger reason was the kindness and justice with which the Colonists had dealt with the Indians. Every foot of land which had been occupied in the different Colonies had been purchased and paid for. The only exception to this statement was the comparatively small territory conquered during the Pequot war. The shield of the law was over the natives, and those who had wronged them were apt to be brought to justice. The trade in furs and other commodities which the Indians had to sell had enabled them to live much more comfortably than before the English came to the country. The Indians gained much from the examples of industry and economy in their civilized neighbors. The missionaries had gathered some thousands of

them into reservations which had been set apart
for the exclusive use of the Indians.   There they
had been taught the civilization and the religion
of the Colonists.   Many of them had comfortable
dwellings, and productive farms and orchards.
Some thousands had been taught to read and
write. They had educated teachers and preachers
of their own race.   Vigorous efforts were made
from year to year to extend these advantages to
the larger tribes, which were still living as their
ancestors had lived.   On the part of the whites
there was a genuine desire to win their savage
neighbors to the habits of civilized life.

The time came when the powerful tribes of
southern New England combined under King
Philip to exterminate the Colonists, and to free
themselves from the restraints of a civilization that
was irksome to them.   Many of the Indians had
by that time provided themselves with firearms,
and they had learned much of the art of war.
It was a very formidable conspiracy which the
Colonists had to face in 1675.   They were
thoroughly united against the common enemy.
Losses of the   They met with heavy losses during
Colonists.   the contest. In Plymouth and Massachusetts ten or twelve towns had been entirely
destroyed, and forty others more or less injured
by fire, making more than half the whole number.
One in ten of the men of military age, five or six

hundred in all, had been slain in battle, or had been murdered at their own homes. There was hardly a family that was not in mourning. Large sums of money had been expended, and the people were burdened with debt when the war was over. It was many years before the Colonists recovered from the losses which the war had brought them. It is pleasant to record that a gift of a thousand pounds was sent " by divers Christians in Ireland to such as were impoverished, distressed, and in necessity by the late war." [1] But no such aid came from the King or his court. No such aid was solicited by the Colonists. It was a true saying of one of their friends in England at that time, that they were " poor and yet proud." [2]

XVIII

During the reign of Charles the Second the English government was less friendly to the Colonists than during the time of the Commonwealth. One reason may have been that two of the regicide judges who had sat in the court which condemned Charles the First to death had escaped to New England, and were known to be secreted among the Colonists. Mr. John Davenport of New

Visit of the Royal Commissioners.

[1] New England Historical and Genealogical Register, ii. 304.
[2] Hutchinson's History, i. 279.

Haven received them to his own house, and preached a very bold sermon, in which he advised his people to receive the Regicides, and aid them as far as possible.[1] It was well known in England that the people of New England were not in favor of the restoration of the monarchy, although they had submitted to it, as an accomplished fact, and had proclaimed the new King.

In July, 1664, there arrived in Boston four Commissioners from the King, sent over to visit the several Colonies, to receive such complaints and appeals as should be presented to them, and to provide for the peace and security of the country, according to their discretion. They came with a fleet of four ships of war, and four hundred troops of the royal army. These were the first vessels of the English navy that had ever been seen in the harbor of Boston. There was less talk of armed resistance than there had been ten years before, when Charles the First proposed to send a Royal Governor to Boston, because the kingdom was now tolerably well united, and the Colonies would have no chance in a contest with the power of England. The King desired to have the Colonies take out new charters, which would give to him the appointment of the governors and the command of the militia. He also desired to take possession of the Dutch

[1] Bacon's Historical Discourses, 1838.

settlement at New Amsterdam, by force of arms,
if necessary.

The expedition, with some aid from the Colonies, proceeded to New Amsterdam, took possession of the place with little opposition, and
changed its name to New York. The Federal
Commissioners met that year in Hartford, and
modified the Articles of Confederation so as to
adapt them to the changed conditions on account
of the union of New Haven with Connecticut.
It was now a Confederation of three Colonies
instead of four.

The Royal Commissioners made their first official visit to Plymouth, where they were received
with the respect due to their rank. The Royal
They proposed that the oath of alle- Commissioners
giance should be taken by all house- in the Colonies.
holders; that all men of competent estates should
be admitted to be freemen; that all laws deroga-
tory to the King should be repealed; and also that
the Lord's Supper should be open to all persons
of orthodox opinions, competent knowledge, and
moral life, either in the churches already existing,
or in congregations of their own. All these proposals were readily agreed to except the last; in
regard to which the officers of the Colony said
that they should expect those who desired to
found churches different from those now existing to continue to contribute their due proportion

towards the support of the ministers, until such time as they should have ministers of their own.

The Commissioners were also well received in Rhode Island. While there they issued some very arbitrary orders for changing the boundaries of the Colony, which awakened much opposition. Among the people in Connecticut they were received with respect, and the authorities were quite ready to adopt the measures which they had proposed to the Colony of Plymouth.

Their next visit was to Boston, where they remained about one month. They asked that the law which limited the franchise to members of churches should be repealed. In response to this request, the law was so modified that at the next election seventy men who were not members of any church within the Colony were permitted to vote. The Commissioners also asked that all persons who had been guilty of treason (that is, the Regicides) should be apprehended; that full reports should be made of the laws now in force in the Colony, and of the provisions for the education of the people. They also asked for a map of the territory which the Colony claimed under the charter. These requests were readily complied with.

The Commissioners next attempted to hold a Court for hearing appeals from the decisions of the Colonial Courts. The magistrates informed them that the charter of the Colony gave to the officers of the Colony power to hear and try all such cases, and that such a Court of Appeal as they proposed to set up would be a violation of the chartered rights of the Colony. But the Commissioners gave public notice that they should hold a session, at nine o'clock the following day, at a place which they designated, to hear and determine an appeal from the decision of the magistrates. But the hearing was not permitted to take place. At eight o'clock of the next day, a messenger of the General Court took his stand at the place appointed for the hearing, and published, with sound of trumpet, a proclamation of the General Court, which denounced the intended act of the Commissioners as a usurpation, and declared that they could not consent to it, nor give it their approval.

The Commissioners saw themselves to be helpless in the presence of this resolute assertion of the rights of the Colonists under their charter. They were confronted in 1665, in the town of Boston, by the same spirit of liberty which led to the battle of Bunker Hill and the Declaration of Independence, a little more than a century later. They soon departed from Boston and continued their journey to New Hampshire and Maine. They afterwards returned for a short time to Boston, but failed to accomplish anything there. The King recalled the Commissioners the next year, and required the Colony to send four persons to represent them in England before His Majesty.

The next General Court "gave diligent attention to the preparation of military defences." They also informed the King that it would be useless for them to send representatives to England, and that they could only commit their cause to God, "praying that His Majesty (a prince of so great clemency) will consider the condition of his afflicted subjects, being in imminent danger by the public enemies of our nation, and in a wilderness far remote from relief."[1]

The General Court also sent a present to the King of masts for the royal navy, which had cost the Colony two thousand pounds. This peace offering was very gratefully received in England, and was of great service in equipping the navy for the war with France.

The Federal Commissioners met at Hartford in 1667, representing only the three Colonies of Plymouth, Massachusetts, and Connecticut. Mr. Leete of Connecticut was President of the Congress. The next year the General Court of Massachusetts regained the control of the district of Maine, of which it had been deprived by the action of the Royal Commissioners. In

[1] Massachusetts Records, iv. (ii.) 317.

1674, the General Court of Massachusetts imported sixty pieces of artillery and five hundred firelocks. They also gave orders for the repair of the fortifications of Boston, Charlestown, Salem, and Portsmouth, commissioned two armed vessels, and placed a force of about seven hundred men under command of General Dennison, "for the vindication of our honor, to secure peaceable trade in the Sound, and to repress the insolence of the Dutch."

The difficulties between Charles the Second and the Puritan Colonists were of such a nature that they were likely to become greater rather than less as the years should go by. The Colonists cherished the traditions of the Long Parliament, and of the statesmen who had deposed the Stuarts and had founded the Commonwealth. They had established republican governments on this side of the sea, and they had been accustomed to elect their own officers and to make their own laws. They were quite willing to recognize their connection with the Mother Country and to swear allegiance to the King. But they claimed their rights as Englishmen under the laws of England, and Spirit of Charles under the charters which they had the Second. received. On the other hand, Charles the Second was not the friend of popular institutions, either in England or America. He wished to appoint the Governors of the Colonies, and to draw a revenue from them, to have the command of their militia, and to reduce the people to such a position that they would be pliant under his government.

After all other plans had failed, it was determined by the King to cancel the charter of Massachusetts. In 1682 he gave notice that unless the concessions which he had called for were agreed to, he should direct the Attorney General to bring a writ of *quo warranto* in the Court of King's Bench, for the purpose of making the charter void. When this was made known in Boston a great town meeting was held in the Old South meeting-house, and the Moderator requested all who were for surrendering the charter to hold up their hands. Not a hand was lifted, and then one of the old Puritans exclaimed, " The Lord be praised." [1] The House of Deputies, after full consideration, also refused to surrender the charter, and on the 21st of June, 1684, the English Court of Chancery, to which the business had been transferred, ordered judgment to be entered for vacating the charter. This action destroyed the whole political structure of the Colony, which had been growing for fifty-four years, and placed the people at the mercy of the King of England. The titles to

[1] Beginnings of New England, 265.

lands and other property were disturbed, and the whole civil and ecclesiastical administration, with all rights and immunities based upon the charter, were swept away.

It was some time before any orders came from England for setting up a new government in Massachusetts, and in the mean time the affairs of the Colony were administered in the ancient form. The sudden death of Charles the Second, by apoplexy, delayed still longer the execution of the decree of the Court of Chancery. James the Second was proclaimed King in Boston, April 20th, 1685. In 1686, a Provisional Government was set up by the authority of the King, and the General Court of the Colony abdicated the government, under protest. This was the last act of the charter government of the Colony.

The charters of Rhode Island and Connecticut were set aside by a process similar to that employed against the charter of Massachusetts. Plymouth had no charter. New Hampshire had been constituted a royal Province in 1679, with a Governor and Councillors appointed by the King. Maine was at that time under a provisional government, appointed by Massachusetts; so that the whole of New England was now subject to the control of the King, and on the 20th of December, 1686, Sir Edmund Andros arrived in Boston with a royal commission as Governor

of New England.   His administration lasted two
years and four months, and was brought to an
end by the intelligence that William, Prince of
Orange, had landed in England.   On the 18th
of April, 1689, Boston was aroused by a call to
arms.   The signal fire was lighted on Beacon
Hill, and the militia began to pour in from the
country towns.   The Castle was surrendered, an
English frigate in the harbor was seized, and
Governor Andros was arrested as he was trying
to escape in woman's clothes.   Thus the Revolution in Massachusetts was accomplished.

William the Third was a king of liberal principles, and did not desire to carry out the plans
for depriving the people of New England of a
share in the government of their own Colonies.
It was found on examination that the charters
of Rhode Island and Connecticut had not been
legally annulled, and these Colonies were permitted to resume their old form of government.
New Hampshire continued to be a royal Province.   The Old Colony of Plymouth was an-
nexed to Massachusetts, and these two, with the
district of Maine, made up the Province of Massachusetts, which received a charter in 1692
from William and Mary.   By the provisions of
the new charter, the freemen of the Province
had the right to elect the Legislature, which had
the power to make laws, and to impose taxes.

The Governor was to be appointed by the Crown. All laws were to be sent to England for approval. A property qualification was prescribed for admission to the right of suffrage, and the old restriction to members of churches was swept away.

XIX

It was seventy-two years from the beginning of English settlements by the Pilgrims at Plymouth, when the charter for the Province of Massachusetts was granted. Condition of New England in 1692. The Puritan Colony of Massachusetts Bay was sixty-four years old. The population of the New England Colonies at that time was probably about seventy-five thousand. This estimate gives forty-five thousand to Massachusetts, including the Old Colony and the district of Maine, eighteen thousand to Connecticut, and six thousand each to New Hampshire and Rhode Island. Boston was a prosperous commercial town of five or six thousand people. The settlements were scattered along the coast, from the Penobscot to the Hudson. The most distant were a hundred miles from tide water. There were large groups of towns on the Connecticut River, and in the vicinity of Massachusetts Bay. The native Indians had become very few in the southern half of New England.

The inhabitants of the Colonies were still almost entirely of English blood. A large proportion of them were religious people, who were accustomed to conduct their religious worship in the Congregational way. There were some adherents of the Church of England. King's Chapel was already standing. There were a few Baptists, and a few Quakers. Only a small minority of the people at that time were members of churches, although a large proportion of them were accustomed to attend religious services on the Lord's day. There had already been some departures from the earlier Puritan administration of ecclesiastical affairs, as we shall see when we come to the history of the Great Awakening. The people were for the most part honest and thrifty farmers, of simple manners, who dwelt in framed houses, and who were making their farms and orchards more valuable year by year. Much of the business connected with the collection of taxes, police regulations, the care of roads and of schools, and the settlement and maintenance of ministers, was done in the town meetings. There were schools in all the towns, except the newest settlements, and these were open to all the children of the people. So far as we have any means of information, a large percentage of the population in the various Colonies, of both sexes, were able to read and write.

The people of the second and third generations in New England were below those of the first generation in respect to culture and refinement of manners. They had the habits of those who are dwelling on the borders of civilization. And yet every practicable effort was made to prevent the process of deterioration. Harvard College was founded that the congregations might have men of education for their ministers. The common schools and the grammar schools were a means of keeping up the intellectual standard among the people. The Pilgrims and Puritans were accustomed to speak of their country as more favored than any other, and when Cromwell proposed to transfer them to lands that had an older civilization,. no one was willing to go. The spirit of the people of New England was well expressed in the re- Spirit of the People. markable book entitled, "The Wonder Working Providence of Zion's Saviour in New England," by Edward Johnson of Woburn. It gives a history of the Colonies from 1628 to 1651. It represents the founders as soldiers of Christ, enlisted in a holy war, and guided at every point by a divine hand. "The Lord Christ," the author says, "intends to achieve greater matters by this little handful than the world is aware of." The simple faith of the people was shown very strikingly in times of great trial, such as when they

13

lost the charter of Massachusetts. They refused to make any compromises, but left themselves under the direction of the Power which they believed had brought them to these shores.

In every settlement the minister was the man of greatest importance, unless there were some of the higher magistrates residing there. In that case they were the peers of the ministers. The Puritan minister was a man of education and culture. His library, though not large, was adapted to his work as a preacher and teacher of the Holy Scriptures. The ministers were usually well versed in the original languages of the Bible, and in the works of the Protestant theologians. They published a large number of theological and practical works, from which we can judge of their learning and culture. These books do not indicate that their authors were familiar with the early English writers, or even with those of the age of Elizabeth. They were not literary men in the modern sense. Of course their knowledge of science was quite limited. But they knew a few things well. Especially they knew the Bible. They were gifted with remarkable spiritual insight. They had trained themselves to reason logically and with convincing power. Many of them had a remarkable knowledge of English history. There were great statesmen among them, and the General Court did well to consult them on the most important crises in the history of the Colonies.

In 1672, the General Laws of the Colonies of Massachusetts and Plymouth, and of Connecticut, were published. These laws provided carefully for courts of justice, for trial by jury, for the punishment of crime, for the protection of property, for the registry of deeds and of wills, and for the administration of estates. There were laws designed to restrict the sale of intoxicating drinks, and to prevent intemperance. The able bodied men of the Colonies were enrolled in the militia, and were frequently drilled by their officers. The revenue was derived from direct taxes upon property. There were regulations for shipping and for commerce. The post office arrangements were very incomplete. We know that certain persons had been appointed to receive and to transmit letters to be sent beyond the seas, and to deliver letters that had been brought from abroad.[1] Connecticut and Massachusetts had been divided into counties.

Such systems of laws as these indicate that the Colonies were already well regulated and prosperous states. They show that the rights of the citizen were carefully respected, and that the people had the controlling influence in the administration of the government. The Pilgrims

[1] Massachusetts Records, i. 281.

and the Puritans were successful in planting Colonies on this side of the Atlantic, that have grown in the course of years into free republics, with intelligent and progressive citizens, fitted to be incorporated into this greater Republic.

XX

MORE than two hundred years have gone by since the Colonies came under the reign of William and Mary. At that time a large part even of Massachusetts, as well as of Connecticut and Rhode Island, was unsettled. In New Hampshire there were a very few towns, all in the southern part of the Colony. Maine had a few trading posts, and a small number of settlements on the coast. There were no settlements of white men in the territory that is now Vermont. The greater part of Northern New England was an unbroken wilderness.

Expansion of the Puritan Colonies.

The Puritan Colonists were about a hundred years from that time in filling the vacant spaces in New England, and in developing the distinctive New England character. In Connecticut about thirty towns were incorporated between 1692 and 1745, about as many as were in existence before that date. In 1762 all the territory of that Colony had been divided into townships, and they were beginning

Filling up Connecticut.

to carve new towns out of those already existing. This process continued for some time, as the original townships were too large for the convenience of the inhabitants. Mr. Bancroft estimated the population of New England in 1755 at 133,000. Up to that time, and for fifty years longer, most of the inhabitants were the descendants of the original Colonists.[1]

A similar process was going on in Rhode Island during the eighteenth century, although there was a larger admixture of Rhode Island and families not of the Puritan stock. Massachusetts. In Massachusetts the fifty years that followed the time of the witchcraft delusion saw a great enlargement of the territory under cultivation. A recent writer has said: " It was the great town-planting epoch in New England history. Companies for the purchase and settlement of new townships were formed in every considerable community. To get more and more land was the consuming endeavor of the hour. The anticipatory Western fever was upon them: and to get further into the woods seemed a passion. No modern Oklahoma or Cherokee strip invaders can surpass the eagerness of those New Englanders of that time."[2] It was in Massachusetts

[1] American Commonwealths. Connecticut. Alexander Johnson, 270.
[2] Religious Life in New England. Dr. G. L. Walker, 51–53.

the period of expansion. About one hundred of the towns of this Colony were settled during this period.

New Hampshire was filled up during the same time by people from the other Puritan Colonies.

New Hampshire. At the beginning of the War of the Revolution a large part of that territory was already occupied. In 1719 a hundred and twenty Scotch-Irish families settled in Londonderry and elsewhere in New England. A few French Huguenots came to New Hampshire. But the great majority of the population was of the stock of the English Puritans.

The early settlers of Maine came from a large number of places. There were some towns where

Maine. the Scotch-Irish were in the majority a century ago, and some of the early churches were Presbyterian.[1] Yet the largest number of Colonists came from Massachusetts and New Hampshire, and they have given their distinctive character to the people of Maine.

When Vermont was opened for settlement, at the close of the French and Indian War, there

Vermont. were many people in Southern New England who were eager to push their way into the new and fertile lands of the north. The War of Independence delayed the rush of settlers to the new State. But as

[1] The Puritan in England and New England, 371-388.

soon as the war was over the people came in large numbers from Western Massachusetts and from Connecticut. The names of Connecticut towns reappeared in the new settlements among the Green Mountains. There were Windsor, Wethersfield, Hartford, New Haven, Wallingford, Waterbury, and many more. It was common at one time to call it New Connecticut. The early settlers took with them the ideas, and the institutions, and the religion of the Puritans, so that when Vermont came into the Union in 1791, it was another Puritan State.

After the adoption of the Federal Constitution and the organization of the national government there was the beginning of the memorable Puritan Exodus to the West. Central and Western New York were settled very largely from Massachusetts and Connecticut. A large number went from Vermont into Northern New York. The Wyoming valley, and some other parts of Pennsylvania, were settled from Connecticut. In 1788 a party of New England people began a settlement at Marietta, Ohio. So many people from Connecticut went into the Western Reserve that this also gained the name of New Connecticut. It was found from the census of 1850 that forty-five per cent of the people living in the six States of Ohio, Michigan, Indiana, Illinois, Iowa, and Wisconsin were natives of New England, or of the

States where the New England element in the
population preponderated.[1] The sons of the
Puritans have given character to those States,

New England in the West. so that they are to-day the New England of the West.

As one journeys farther west he finds a great
many people of Puritan blood in the States in the
Rocky Mountain region and on the Pacific coast.
A large proportion of the public men who have
had a leading part in moulding the educational,
social, and religious institutions of those States
had their training in New England.

There was only one college in the Puritan
Colonies in 1691, and many of the people in the
distant towns were accustomed to contribute regularly towards its support. Yale was founded a little later. Williams, and Dartmouth, and Bowdoin,
and the University of Vermont, and Middlebury,
and Amherst, are all daughters of Harvard and
Yale. The scores of colleges and universities
in the newer States are near of kin to these.

The Greater New England stretches from ocean
to ocean. The hopes of the founders have been
realized, not only in the small States which grew
up under their intellectual and religious influence,
but in the greater Commonwealths that have been
moulded by their descendants. The last census

[1] Congregational Quarterly, 1861, pp. 20, 21.

shows that even as late as 1890 more than a quarter of those who were born in New England were living outside of New England. These Eastern States are even now the places where the great scholars and divines, the authors and statesmen of the nation, have had their education. They are, like the small states of Greece, the training schools for the artists and poets and philosophers of the world.

III

John Eliot, The Apostle to the Indians

John Eliot, the Apostle to the Indians

THE Puritan was a many-sided man. The Puritan divines were in many respects the best representatives of this great body of English Protestants. But their theology was not original with them. It was borrowed from Geneva and from Scotland. The Puritan was a statesman as well as a preacher, and English and American liberty owes a great debt to the Puritan fathers. He was a soldier, as well as a preacher and a statesman. The Puritan was a poet also, and a philosopher, — a discoverer and an inventor.

The Puritan was a missionary. The same religious spirit which inspired the author of Paradise Lost, and gave invincible force to Cromwell's Ironsides, — which led the Pilgrims and the Puritans to seek a home in the wilderness where they should be free to worship God, — this spirit led them to plan not only for themselves, but for the pagan aborigines. Governor Bradford in his History of Plymouth, speaking of the Pilgrims while yet in Holland, says that

they began as early as 1617 to think of a removal to America for several weighty reasons,
among which he mentions "an inward zeall, and
great hope of laying some foundation, or making
way for yᵉ propagating and advancing yᵉ Gospel
of yᵉ kingdom of Christ to the remote ends of
the earth, though they should be but stepping-
stones to others." [1]

The Pilgrim fathers certainly cherished this
"inward zeall and great hope," and they did what
they could to lead the Indians to the Christian
faith. During the early years of Plymouth
Colony a number of the Indians became Christians. Amid the labors and privations of their
pioneer life the Pilgrims found time to teach
the natives, and to recommend to them the
religion of Christ.

The same was true of the Puritans. The
charter of the Colony of Massachusetts Bay
states that it is the principal end of the plantation to "Winn and incite the natives of the
country to the knowledge and Obedience of the
onlie true God and Saviour of Mankinde, and
the Christian Fayth." The original seal of the
Colony of Massachusetts Bay had on it the fig-
ure of an Indian, with the words, "Come over
and help us."

[1] Bradford's History, 24. Massachusetts Historical Society's
Collections, 4th series, vol. iv.

I

IN the earlier years of both Colonies it was not practicable to establish missions among the Indians. The people were too poor, Early Missionary and the struggle for existence was Efforts. too intense. But their relations with the Indians were generally friendly. The Indians came every day into their settlements and into their cabins. Sometimes they had articles to sell. They were an imitative race. They were disposed to do as the English did. They were not slow to perceive some of the advantages of civilization. The religion and the civilization of the English seemed to these children of the forest to be closely related to each other. They were very susceptible to kindness from their white neighbors. The seeds of truth were scattered among them, and there was increasing encouragement to engage in direct missionary work. In 1636, the Plymouth Colony enacted laws to provide for the preaching of the Gospel among the Indians. This led to a number of efforts within the Plymouth Colony to bring the Indians under religious instruction. As early as 1632, Roger Williams, while a pastor at Plymouth, began to study the language of the Indians of that vicinity. He took pains to become familiar with Indian life, so as to be able to influence

them.   He was frequently engaged in direct missionary work among their tribes.

The most important movement for the conversion of the Indians was initiated by the General Court of Massachusetts. In November, 1644,
the Court expressed its desire that some more
direct means should be used for the religious instruction of the Indians.   It asked the ministers
to express their opinions as to the best methods.
In 1646, the same body directed the ministers
to choose two of their number at the annual
election every year, to engage in missionary work
among the Indians.   This called general attention to the matter.   But a great preparation had
already been made for this work.   The Pequot
War had been so long over that there seemed to
be a reasonable prospect of permanent peace, at
least with the Massachusetts tribe of Indians.
The policy of the two Colonies had always been
to cultivate peaceful relations with the aborigines. They had never engaged in war with
them, except in defence against hostile attacks.
In 1646, the English and the Indians were
dwelling together as neighbors and trusting
friends.

A number of the ministers in the New England Colonies had been studying the languages
of the natives and cultivating an acquaintance
with them.   In 1643, Thomas Mayhew, a mer-

year of our Lord God 1604." That church is a very ancient structure. Parts of it are probably eight hundred years old. The tower, which is five hundred years old, contains a peal of bells of exceptional sweetness and purity. A memorial window to commemorate John Eliot has been placed in the chancel of the church, at the expense of his descendants in this country, and was dedicated with appropriate ceremonies, May 21, 1894.[1]

We have very little knowledge of the childhood and youth of John Eliot. He was the third child in a family of seven. "It was a great favor of God to me," he said at a later time, "that my first years were seasoned with the fear of God, the Word, and prayer." Before he was six years old, his father removed to Nasing, Essex County, a place that was distinguished above almost any other in England for the number of Puritan families that

Childhood and Youth of John Eliot.

Essex, because the younger children of the family were baptized in the church in that parish. For the record see the New England Historic Genealogical Register, 1894, p. 402. Also the Boston Evening Transcript, October 21, 1893. The present rector of the church, Rev. John T. Lockwood, writes, " The entry here copied is, fortunately, one of the few in Widford Parish which remains clear and distinct after the lapse of 289 years."

[1] See the Boston Evening Transcript, June 16, 1896; and the N. E. H. Genealogical Register, 1894, p. 80. Dr. Elliot secured about $1000, from the Eliots of the United States toward the expense of this memorial window.

went from it to New England.[1]   He grew up in
a community in which the Non-Conformists were
so numerous as to exert a strong influence.   He
was matriculated as a pensioner in Jesus College,
Cambridge, March 20, 1618, and received the degree of Bachelor of Arts in 1623.[2]   He was distinguished at the University for his love of the
languages, Greek and Hebrew especially.   He
was also well versed in the general course of
liberal studies that were pursued at that time in
the English Universities, and was noted for his
discriminating knowledge of theology.   He was
fond of philological inquiries, and was an acute
grammarian.[3]

III

On leaving the University, he was employed
as an Usher in the Grammar School of Thomas
Hooker, at Little Baddow, near Chelmsford, in
Essex County.   The influence of Thomas Hooker,
who was eighteen years older than Eliot, was the
leading influence in forming his religious character.   He always spoke of the time of his resi-
dence with this great Puritan divine as the begin-

[1] Memorials of the Pilgrim Fathers, by W. Winters.   1882.
[2] Original Record, Cambridge University.
[3] Eliot Genealogy, 34.   Memorials of the Pilgrim Fathers, 26.
Life of John Eliot in Sparks's American Biography, by C. Francis,
4, 5.   Will of Bennett Elliott, New England Historical and Genealogical Register, 1894, pp. 366, 367.

ning of his religious life. "To this **Beginning of his** place was I called," he said, "through **Religious Life.** the infinite riches of God's mercy, — for here the Lord said unto my dead soul, 'Live'; and through the grace of Christ I do live, and I shall live forever. When I came to this blessed family, I then saw, and never before, the power of godliness in its lively vigor and efficacy."[1] Under the influence of Mr. Hooker, he was led to devote himself to the Christian ministry.

We know comparatively little of his life during the eight years that followed the date of his graduation. A part of the time was occupied by his work of teaching at Little Baddow. But those were years of persecution for the Non-Conformists. Neal tells us, in his "History of the Puritans," that "Elliot was not allowed to teach school in his native country."[2] Mr. Hooker was compelled to flee into Holland. Mr. Eliot saw very little opportunity to preach the truth as he understood it in England, and he made preparations to go to New England. A number of his personal friends, including some of his near relatives, had engaged to follow him as soon as the way should be open, and he had given a conditional promise to become their minister. Some of this company had been his neighbors at Nasing.

---

[1] The Life of John Eliot, by Dr. Nehemiah Adams, 1870.
[2] Neal's History of the Puritans, i. 305, Harpers' edition, 1858.

IV

HE sailed for New England in the ship Lyon, "in the ninth month," we are told, and "landed in Boston, November 4, 1631." He had as fellow passengers Mrs. Margaret Winthrop, the wife of Governor Winthrop, "with his eldest son and other of his children,"[1] and more than fifty other people, who went to join the Massachusetts Colony. Mr. Eliot was now twenty-seven years of age, and he must have been already prepared for his work as a minister, although it is not certainly known that he had been ordained in England. He immediately united with the First Church in Boston, and was at once invited to be their minister until the return of their pastor, Mr. Wilson, from England. His services were very acceptable to that congregation, and they set their hearts on securing him as the teacher of the church, in connection with the pastor.[2]

The next year, however, his friends from Essex County came over and settled in Roxbury. They claimed the fulfilment of his promise to devote himself to their service. In accordance with this understanding Mr. Eliot declined to listen to the proposals of the church in Boston, and accepted

[1] The Puritan in England and New England, 232.
[2] Winthrop's Journal, i. 93.

the call to settle in Roxbury. He was ordained at Roxbury, November 5, 1632, as teacher of the church, and continued in that office until his death. He had been married about a month before his ordination to Hannah Mumford, or Mountford, a lady of about his own age, to whom he had been betrothed in England. She had come to him under the care of friends as soon as he could promise her a home, and they labored together with one heart and mind until her death, more than fifty years afterwards.

The ministry of Mr. Eliot in Roxbury was like that of the other Puritan pastors of his time in New England. He was a very able and well read man, — a student of the *His Ministry in Roxbury.* principles of government, as well as of theology. He was in sympathy with the advanced political views of the Puritans. He believed in a republican form of government, while he was willing to submit to any other form which was established. He rejoiced in the overthrow of the Stuarts, and in the establishment of the Puritan Commonwealth. He guarded with jealous care the rights of the people in the Colony to representation in the government. He blamed the Governor and the Council because they had concluded a treaty with the Indians, without consulting the representatives of the people. He was the author of a political work called "The Christian Commonwealth," which set forth, among other things, the right of the people to elect their own rulers. The leading principle of the book was accepted, in the time of Cromwell, by the Puritans in England and America. After the restoration of the Stuarts, however, such principles were considered "seditious, and subversive of the government established in" England. The General Court of Massachusetts took measures to suppress the book, and obtained from Mr. Eliot a retraction of so much of the book as treated the government of England by King, Lords, and Commons as antichristian. He acknowledged the restored government of England as "not only a lawful, but eminent form of government," and declared his readiness to subject himself, for conscience' sake, to any form of civil polity which could be deduced from Scripture as being of God, and abjured everything in the book inconsistent with this declaration.[1]

But although Mr. Eliot was interested, as all the Puritans were, to secure the rights of the people, he was, above all other things, a minister of the Gospel. He was, all his life, a close student of the Bible, and an earnest and faith-

[1] Republished in the Mass. Hist. Soc. Coll., viii. 29. Francis, Life of Eliot, 210–212.

ful preacher, as well as an affectionate and devoted pastor. He held the Puritan theology, and preached it, and defended it. His church had two ministers a part of the time of his ministry,— a pastor and a teacher, — but there was work enough for both of them. He was regarded as a minister of unusual gifts, as is shown by the fact that the church in Boston desired him to take the place that was soon afterwards filled by that eminent man, John Cotton.

He was so fond of the Hebrew language that he used to say that it was better fitted than any other language to be the universal language. He was quite sure that Hebrew would be the language of heaven.[1] He was interested especially in the progress of medical science, and he believed that human life would be much longer when the physicians should have gained a knowledge of all the medicines that nature has provided, and should have skill to use them. He was sure that the time was coming, according to one of the prophecies, when "the child shall die an hundred years old,"[2] and when those who were aged should count their years like the patriarchs.

"He was distinguished," says one of his biographers, "for facetiousness and affability." His

---

[1] See Eliot's Communion of Churches, chap. iii. 17. Francis, Life of Eliot, 306–308.

[2] Isa. lxv. 20.

conversation was sprinkled with wit. He had a strong interest in young people. The little children loved him. He was interested in the public schools, and was the means of establishing a free school in Roxbury, for the support of which he bequeathed a considerable part of his estate. Cotton Mather states that in his day Roxbury furnished more scholars for the College than any other town of its size in New England. His preaching was distinguished by great simplicity and plainness, so that, as Cotton Mather says, in his quaint way: " The very lambs might wade into his discourses, on those texts and themes wherein elephants might swim. . . . His manner was usually gentle and winning, but when sin was to be rebuked, or corruption combated, his voice swelled into solemn and powerful energy. . . . On such occasion there were as many thunderbolts as words." [1]

V

WHEN Mr. Eliot began in earnest to learn the Indian language, he found an Indian living in

Learning the Language of the Indians.

Dorchester who was exactly fitted to become his teacher. He says: " God first put into my heart a compassion over their poor souls, and a desire to teach them to

[1] Francis, Life of Eliot, 309–315.

know Christ, and to bring them into His king-
dome.   Then presently I found out a pregnant
witted young man, who had been a servant in an
English house, who pretty well understood our
language, and well understood his own language,
and hath a clear pronunciation: Him I made my
interpreter."   In another place he tells us that
this Indian belonged to Long Island, and that he
had been taken prisoner, and had lived with Mr.
Colicott of Dorchester.   " This Indian," he says,
" can read, and I taught him to write, which he
quickly learnt.   He was the first one I made use
of to teach me words, and to be my interpreter.
. . . By his help, I translated the Commandments,
the Lord's Prayer, and many texts of Scripture :
also I compiled both exhortations and prayers by
his help.   I diligently marked the difference of
their grammar from ours.   When I found the way
of them, I would pursue a Word, a Noun, a Verb,
through all the variations I could think of.   We
must not sit still and look for miracles.   Up, and
be doing, and the Lord will be with thee.   Prayer
and pains, through faith in Christ Jesus, will do
anything." [1]

If we follow the latest authority, this interpreter
was an Indian from Long Island, who was well
known there, in subsequent years, as a very intel-

[1] See a note at the end of his Indian Grammar, printed in Cambridge in 1664.   See also a letter of John Eliot, dated February 12,
1649, quoted in Cockanöe, 1896.

ligent interpreter. His name is variously written, as Cockoo, Cocköe, or Cockenöe.[1] We can imagine the enthusiastic student of the Indian language, calling in this " pregnant witted " young Indian to help him in the long evenings. The minister was now forty years of age, and it was not so easy for him to learn a new language as it would have been twenty years earlier. The language was unlike any other with which he was acquainted. Some of the words were of enormous length. Four or five syllables make a long word with us, but on the title page of Eliot's Indian Bible there is a word of eight syllables. In the second verse of the first chapter of Genesis there is one of nine syllables, with twenty-four letters. I have counted sixteen syllables, with forty-two letters, in an Indian word. The reason of this long drawing out of words is that they express by one word what we express by several words. The pronoun, and the adjective, and the verb, and sometimes the noun, are all in one word.

Mr. Eliot had another interpreter, an older man, Job Nesutan. Both of these Indians became Christians.[2] It is probable that he had the help of several other Indians in his study of their lan-

[1] John Eliot's first Indian teacher, Cockenöe, 1896, Harpers.
[2] Francis, Life of John Eliot, 40, note. " This young man was then about to join the church in Dorchester." Cockenöe, 16, note.

guage. He would get a word here, and another there, and would learn how to use them. His method seems to have been this: Having an English sentence, he would find out the Indian words that make up that sentence. In that way he would learn the order of the words, and the inflections, as well as the words themselves. It is plain that he could not have learned the language so well, if he had not been a well trained grammarian. He had a genius for acquiring languages, and a love for the study of new languages. He gradually gained the power, not only to write the Indian language but to speak it. The other pastors of the vicinity were perhaps as much interested as he in the work among the Indians. Several of them had some knowledge of the language. But they all looked to Mr. Eliot as their leader, because he could use the language so much better than they. At that time Protestant missions were in their infancy. For a hundred years after the death of Luther, the Protestant churches were not prepared to establish missions among the heathen. The Dutch Protestants sent a few missionaries to the East Indies, and established a missionary college. But when the Pilgrims came to America there was not a Protestant missionary society in the world.

VI.

THE first effort was made about the middle of September, 1646, not at Nonantum, but at Dorchester Mill.   Mr. Eliot says himself,

Preaching to the Indians. " When I first attempted it, they gave no heed unto it, but were weary, and rather despised what I said."   He writes in another place that the Indians of Dorchester Mill did not regard any such thing, at first, though they afterwards desired to be taught to know God.[1]

[1] Letter of John Eliot to T. S., September 24, 1647, in the Mass. Hist. Soc. Collections, 3d series, iv. 50.   It was in the wigwam of Cutshamakim, the sachem of Neponset, within the limits of Dorchester : —

" When I first attempted it, they gave no heed unto it, but were weary, and rather despised what I said.   A while after God stirred vp in some of them a desire to come into English fashions, and live after their manner . . . which when I heard, my heart moved within mee, abhorring that wee should sit still and let that work alone, and hoping that this motion of them was of the Lord, and that this mind in them was a preparative to imbrace the Law and Word of God ; and therefore I told them that they and wee were already one," etc.   " I told them that if they would learn to know God, I would teach them : unto which they being very willing, I then taught them, (as I at sundry times had indeavored afore,) but never found them so forward, attentive, and desirous to learn, and then I told them I would come to their Wigwams, and teach them, their wives and children, which they seemed very glad of : and from that day forward I have not failed to doe that poore little which you know I doe.   I first began with the Indians at Noonantum, as you know ; those of Dorchester Mill not regarding any such thing."   The Cleere Sun-Shine of the Gospel, Eliot's Letter to T. S., Mass. Hist. Soc. Coll., 3d series, iv. 50.

His next effort was at Nonantum.[1] There had been great solicitude about the result of this second attempt, and much prayer had been offered. He did not go alone, nor without an appointment. There were four in the missionary party. Eliot of course was one; Thomas Shepard, minister in Cambridge, was another; John Wilson, minister in Boston, was probably the third; and Major Daniel Gookin was probably the fourth. We have an account of this meeting, written by one who was present. It is plain from the narrative itself that it was not written by Mr. Eliot. Perhaps it was by Mr. Wilson.

"Upon October 28, 1646," so the record runs, "four of us, having sought God, went unto the Indians inhabiting within our bounds, with desire to make known the things of their peace to them. A little before we came to their Wigwams, five or six of the chief of them met us with English salutations, bidding us much wel-

[1] It is not easy to fix the exact location of Waban's tent. Gookin says (Mass. Hist. Soc. Coll., 1st series, i. 168): "The first place he began to preach at was Nonantum, near Watertowne Mill, upon the south side of Charles River, about four or five miles from his own house, where lived at that time Waban, one of their principal men, and some Indians with him." This, so far as we know, is the only contemporary authority. Tradition, which runs back a number of generations, has fixed upon a spot on the southeastern slope of Nonantum Hill. Here a terrace has been constructed, bearing an inscription which states that near this spot Eliot first preached to the Indians. See also Drake's History of Middlesex County, ii. 443.

come: who, leading us into the principall Wigwam of Waauban, we found many more Indians, men, women, children, gathered together from all quarters round about, according to appointment, to meet with us and learn of us."[1]

It was a great historic occasion. It was in obedience to the requirement of the General Court of the Colony for one thing. Four representative Puritans were there to express the "inward zeall and great hope" they had of winning "the natives of the country" to the "Saviour of Mankind." It was almost the earliest of Protestant missions, and so it was very nearly the beginning of that great missionary movement which has since extended over the world.[2] Eliot and Mayhew, and a very few more, stand almost at the head of that great multitude of missionaries who have been going out from Christian lands these last two hundred and fifty years.

VII.

When all were assembled, in that "principall Wigwam of Waauban," Mr. Eliot began the service with prayer. He prayed in English, because his command of the language of the Indians was

[1] The Day-Breaking of the Gospell with the Indians in New England, in Massachusetts Historical Society's Collections, 3d series, iv. 3.

[2] Protestant Missions, Dr. A. C. Thompson, 22–81.

so imperfect that it seemed hardly The First Meet-
reverent to address the Lord with ing at Nonantum.
such broken words.[1] Then Mr. Eliot preached
to that attentive company, as the old chronicler
tells us, " the blessed word of Salvation, for
an hour and a quarter." He began, in the
only way in which it was possible for him to
begin with any prospect of success, by telling
the Indians of the law of God. He repeated the
ten Commandments, and explained the meaning of each one of them. He showed them in
what ways they were breaking these commandments of God every day of their lives. He made
his address very plain and practical, for he knew
very well what the sins of the Indians were. He
told them that the great God was angry with
them every day because they were every day
breaking His commandments. He told them
further, that he had come, with their English
friends, to make known to them a Saviour who
had come into the world to seek and to save lost
men. He made it plain to them that, if they
would repent of their sins, and pray to God for
forgiveness, if they would worship God, and obey
His commandments, — His anger would turn away
from them, and He would make them His dear
children.[2]

[1] Francis, Life of Eliot, 49.
[2] The Day-Breaking of the Gospell with the Indians, 4

The effect of his address upon the Indians was very great, just as the effect of these truths has always been very great wherever they have been preached. Mr. Eliot then inquired whether they had understood what he had said. They answered that they had. He then said, " Have all of you in this Wigwam understood, or only some few? " and they answered, " with multitude of voyces, that they all of them did understand all that which was then spoken to them." After this, the old record tells us, we invited them to ask questions "for the more clear understanding of what had been delivered." Whereupon one inquired, " How may we come to know Jesus Christ? " After this had been answered, another inquired, "Whether Jesus Christ did understand, or God did understand Indian prayers, when they spoke in their own language." They were told that " God made Indian men, just as He made Englishmen, and He knew the words and even the thoughts of Indians because He had made them. After a number of other inquiries had been answered by us, we also asked a number of questions of them, which they answered as well as they could. . . . After three hours' time thus spent with them, we asked them if they were not weary, and they answered, No. But wee resolved to leave them with an appetite. The chiefe of them, seeing us conclude with prayer, desired to know when we would come againe; so wee appointed the time, and having given the children some apples, and the men some tobacco, and what else we then had at hand, . . . wee departed with many welcomes from them." [1]

Two weeks later Mr. Eliot and his three friends came to Nonantum again, and found a larger number of Indians, and, what was very significant, that the Indians had provided seats for the English visitors. He began this time with the children. He taught them a short catechism with three questions: —

"Who made you and all the world?
"Who shall redeem you from sin and Hell?
"How many Commandments hath God given you to Keep?"

After the children had learned this catechism, Mr. Eliot preached to the Indians "by the space of an hour," going over once more with the principal facts and doctrines of the Christian religion. A number of Indians were melted to tears by what they were told of the love and grace of God, and of their sin against Him. An old Indian inquired whether it "was too late for such an old man as hee, who was neare death, to repent, or seeke after God?" Another asked how the

[1] Day-Breaking of the Gospell, 5–8. Winthrop, ii. 304.

English came to differ so much from the Indians in the knowledge of God, seeing we all have one Father. Another wished to know how we may come to serve God. They spent the whole afternoon in this way. Mr. Eliot prayed this time in the Indian language, to the great joy and wonder of his dusky congregation.[1] They were now certain that the God whom Mr. Eliot worshipped could understand Indian prayers.

VIII

Mr. Eliot continued to go to Nonantum once a fortnight, to catechise the children,[2] and to preach to the people. He had the co-operation of the men of greatest influence in the Colony. Governor Winthrop was sometimes there, and President Dunster of Harvard College, and Major Gookin, and Mr. Heath, and Mr. Edward Jackson. Of the ministers, we find the names of Shepard, and Wilson, and Richard Mather, and Allen of Dedham, and others.[3] The work spread rap-

[1] Day-Breaking of the Gospell, 8–17.

[2] He extended his catechism for the children so as to include the most important points of the Christian faith. This was afterwards printed, and was an important part of the means used by Mr. Eliot in teaching the Indian children. He also prepared, and printed in the language of the Indians, a larger catechism which he used for the older members of the Indian communities. See Mass. Hist. Soc. Coll., i. 169, Gookin.

[3] Day-Breaking of the Gospell, 41.

idly. An Indian sachem who lived near Concord came to Nonantum to hear the missionary, and he desired Mr. Eliot to go and preach to his people. Another sachem at Neponset, Cuts-ha-ma-kim, who had formerly opposed the work, desired to have a meeting in his cabin. For a long time Mr. Eliot went regularly one week to Neponset, and the next week to Nonantum. He had a number of other preaching places in this vicinity, such as Pawtucket, "where is a great confluence of Indians every spring"; Wamesit near Tewksbury, Concord, Nasha-way (now Lancaster), and Punkapaog (now Stoughton).

He went sometimes as far as Yarmouth toward the east, and nearly as far toward the west. There was some difference in the dialects, yet the Indians were almost always able to understand Mr. Eliot, and many received his message with great joy. He wrote the following sentence in the record book of his church, at the close of the first winter: "This winter was one of the mildest that ever we had: no snow all winter long, nor sharp weather. We never had a bad day to go and preach to the Indians all this winter: praised be the Lord."

All the accounts that have come down to us indicate that there was a genuine religious work at that time among the Indians. Among

Permanent Effects of this Work. the results were such as these: The Indians forsook their former religion and worship, — they began to pray not only by themselves, but in their families, morning and evening, and to return thanks at their meals. They taught their children as far as they were able, and they asked earnestly for teachers and schools. They began to keep the Lord's day as a day of rest and of worship. They met by themselves, when the missionary could not be present, to pray, and to speak of the things they had learned from God's word.[1]

Waban, the leading man at Nonantum, soon began to pray, and to teach his company the things he had so recently learned. After the third meeting at Nonantum, there came to Mr. Eliot's house in Roxbury one Wampas, "a wise and sage Indian." He took with him his own son, and three other children, and asked permission to leave them with the English, that they might be educated to know God, for, he said, if they remain at home they will grow up in rudeness and wickedness. Wampas also brought two young Indians, who wished to find employment in English families, that they might be in the way of knowing the true religion, in which they already felt a deep interest.

[1] Eliot's Letter to T. S., Mass. Hist. Soc. Coll., 3d series, iv. 51.

Mr. Eliot believed that civilization must go with Christianity. "I find it absolutely necessary," he says, "to carry on civility with religion."[1] The savage must form habits of regular industry before he can have strength of character to live an honest and virtuous life. He believed that "cleanliness is next to Godliness." He pointed out that there could be no delicacy in the family life so long as all lived by day and by night in one apartment. So he sought to gather the families of praying Indians into a community, where they could build better houses, and could labor in the fields as the English did. The General Court "purchased land for them to make their towne,"[2] at the same time that the Indians were consulting about laws to govern themselves. Under the lead of Waban they adopted ten laws, as many as there were Commandments. These laws were intended to secure habits of industry and of virtue, and to lead to a cleanly and decent way of living. The Indians set about enclosing the ground that had been given them, — some hundreds of acres, — with ditches and a stone wall. Mr. Eliot had provided for them "mattocks, shovels, and crowes of iron," and he promised to give them sixpence a rod for all the wall they

---

[1] Mass. Hist. Soc. Coll., 3d series, iv. 88.

[2] Day-Breaking of the Gospell, Mass. Hist. Soc. Coll., 3d series, iv. 20, also 31, also 88.

would build.[1]   The Indians desired to know
what name their town should have, and they
were told it should be called Noonatomen, or
Nonantum, which signifies rejoicing.   These
people built their houses with partitions for separate rooms, so that, we are told, "the meanest of
them were equal to those of any sachem."   They
were provided with cloth by their English friends,
and in a little time they were able to go to the
religious services decently clothed.   Some remains of their walls were to be seen a century
ago.   It was a great uplift for those poor people.
Mr. Eliot promised to give them many hundred
trees, for orchards.   The women desired to learn
to spin, and he procured wheels for them.   They
began to form habits of industry, and to find
something to sell at market, at all seasons of the
year.[2]   Mr. Shepard states that when he came
to Nonantum, late in the summer of the next
year, he "marvailed to see so many Indian men,
women, and children in English apparell, they
being generally clad, especially upon Lecture
dayes, which they have got partly by gift from
the English, and partly by their own labours, by
which some of them have very handsomely ap-
parelled themselves, and you would scarce know
them from English people." [3]

[1] Clear Sun-Shine, Mass. Hist. Soc. Coll., 3d series, iv. 61.
[2] Ibid., Eliot's Letter, 59.   [3] Ibid., 45.

On the 8th of June, 1647, the Cambridge Synod met for its second session at Cambridge. It was thought best that the missionary work among the Indians should be brought before the representatives of all the churches of New England. Accordingly, Mr. Eliot called together a great number of the Indians, and preached to them in their own language, in the presence of the Synod. He set before them the teachings of the Bible in regard to sin, and to the need of a Saviour. He catechised the children also, and the ministers were delighted, not only by the careful attention of the people to the word, but especially by the " readiness of divers poor naked children to answer openly the chief questions which had been taught them."[1] From that time the work among the Indians had a large place in the sympathies and the prayers of good people not only here but in England.

Eliot's Sermon to the Indians at Cambridge.

IX

Thus, in less than a year, the work of this Apostle among the Indians had reached a point where it was necessary to ask for regular and generous contributions for carrying it forward, and those contributions must come from England. Mr. Eliot

Need of large Missionary Contributions.

[1] Ibid., 45. Winthrop, ii. 376.

himself was a man of slender resources. His salary at Roxbury was only £60 a year, which was smaller than that of some other ministers in the vicinity, and with that he was to support and educate a family of six children. The General Court voted him the first year a gratuity of £10, but this would not have paid for the articles which he procured for the Indians during that year.

The settlements about him were very new, and the people were poor. Boston was only sixteen years old, and the time of log houses with thatched roofs had not gone by. Dorchester, with the other towns south of Boston, was infested by wolves, and it was paying a bounty of thirty shillings for every wolf's head. "The place that is now Walnut Avenue was then called The Fox Holes, and a little further on toward Grove Hall was The Bear Marsh, and The Wolf Traps."[1]

There was not a Protestant Missionary Society in the world at that time. Mr. Eliot and his co-laborers set themselves to *create* such an organization on the other side of the sea. Very careful and particular accounts of the work among the Indians were written by those who had a part in it, such as "The Day-Breaking," "The Cleare Sun-Shine," "The Glorious Progress by the Gos-

[1] Dr. A. C. Thompson's Protestant Missions, 56–58.

pell," and others. Governor Edward Winslow, the agent of the Colonies in England, published in London a number of the letters of Mr. Eliot, in which, in the most simple and modest way, he told of what God was doing for the Indians. This was dedicated by Governor Winslow to the Parliament of England. The statements which the praying Indians made before the elders in regard to their religious exercises were all taken down in writing by Mr. Eliot, and these, with the names of the Indians, were published and read in England. Mr. Eliot wrote to England, "We need some annual revenue to purchase tools for the Indians, to pay teachers for their schools, to pay for printing in their language a primer in which they may learn to read, and to pay for such help as I need in translating the Scriptures, which I look upon as a sacred and holy work. We shall also need to pay for printing such a translation when it shall have been made." His plans were even larger than that. He said, "There be sundry pregnant witted youths, which I desire may be wholly sequestered to learning and put to school." These youths he desired to train up as preachers.[1]

These appeals to English Christians were not in vain. Oliver Cromwell, who was then Lord

[1] Eliot's Letter, Mass. Hist. Soc. Coll., 3d series, iv. 123.

Protector, is said to have had a plan for the universal diffusion of the Gospel, and his influence was in favor of every missionary enterprise. By his aid a corporation was established by act of Parliament, entitled " The President and Society for the Propagation of the Gospel in New England." It was ordered that a general contribution for the object should be made in all the churches through England and Wales. The results, at first small, became in a few years very generous. The whole amount that was sent to New England from this Society cannot be stated in definite terms, but it is known that it amounted to several thousand pounds sterling.[1] The charter was renewed in 1660, after the restoration of Charles the Second, and Sir Robert Boyle, one of the founders of the Royal Society, was its President.

It appears from notices in various letters of Mr. Eliot, and of Major Gookin and others, that the funds received from this society were used in paying the expenses of the education of a number of young Indians, who became preachers to their people ; in building the Indian College at Cambridge ; in printing Eliot's Indian Bible, and other books in the language of the Indians ;

---

[1] Mass. Hist. Soc. Coll., 1st series, i. 218 ; iii. 180, Letter iii., also Letter vii., to Sir Thomas Boyle. See Francis, Life of Eliot, 228–230.

in providing tools and instruments of various kinds for their use; and in the payment of salaries to missionaries, and native preachers and teachers.[1] Thus the way was prepared for securing the pecuniary support of this work among the Indians, not only in Massachusetts, but in the other New England Colonies, and this Society was the pioneer of the great number of Foreign Missionary Societies, which have been formed and supported by English and American Christians.

X

THE time had now come to carry out Mr. Eliot's plans for a larger and more permanent settlement for the Christian Indians. Settlement of Nonantum was found to be too small, Natick. and too near the English towns. The missionary work was making rapid progress among the Massachusetts tribe of Indians, and it was expected that it would extend to the more numerous and powerful tribes, — to the Narragansetts and the Mohegans, and to other branches of the great Algonquin family in New England. The missionaries in the Colony of Plymouth were also encouraged by their success among the Pokanokets, or Wampanoags, to expect the con-

[1] Mass. Hist. Soc. Coll., 1st series, i. 212.

version of the Narragansetts. The plans of Mr. Eliot were made in the expectation of bringing the entire Indian race under the influence of the Gospel. In November, 1648, he wrote to Governor Winslow in London: " The Indians are not willing to come to live near the English, because they have neither tools, nor skill, nor heart to fence their grounds, and if it be not well fenced their Corne is spoyled by the English cattell, which is a great discouragement to them and to me. A place must be found somewhat remote from the English, where they must have the word constantly taught, and government constantly exercised." There should be " incouragements for the industrious, and means of instructing them in Letters, Trades, and Labours, as building, fishing, Flax and Hemp dressing, planting orchards," etc. " Such a place will draw many from divers places who desire to be taught the knowledge of God."[1]

These were the plans of Mr. Eliot for an Indian town. The matter was under consideration two or three years. He made a number of excursions into the wilderness in the hope of finding the right place. This matter was made the subject of prayer by the friends of the work among the English, as well as among the Indians. At length a place was selected, on the banks of

[1] Mass. Hist. Soc. Coll., 3d series, iv. 81.

Charles River, eighteen miles southwest from
Boston. They called it Natick, "a place of hills."
It was granted to the praying Indians by the people of Dedham, at the request of Mr. Eliot. This
grant was confirmed by the General Court. It
is also recorded at Natick, that two families
which were supposed to have some claim upon this land, gave a quitclaim of all their right
and interest in the land in Natick "unto the
publick interest of the Towne of Naticke, that
so the praying Indians might there make a
Towne."[1]

When the land had been secured, Mr. Eliot
induced a considerable number of the praying
Indians to remove from Nonantum, and from
some other villages, to Natick. The settlement
was begun in the spring of 1651. The town was
laid out in three streets, two on the Boston side
of Charles River, and one on the other side. A
foot-bridge had been built across the river the
year before by the Indians, under the direction
of Mr. Eliot. This bridge was eighty feet long,
and nine feet above the water in the middle, with
strong supports of stone. This bridge is said to
have answered its purpose well, and to have stood
against the floods longer than some of those built
by the English.[2]

[1] Biglow's History of Natick, Boston, 1830, p. 23.
[2] Mass. Hist. Soc. Coll., 3d series, iv. 138 and 178.

Lots of land were measured and divided. A house lot was assigned to each family. The fields were sown for a crop, apple trees were planted, and dwellings were erected. The Indians at first built wigwams, because, as Mr. Gookin says, they had more skill in such building, and because they were less costly, and warmer.[1] In the course of time, however, the Indians built houses like those of the English Colonists, with partitions and with cellars underneath. They also built a fort of the trunks of trees set in the ground, in circular form. This stockade covered a quarter of an acre of ground. They also built, with a little assistance from an English carpenter, a large framed house, fifty feet long, and twenty-five feet wide, twelve feet between the floors. This building was for the common use. The lower part was a place for worship on the Lord's day. On other days it was used as a schoolroom. The second floor was a storehouse for furs, and other goods. One corner of this storeroom was separated from the rest by a partition, for the use of Mr. Eliot. Here he had a bed, which he occupied as often as he had occasion to remain over night. Governor Endicott praised the ingenuity and the industry of the Indians, " in hewing and squaring their timber, the sawing of the boards, and making a chimney, making also the ground-sells, and wall-

[1] Mass. Hist. Soc. Coll., 1st series, i. 181.

plates, mortising, and letting in the studds into them, — there being but one Englishman to show them, and he only two days."[1]

XI.

THE next business was the organization of the Indian Community. Mr. Eliot induced them to adopt the plan of government which he had recommended in his book, "The Christian Commonwealth"; a plan which he had borrowed from the eighteenth chapter of Exodus. The people elected their own rulers. They chose first a ruler of a hundred; then two rulers of fifties; and then rulers of tens, whom they called tithing men. They also entered into a civil compact, which they called a Covenant. It was written by Mr. Eliot, and the record of it is probably the earliest public record in existence in the language of the Massachusetts Indians. It is dated September 24, 1651. and is in these words: —

Organization of the Indian Community.

"We doe give ourselves and our children unto God, to be His people. He shall rule us in all our affairs, not only in our religion, and affairs of the Church, (these we desire as soon as we can, if God will,) but also in all our works and affairs of this world. God shall rule over us. The Lord is our Judge. The Lord is our Law-

[1] Mass. Hist. Soc. Coll., 3d series, iv. 190, also 1st series, i. 181.

giver. The Lord is our King. He will save us. The Wisdome which God hath taught us in his Booke, that shall guide us and direct us in the way. O Jehovah, teach us wisdome to find out thy wisdome in thy Scriptures. Let the grace of Christ help us, because Christ is the wisdome of God. Send Thy Spirit into our hearts, and let it teach us. Lord take us to be thy people, and let us take thee to be our God." [1]

Two weeks later, Governor Endicott, Mr. Wilson, and many others, attended the religious services at Natick, and they have left an account of what they saw. The Governor was much pleased by the exhortations and prayers of the Indians, and by the attention and seriousness of the congregation, which numbered about one hundred, and especially by the singing of a psalm by the Indians in their own language. Mr. Wilson described the appearance of the village, the circular stockade, the framed common house, the dwellings of the people, "the firme high foot-bridge over the River,—archwise." He spoke of the appearance of the assembly, the men seated by themselves, and the women by themselves; of the sermon of Mr. Eliot, for an hour more, about "Coming to Christ, and bearing his Yoke." They found the Indian school then in progress, and many other agencies that belonged to this missionary settlement.

[1] Mass. Hist. Soc. Coll., 3d series, iv. 172.

The laws of the Colony of Massachusetts were extended over this Indian town, with certain limitations. The Indians were left free to manage their local affairs in their own way. The chief of their officers was Waban, who was a man of great discretion as well as piety. He was the natural leader of the settlement. Two constables were chosen each year. The General Court appointed Major Gookin to superintend the various Indian communities. He was empowered to hold a court, of which he was to be the presiding judge, and of which certain officers chosen by the Indians were to be members. The powers of this court were such as county courts among the English exercised.[1] The Indian settlement had the full and hearty good will of the white people of the vicinity. Natick was the model for a number of other Indian communities, which were organized within the next thirty years by Mr. Eliot. There seems to have been in these communities a combination of the private ownership of houses and house lots with the tribal ownership and use of those buildings and lands that belonged to the community. Major Gookin, while he was the Indian Commissioner, made visits to all the towns of praying Indians, in company with Mr. Eliot. He has left an interesting account of three such visits, made in 1673 and

[1] Mass. Hist. Soc. Coll., 1st series, i. 177–184.

1674, which contains the only definite information of the Indian communities that has come down to us. He found fourteen of these communities. Each of the older communities had its Indian reservation, consisting of from two thousand to six or seven thousand acres of land. Each had its place of worship, its school, and its teacher. Mr. Eliot had trained a number of young Indians as preachers for these congregations, and he went, from time to time, to the people to introduce preachers, who were accepted by them with great joy. They were in the habit of observing the Lord's day, and of meeting for worship and religious instruction on that day. The Indians to whom Mr. Eliot had preached at Neponset had removed to Pakeemitt, within the present limits of Stoughton. They had a ruler, a constable, and a schoolmaster. Mr. John Eliot, Jr., preached to them once a fortnight for a number of years, until his decease. Pawtucket, on the Merrimac, where Mr. Eliot began to preach very early, was a community of about seventy-five praying Indians. Their teacher was Samuel, who had been educated at the expense of the English Society. Once a year there was a great gathering of Indians from a large extent of country to fish at the falls of the Merrimac. This was the time when Mr. Eliot was able to reach a large number of strangers.

Other communities were in the vicinity of Concord, Marlborough, Grafton, Uxbridge, Woodstock, Lancaster, Worcester, and Brookfield.

Mr. Gookin found about eleven hundred Christian people in these fourteen towns in 1674. Many of them had been baptized, and a much smaller number had been gathered into churches.[1]

XII

IN connection with these communities, I should speak of the earliest Indian churches. Mr. Eliot desired to gather the Christian Indians into churches as soon as they were prepared for membership. This wish was shared by a large number of the praying Indians. But Mr. Eliot was a cautious man, though bold and decided when he was sure that

Formation of Indian Churches.

[1] Mass. Hist. Soc. Coll., 1st series, i. 180–195. The following are the names of the towns mentioned by Mr. Gookin: —

Naticke,	6,000 acres,	29 families,	145 persons.	
Pakeemitt, or Punkapaog,	6,000 "	12 "	60 "	
Hassanamesitt,	8,000 "	12 "	60 "	
Okommakamesit,	6,000 "	10 "	50 "	
Wamesit or Pawtucket,	2,500 "	15 "	75 "	
Nashobah,	2,600 "	10 "	50 "	
Magunkaquog,	3,000 "	11 "	55 "	
Manchage,	Unknown,	12 "	60 "	
Chabanakongkomun,	"	9 "	45 "	
Maannexit,	"	20 "	100 "	
Quantisset,	"	20 "	100 "	
Wabquisset,	"	30 "	150 "	
Pakachoog,	"	20 "	100 "	
Waeuntug,	"	10 "	50 "	

the time for action had come. There were reasons for special care in this matter. The Indians, although sincere in their professions, were easily led astray by those who lived by pandering to their weaknesses. Although it was contrary to the laws of the Colony to sell strong drink to them, the laws were constantly violated, and the work of the missionary was hindered by the lapses of his people into intemperance. After the Indians had orchards of their own, and fields of grain, they learned to distil strong liquors for themselves. Intemperance was sure to lead these weak people into other forms of evil. The consequence was that some, who had run well for a time, became apostates, and went back to the vices of the pagans.

It appears from a number of circumstances that public opinion in the Colony was never quite favorable to the formation of Indian churches, because the majority of the people did not trust the Indians. There were many who believed that it was enough to gather them into communities like the one at Natick, where they could have regular instruction from their ministers, without organizing them into churches. Mr. Eliot did trust the Indians, because he knew them so well, but he accepted the Puritan doctrine of a converted church membership, and he did not think it would be wise to admit them to full communion

in the churches until they had been sufficiently
proved.

So he acted with great caution. He taught the
praying Indians very carefully the larger catechism
which he had prepared. For a number of years
he had a class of catechumens which he met regularly, and to which he gave a great deal of time.
In August, 1652, he called together the pastors
of the churches to hear the statements which the
Indians might make of "their experience in the
Lord's work upon their hearts." Two years later
the Indians were called a second time before a
council of the ministers to give a reason for the
hope that was in them. The questions and the
answers were taken down, and they are in print.
They show the care that was used to test the Indians as to their knowledge of religious truth, and
as to the sincerity of their religious professions.
They showed that they had made great progress
in the knowledge of the Bible, and in spiritual
discernment. But it was not until 1660 that the
first church among the praying Indians was
formed at Natick. Mr. Eliot baptized the catechumens, and administered to them the Lord's
Supper. From that time the church at Natick was
recognized as a regular Congregational church,
with its own officers and its regular worship, and
with the Christian sacraments. It is not known
how many members it had in the beginning, but

in 1670 it had between forty and fifty communicants. In 1671 the second Indian church was gathered at Hassanamesett, within the present town of Grafton. " This church had a meeting-house for the worship of God after the English fashion of building." It had a native pastor, and a ruling elder, and a deacon. There were sixteen members of the church living in the town, and several others living in other places. There were in the community about thirty baptized persons.[1] A few other Indian churches were organized, but the number was never large. Some Indians were members of the English churches in the Colony. They preferred to be admitted to such churches, and they were welcomed.

In the training of Indian preachers, Mr. Eliot was very successful. It was his opinion that native Indians were better fitted to preach to their own people than others can be. He lived to see twenty-four such preachers raised up, and prepared for their work, many of them by his own instrumentality. We have the authority of Dr. A. C. Thompson for the statement that, after all that has been done for Indian missions during the present century, it is not certain that there are as many well qualified Indian preachers to-day as there were two centuries ago.[2]

[1] Mass. Hist. Soc. Coll., 1st series, i. 184, 185.
[2] Protestant Missions, 71.

XIII

In addition to the care of these settlements of praying Indians, Mr. Eliot was engaged for almost forty years in preparing to translate the Bible into the language of the Massachusetts Indians, and in the translation itself. He was at work upon it as long as he lived. This was his greatest work. He held the opinion that the people could not become intelligent and stable Christians until they had the Sacred Scriptures in their own language, and were able to read them. For years after he was able to speak the language himself, and to teach the Indians to read it, he did not venture to hope that he could put the Bible in printed form into their language. But when he found that it was possible for him to do it, he accepted it as the crowning work of his life. The language was at best that of a barbarous people, — a language, we are told, without poetry or song. To put the great mass of inspired thought, which came to him in the forms of Hebrew and Greek speech, into a language so barren of words to express spiritual truth was a most difficult task. The word "book," for example, did not exist in the Indian speech, for they had no books. So he must borrow the word from another language. They had no word for Testament, or for Christ,

The Translation of the Bible.

and no fit word to be used as the name of God; and so all these English words were transferred in order to make *the title page for the Indian Bible.* Even the word "salt" had to be put into the language, and with that a great many other words to stand for things that are commonplaces among civilized people, but are strange to people without culture.

Our present Revised Version of the Bible was the work of almost one hundred of the selected scholars of England and America. But it was only a revision of an English Version that was itself the work of many minds, two centuries and a half earlier. Almost every one of the great translations of the Bible has been made by the help of a large number of men trained to scholarly investigation. But Eliot had no companions in his work except such Indian interpreters as he had first taught to read and to write. But he labored at his desk early and late, year after year, amid the calls for preaching and parochial work among his own people; — the calls for preaching and teaching, and training preachers and teachers for his Indian congregations; — the care of his family, the care also of that Society in England from which all his funds must come, and the care of all those communities of praying Indians. How wonderful that the translation got itself done at last! It is, by the concession of all, one of the wonders of literary history.

The translation of the New Testament was published in Cambridge in September, 1661, about thirty years after Mr. Eliot landed in New England, and fifteen years after he began preaching to the Indians. That of the Old Testament was published in 1663. The printers, and the printing press and types, and all the materials necessary for the printing, were sent over from England by the Society for Propagating the Gospel in New England, which Society paid the expenses of the publication. The number of copies in the first edition was probably fifteen hundred.[1] The expense was not far from £1,000. It was the first Bible printed in America. It was not till the middle of the next century that the Bible in English was printed in this country. This edition lasted about twenty years. A large number of the younger Indians were able to read it. It was the household book in hundreds of cabins in the wilderness. It was the most effective means which the missionary was able to employ in his work.

In 1680, a second edition of the New Testament was printed, and five years later the second edition of the Old Testament was also printed. Mr. Eliot was assisted in the revision by John

[1] Francis, Life of Eliot, 225.

Cotton, Jr., of Plymouth, who had acquired a good knowledge of the language. Mr. Eliot was eager to have the revision completed. " My age," he says, "makes me importunate. I shall depart joyfully may I but leave the Bible among them, for it is the word of life. . . . I desire to see it done before I die, and I am so deep in years that I cannot expect to live long."

But the two Testaments were bound up together; the Psalms in Indian meter, with a catechism, were added; and this second edition of two thousand copies was in use three or four years before the death of the translator. The cost of this edition was £1,000. It is interesting to learn that one of the printers was an Indian. These two editions made about thirty-five hundred copies in the language of this tribe. It was the most precious book in many Indian homes. It served to keep alive the piety of the Indians in the dark days that were before them.

It is a rare and curious book now, the only memorial of a language that has passed away with the people who used it. It is the most valuable means for studying the dialects of the Algonquin tongue. About one hundred copies remain in libraries in this country and in Europe. It commands a higher price at auction sales than almost any other book. Only a very few now living can read it. One word, at least, has been adopted into our language from Eliot's Bible. The great leaders among the Israelites, like Joshua and Gideon and Samson, were called in that Bible Mug-Wumps, and this is a good name for the independent leaders and voters among our citizens.[1]

XIV

WHILE Mr. Eliot was securing the formation of a Missionary Society in England for the support of Indian Missions, and in gathering the praying Indians into communities and churches, and translating the Bible into their language, he was laying a broad foundation for permanent work among them. He confidently expected that the race would become a civilized and a Christian people. Some of the "wise and sage" Indians were accustomed to say, at that time, that within fifty or a hundred years all the Indians would become like the English. The exceptionally rapid progress of the missionary work, during the first thirty years, under the Mayhews and others in the Plymouth Colony, and under Eliot in Massachusetts, made this seem very probable. The "great hope and inward zeall" of the Pilgrims

Progress of the Work among the Indians.

[1] The Indian title to the second edition of the Bible is this: "Mammusse Wuneetupanatamwe, Up-Biblum God Nanesswe Nu-kone Testament kah wonk Wusku Testament."

and the Puritans led them to labor and pray very earnestly that it might be accomplished.

Mr. Eliot made efforts from year to year to obtain a hearing for the Gospel among the Mohegans and the Narragansetts, those more powerful tribes, of whom the Massachusetts and the Pakonoket tribes were afraid. He petitioned the Commissioners of the Colonies to provide for the "instruction of all the Indians in all parts," and he told the Indians that he had done so. "The Mohegans," he says, "were much troubled lest the Court of Commissioners should take some course to teach them to pray to God," and their sachem went to Hartford to express "his great unwillingness thereunto."[1]

This opposition of the sachems to missionary work among their people was very decided. Mr. Eliot tells us that one of them came to his religious service, and, after the Lecture, protested against his "proceeding to make a Town," and told him "that all the sachems in the country were against it." He was so violent that all the Indians "were filled with fear, their countenances grew pale, and most of them slunk away." But Mr. Eliot replied to him with equal boldness. "*I told him,*" he says, "*that it was God's work I was about, and that God was with me. . . .* I do not fear you," I said, "nor all the sachems in the

[1] Mass. Hist. Soc. Coll., 3d series, iv. 139.

country. . . . I am resolved to go on with my work; and do you touch me if you dare. . . . And it pleased God," we read in Mr. Eliot's record, "that his spirit shrunk, and fell before me." So it was that this humble man of God, "whose heart was full of love, and who with the most winning gentleness would interest himself in the wants of the little children in the wigwam," was able, when the occasion demanded, " to face without dismay the savage chiefs, and answer their violence with a firmness before which the stoutest of them quailed."

Still, the missionary was often in great personal danger, for the sachems and the Powwows, or medicine men, believed that they should lose their power over the people if the religion of the English should make progress among them. The sachems would sometimes drive him out with violence, and would tell him that, if he came again, it would be at his peril. Still he continued his work, and planned as wisely as he was able for its extension. He sent two discreet Indians at one time with a generous present to the most powerful sachem among the Narragansetts, with the purpose of teaching his people the Bible. The sachem accepted the present, as Indians generally do, but refused to receive religious instruction. But the young Indians went about among the people, and found them willing and eager to receive what they had to tell them of the Gospel. He was continually sending his trained native helpers on missions among the pagan Indians, and they found the way open to do good among the people, though they seldom had any favor from the chiefs.

There is a story mentioned by a number of the earlier biographers to this effect: that Mr. Eliot once met King Philip himself, and urged him to accept the Christian faith, and to encourage the teaching of the Bible among his people. It is said that the chieftain rose to his feet, and, taking hold of a button on Mr. Eliot's coat, said with vehemence, "*I care no more for your Gospel than I care for that button.*" This story, if true, shows some of the causes of King Philip's War.

Mr. Eliot pushed his work forward wherever he was permitted. During the twenty-five years from 1650 to 1675 he was enlarging the circle of his influence every year. He made Natick the centre of his operations, but he went himself to a great number of Indian villages, some of them far away. Sometimes it was necessary for him to send Indians over the path to mark the trees, or to cut a path for the missionary through the thick trees.[1] He went four times in one year to Nashaway, now Lancaster, though it was forty miles away. He went generally by invitation.

[1] Mass. Hist. Soc. Coll., 3d series, iv. 123.

The aged sachem at Quaboag (now Brookfield), sixty miles away, asked him to come and teach him and his people. But there had been hostilities between the Narragansetts and the Mohegans, and the road was unsafe. So the sachem at Nashaway came, with twenty armed men, to escort the missionary. He took some of his English friends as an additional guard. But the journey proved to be a hard one. There was continual rain, and they had no protection from the storm by night or by day. "I was not dry, night nor day," he says, "from the third day of the week unto the sixth, but so travelled and at night pull off my boots, wring my stockings, and on with them again, and so continued. . . . The rivers also were raised, so that we were wet in riding through. But that which added to my affliction was, my horse tyred, so that I was forced to let my horse go empty, and ride on one of the men's horses, which I took along with me. Yet God helped me. I considered that word of God, 'Endure hardness as a good soldier of Jesus Christ.'" [1] At the end of the journey, the missionary found "sundry who were hungry after instruction," so that he was well paid for his journey. He records with thankfulness that neither himself nor any of his company were hurt, but came home in safety and in health.

[1] Mass. Hist. Soc. Coll., 3d series, iv. 125.

I do not know where to look for more interesting journals of missionary work than we have in Major Gookin's narrative of an official tour which he took with Mr. Eliot through the country of the praying Indians the year before the great war. They went on horseback, through the forests, Major Gookin as the magistrate, and Mr. Eliot as the apostle to the Indians, both acting under the authority of the General Court. The Law and the Gospel, civilization and religion, went together. Setting out from Natick, they visited Stoughton, Pawtucket, Littleton, Hopkinton, Lancaster, Dudley, Uxbridge, Woodstock, and Brookfield. Eliot spent the days in journeying and in preaching. In the evenings he met his old friends in their wigwams, and heard and answered their questions, talked with the little children, comforted the sick and the afflicted, and led them all to a closer fellowship with the Master.

XV

THE good work among the Indians continued to increase up to the beginning of King Philip's War, in 1675. There were at that time **Results of the Work among the Indians.** about eleven hundred praying Indians on the mainland in Massachusetts, who were distributed in fourteen towns, seven of which had tracts of land secured to them by the

General Court. Schools for the children of Indians had been in operation in most of these towns for many years, and a large proportion of the younger Indians were able to read, and a smaller proportion were able to write. The preachers and the teachers in these villages were nearly all Indians. There were two organized churches within this field, with not quite one hundred members.

Outside the field of Mr. Eliot's direct labors a more extended missionary work had been carried on within the Old Colony, and on the Islands, and in Rhode Island and Connecticut. This work probably began a little earlier than that on the mainland in Massachusetts.[1] It was prosecuted by a number of enterprising and devoted missionaries, among whom were the Mayhews, father, son, and grandson, Richard Bourne, Thomas Tupper, John Cotton, Jr., and Samuel Treat; and in Rhode Island and Connecticut, Roger Williams, Abrahan Pierson, and James Fitch. Some of these missionaries were in charge of English churches; others gave their whole time to the work among the Indians.[2] In 1675 there were about twenty-five hundred praying Indians in the Old Colony, and on the Islands.

[1] Mass. Hist. Soc. Coll., 3d series, iv. 109. New England Memorial, 379, 384.

[2] Mass. Hist. Soc. Coll., 1st series, i. 196–210; 3d series, iv. 107–118. New England Memorial, 379–400.

Mr. Eliot states that there were four churches on the same ground at that time.[1]   Many of these Indians had been civilized, and gathered into towns, which towns had tracts of land, larger or smaller, secured to the Indians by the government of the Colony.   Most of the Indian congregations had native pastors.   A large number of the people were able to read and write their own language.

These missionaries received salaries from the Society in England.   Mr. Eliot had £50 a year, Mr. Mayhew £30, and Mr. Bourne £25.   There was a constant interchange of fraternal greetings, and of labors.   Mr. Mayhew assisted at the organization of the church at Natick, and Mr. Eliot at the organization of the church at Marshpee, and at the ordination of a number of pastors.

An interesting incident has been preserved which shows the liberal spirit of Mr. Eliot, in connection with the account of the well known visit to Boston of Father Gabriel Druillette, a Jesuit missionary from Canada, in 1650.   During his stay in Massachusetts, he called at the house of Mr. Eliot in Roxbury.   He writes in his journal that Eliot invited him to lodge with him, as the night had overtaken him.   These two missionaries — the Jesuit and the Puritan — had much discourse concerning their work among

[1] Mass. Hist. Coll., 1st series, i. 196–210; 3d series, iv. 107–118. Also Francis, Life of Eliot, 263–265.

the Indians. The priest wrote in his journal that Eliot treated him with respect and affection, and invited him to pass the winter with him. The morning and evening devotions of the Puritan household must have kept their wonted course, — while the faithful priest had his oratory, his orisons, and his matin mass before breaking his fast. So easily do good people of different faiths approach each other, when they are devoted to the service of the one Lord, and to the salvation of their fellow men.

XVI

IF peaceful relations could have been continued between the Colonists and the aborigines, it is probable that these efforts King Philip's to civilize and Christianize the In- War. dians would have been so far successful that the great body of them would have accepted the religion and the civilization of the English settlers. That, as we have seen, was the expectation of some of the more enlightened Indians. Still, the method of separating the Christian Indians from their countrymen may not have been as wise as it seemed to Mr. Eliot. It is not the method of modern missionaries. The love of independence was a strong sentiment among the savages. The settlements of the

English were crowding upon their hunting grounds, and the leaders among the more powerful tribes, especially the Mohegans and the Narragansetts, believed that they should become a subject race if they permitted civilization and Christianity to change the habits of their people. These pagan chiefs had a powerful leader in King Philip, the son of Massasoit, chief sachem of the Wampanoags. In him the highest spirit of his race was impersonated, and he led the pagan Indians in a desperate war, in which their watchword was victory or death. The war covered all New England. For almost three years there was a reign of terror. All the New England Colonies united their forces. From the beginning the war was cruel and desperate. The burning of Lancaster and Medfield and Brookfield and Groton and Marlborough and Warwick and Providence, — the massacre of helpless women and children, — the scalping of husbands and brothers, — the infernal torture of prisoners, — roused the whole of New England to a vigorous, and in the end a successful war.

But the war swept away the largest number of the praying Indians, in that part of Massachusetts which was the field of Eliot's labors. Their towns were located where the contest raged most fiercely. They were not trusted by either party. Philip suspected them all, because they had already yielded themselves to the laws and the religion of the Colonists. The English did not trust them because they believed that, with the Indians, the ties of blood would be stronger than the obligation to their new friends. This distrust was strengthened by the fact that some of the praying Indians, from the newer towns were induced to fight with Philip on the side of their race. At the same time, the great body of the Christian Indians were entirely loyal to the English. Several hundred of them enlisted in the army, and taught the English how to cope with the tactics which the Indians always follow. Many times the army was saved from a treacherous ambush by the skill of these allies. "I contend," says Major Gookin, "that the small company of our Indian friends have taken and slain of the enemy, in the summer of 1676, not less than four hundred, and their fidelity and courage are testified by the certificates of their captains."

And yet, amid the excitements of the time, the friendly Indians were suspected. The slightest occurrence was enough to kindle the passions of the people. A barn was burned. It was afterwards discovered that it was set on fire by the hostile Indians. But the inhabitants at once imputed the crime to the Christian Indians, and a number of them were shot down before their own doors. Mr. Eliot, now more than seventy years of age, defended the Indians when they were unjustly accused. In some instances Mr. Gookin and Mr. Eliot proved before a court of justice that the charges against the Indians were unjust, and secured their release. This made them unpopular with the people, who accused them of being in sympathy with robbers and murderers.

In October, 1675, the General Court passed an order that the Indians at Natick should be forth-with removed to Deer Island for safe keeping. There were at that time some two hundred of them, and their removal would break up the settlement, which had been their home for twenty-four years. No charge was made against them, except that it was feared they might become traitors. They sadly but quietly sub-mitted. Their venerable missionary met them on the banks of Charles River, and exhorted them to submit patiently, and to remember that " through much tribulation they must enter into the kingdom of God." All who witnessed the scene were deeply affected by the quiet resigna-tion " of the poor souls, encouraging and ex-horting one another with prayers and tears." Later, the Christian Indians of Punkapog, and of a number of other towns, were also removed to Deer Island and Long Island, so that the whole number in captivity was more than five hundred. They were exposed to much suffering from the lack of food and proper care, and many of them died during their confinement. Eliot and Gookin, and other friends, visited them frequently, encouraging them and ministering to their wants.

When the stress of the war was over, the Indians were removed to Cambridge. Many of them were very ill at the time of their removal. Mr. Eliot and Major Gookin devoted themselves to them, securing for them wholesome food, and such care and medicine as their condition required, so that the most of them recovered. Before winter, they removed from Cambridge. Most of them returned to Natick, and the other settlements from which they had been taken. But they had suffered great losses by the breaking up of their homes. A large number had lost their lives during the war. They came back in poverty, with diminished numbers, without heart or hope. The sympathy and confidence which they had begun to cherish toward their white neighbors had received a rude shock. They felt that, in any emergency, they were powerless, and that they had no means of securing redress. All these things tended to limit the progress of the missionary work which had been so auspiciously begun.

XVII

M R. E LIOT resumed his regular missionary labors as soon as the war was over. He endeav-
ored to gather such as remained of the Indians into their old villages

The Closing
Years.

and places of worship. He was busy preaching to his own people, and visiting them at their homes, and encouraging schools. His latest years were busy years.

It is easy to understand why his work for the Indians did not secure larger and more permanent results. He laid, as we have seen, a broad foundation for a great missionary enterprise. Under favorable circumstances, the churches which were gathered by Eliot, and the Mayhews, and their associates, would have grown to such numbers and influence that they would have evangelized the entire race of Indians. But those churches were planted among a small and decaying people. Mr. Bancroft estimates the whole number of Indians in New England, west of the St. Croix, in 1675, at thirty thousand, a number less than the population of a small city. About four thousand of this small number, more than one eighth, had already been evangelized. The Indian population had been declining for some time before Europeans came to settle on

these coasts. It continued to decline. King
Philip's War was fatal to the Indian race in
these Eastern Colonies. The tribes were broken
up and scattered among the other tribes, so that
the Indian no longer appears as an important
element of population here.

Everything was done that could be done to
preserve and enlarge the Indian churches. In
1684, Mr. Eliot wrote that the number of villages of praying Indians had been reduced to
four : — viz. Natick, Pawtuckett, Stoughton, and
Dudley. In the Old Colony and on the islands,
the number was considerably larger. There was
some religious growth in these communities.
The native preachers were earnest and diligent
in their work. They were assisted by the English ministers, who had planted the churches, and
by their successors. But the Indian race faded
away, year by year, and the churches of necessity became smaller and weaker. The reason
was not that the English crowded them out.
They had set apart reservations of land which
were secured to the Indians, and they taught
them how to cultivate the land. The Indian
lacked iron in the blood, strength of purpose,
power to resist temptation to intemperance and
to other vices. Even Christianity, as set forth
by Eliot and Mayhew, and the other apostles
to the Indians, could not secure the continued

existence of the race. " There is a cloud," said Mr. Eliot in his old age, — "a dark cloud upon the work of the Gospel among the poor Indians. The Lord revive and prosper that work, and grant that it may live when I am dead."

Mr. Eliot had a serene and beautiful old age. His mind was vigorous and active. At the age of seventy-four, he published " The Harmony of the Gospels," a work to which he had devoted a great deal of study. He wrote frequently to England in regard to the printing of his revised version of the Bible. " Our praying Indians," he said, "both on the islands and on the mainland, include thousands of souls, and all of them beg, cry, and entreat for Bibles. He carried the revised edition of the Indian Bible through the press when he had passed his eightieth year. He was still interested in the progress of medical science, and in the study of theology. He continued to preach as long as his strength lasted, and then he asked his people at Roxbury to make no delay in selecting his successor. He outlived nearly all his old friends in the ministry, and he used to say that Richard Mather, and John Cotton, and the other dear friends who were waiting for him in heaven, would think he had gone the wrong way. His last words were, " Welcome joy! " and then, " Pray, pray, pray!"

He died on the 20th of May, 1690, eighty-five years of age, one of the last of that generation of great and holy men.

He was buried in the parish tomb, in the old burying ground, at the corner of Washington and Eustis Streets, Roxbury (now Boston).

Mrs. Eliot had died three years before, March 24, 1687. Their children were:—

HANNAH, born September 17, 1633.
JOHN, born August 3, 1636, H. C. 1656.
JOSEPH, born December 20, 1638, H. C. 1658.
SAMUEL, born June 22, 1641, H. C. 1660.
AARON, born February 19, 1644. Died 1655.
BENJAMIN, born January 29, 1647, H. C. 1665.

The following is an incomplete list of his publications, in addition to the Indian Bible:—

An Indian Catechism, 1655.
The Christian Commonwealth, 1659.
Baxter's Call to the Unconverted (Translation), 1664.
The Indian Psalter, 1664.
The Communion of Churches, 1665.
Bayley's Practice of Piety (Translation), 1665.
The Indian Primer (Indian), 1669.
The Logic Primer (Indian), 1672.
Harmony of the Gospels, 1678.
Shepard's Sincere Convert (Translation), 1689.

The following inscription was placed upon his tomb.[1]

HERE LIE THE REMAINS
OF
JOHN ELIOT,
THE APOSTLE TO THE INDIANS,
ORDAINED OVER THE FIRST CHURCH,
NOVEMBER 5, 1632.
DIED MAY 20, 1690,
AGED
LXXXVI.

[1] See Genealogical Register, xiv. 220.

IV

Jonathan Edwards, and the Great Awakening

Jonathan Edwards and the Great Awakening

Jonathan Edwards, and the Great Awakening

THE Great Awakening of which so much is said in the books published in New England about the middle of the eighteenth century, was connected with a remarkable declension of the religious life in the Puritan churches. The fathers of New England had come here especially to plant pure churches, on the basis of a membership made up of those who had a genuine religious experience. All who became communicants in those churches during the first generation were required to give an account of their religious experiences. It was the confident expectation of the Pilgrims and the Puritans, that they should be able to develop a church life in this new country that would be much nearer the standard of the New Testament than any that had been known since the time of the primitive churches. They were confident that, in leaving the methods of organization and of worship to which they had been accustomed in England, they had escaped from the influences that tended towards a weak and formal spiritual life.

I

IN this expectation they were for a time disappointed. It is true a high standard of piety was maintained in their churches for thirty or forty years. But the second generation fell below the standard of the fathers. We have the well known statement of Thomas Prince, that "a little after 1660 there began to appear a Decay; and this increased to 1670, when it grew very visible and threatening, and was generally complained of and bewailed bitterly by the Pious among them; and yet much more in 1680, when but few of the first Generation remained."[1] This state of things

The Reform- led to the calling of the Reforming ing Synod. Synod, which met in Boston in 1678. It was made up of delegates from the churches of Massachusetts. This Synod, after a careful examination of the religious condition of the congregations, set forth a statement which, as it is read now in the pages of Cotton Mather, is simply appalling. They lamented the neglect of public worship; the desecration of the Lord's day; the lack of family government; an alarming increase of worldliness among the people, accompanied by dishonesty, extravagance, lying, intemperance, profanity, and a general decay of godliness in the land. The change was

[1] Christian History, Boston, 1743, i. 84.

certainly very great from the time when Hugh
Peters, in a sermon preached in 1646 before
Parliament, the Westminster Assembly, and the
Corporation of London, stated in respect to
Massachusetts, " I have lived seven years in a
country where I never saw a beggar, nor heard
an oath, nor looked upon a drunkard."

The evidence that there was a decline in the
religious life in New England at that time is
too decisive to be questioned. The Election
Sermons preached before the General Court of
Plymouth Colony, and of the Colony of Massachusetts Bay, and of that of Connecticut, show
that the change in the churches had been such
as to cause very great alarm. In Plymouth,
Thomas Walley said in 1669, " How is New
England fallen ! The land that was a land of
Holiness hath lost her holiness." In Massachusetts, William Stoughton said to the Legislature
in 1668 : " O what a sad metamorphosis hath of
later years passed upon us in these churches and
plantations ! Alas ! how is New England in danger to be buried in its own ruins." Dr. Increase
Mather said in 1678 : "Clear, sound conversions
are not frequent. . . . Many of the rising generation are profane, Drunkards, Swearers, Licentious,
and scoffers at the Power of Godliness." Rev.
Samuel Whitman said in Connecticut in 1714 :
" Religion is on the Wane among us. . . . We are

risen up a Generation that have in a great
Measure forgot the errand of our Fathers."[1]

There were a number of reasons for this appar-
ent failure of the early churches of New England
to realize the hopes of their founders.
Reasons for the Decline of Religion. These reasons were not such as to
cast any discredit upon the sincerity
or the piety of the founders. Some of the reasons were connected with the weakness and iso-
lation of the settlements. The second generation
had not enjoyed the pleasant social life of Old
England. They were ruder in manners than
their fathers, with less of education and of culture. The struggle of life in the wilderness was
a severe one, and there was a tendency to give a
subordinate place to the things that are religious. The first settlers had come here fresh
from the struggle for freedom to worship according to their own consciences. Their children had
no such experience of conflict.

There was also an element in the population
made up of the children of those who had come
to New England in the condition of servants to
the original planters. These persons were never
in full sympathy with the ideas of the Puritans,
and their descendants were only too likely to
fall away from the religious habits of the earlier

[1] See the Election Sermons preached in these three Colonies
between 1668 and 1714.

generations. " They were," says Dr. Walker, "rela-
tively a numerous and positively a debasing factor
in the life of the Colonial towns and villages." [1]

Besides these natural causes of the decline of
religion in the Colonies there were other causes
connected with the methods that were adopted
by the leaders among the New England Puritans. It is common to say that "they builded
better than they knew." The statement may be
correct as to the main part of the policy of the
founders. And yet they had established an ecclesiastical system in their plantations that was
comparatively untried in modern times. It was
inevitable that some mistakes should be made,
even by men as wise and devout as the founders
of these Colonies.

The close union of Church and State in Massachusetts and some of the other Colonies was
shown by the results to be one of these mistakes.
Such a union was especially unfavorable to the
development of Congregational Churches. While
it lasted it limited very much the development of
the religious life among the people. It was not
in harmony with the free spirit of the churches
that were here established. Experience has
shown that it is better for Congregationalists not
to be " The Standing Order."

[1] Some Aspects of the Religious Life of New England, p. 49.
Dr. George L. Walker.

The Half Way Covenant was another of the mistakes of the early Congregationalists. It was, at best, a compromise between the methods of the Established Church of England, and those of the free churches of New England. In the course of time it did away with the Puritan principle of a church made up of regenerated persons. The Episcopal Church, with its methods of government, and its Prayer Book, is much better fitted than the Congregational churches to train a class of communicants who have come into the church by reason of their baptism in infancy.

In addition to these causes of declension, we should recognize *the methods of presenting religious truth in the pulpit*. The early ministers of New England were extreme Calvinists. They had not learned in the seventeenth century how to preach the sovereignty of God in such a way as to develop a sense of personal freedom and responsibility. We have but to read the treatises that were given to the press during the first century of the history of New England by the Puritan divines to learn that they were not " wise to win souls " by presenting the " sweet reasonableness " of the Gospel. The sermons of those preachers made the impression upon some minds that all things were so arranged in the Divine economy

Preaching in the Seventeenth Century.

that impenitent men had very little to do towards securing their salvation.

For example, Thomas Shepard said : " Thou mayest see the land of Canaan, and take much pains to goe into Canaan, and mayest tast of the bunches of Grapes of that good land, but never enter into Canaan, into Heaven, but thou liest bound hand and foot in this woful estate, and here thou must lie and rot like a dead carkasse in his grave untill the Lord come and rowle away the stone, and bid thee come out and live." [1] In another place he says : — " Now doe not thou shift it from thy selfe, and say, God is Merciful. True, but it is to very few, as shall be proved. 'T is a thousand to one if ever thou bee one of that small number whom God hath picked out to escape this wrath to come." [2]

President Willard said : " Election is an act of grace. Redemption is an act of pure grace. Election is absolute, not hypothetical. The subjects of election are a definite number of men. . . . There are some men to whom God doth not afford the means and offices of Salvation, and they must needs perish." [3]

These quotations are sufficient to indicate the sort of instruction that used to be given in

---

[1] Sincere Convert, 1646, p. 71.

[2] Ibid., p. 98.

[3] Willard's Body of Divinity, 196, 197.

many of the congregations during the Puritan age in New England. There was a variety in the methods of preaching at that time. Thomas Hooker gave more emphasis to the truth of personal freedom and responsibility than John Norton did. Some of those preachers found the substance of their messages in the parables of the Prodigal Son, and of the Great Supper, and in the free and gracious invitations of the Saviour. But the prevailing tone in the pulpit was fatalistic. It discouraged human effort. Great multitudes were waiting for God to come and save them. They persuaded themselves that they were not responsible for their continued impenitence. They were using the means of grace, and they were taught that they could do no more until God should be pleased to pluck them as brands from the burning.

After the time of the Reforming Synod the decline of religion was checked for a few years, **Efforts to check the Religious Declension.** and earnest efforts were made in Massachusetts and Connecticut to bring about a general awakening among the people. These efforts were not in vain. There were some revivals of religion in the churches. We have an account of a remarkable religious work in Taunton in 1704, and of a number of revivals in Northampton during the long ministry of Rev. Solomon Stoddard. The list might easily be extended. But on the whole the ministers and churches of New England at that time were very far from the ways of the fathers. The Half Way Covenant had brought into the churches large numbers of people who were not, even in their own judgment, true Christians. The need of regeneration was not made prominent in the preaching of that time. The ministers were preaching morality, and the people were becoming more immoral every year. Many were trusting to their good works to save them, but they were not careful to do such works as God had required. "And yet," said one of the old writers, "never had the expectation of reaching heaven at last been more general or more confident."

The Protestant churches in Great Britain at that time were no better than those in America. There had been a decided reaction from the intense religious spirit of the seventeenth century. Bishop Butler remarks, in the Preface to the Analogy (1736), that "it has come to be taken for granted that Christianity is not so much as a subject of inquiry; but that it is now discovered to be fictitious." The same writer stated that the characteristic of that age was "an avowed scorn of religion in some, and a growing disregard of it in the generality." Addison declared that there " was less appearance of religion in England than in any neighboring state or kingdom." "In the higher circles of society," said Montesquieu, "every one laughs if one talks of religion." Bishop Burnet, in 1713, wrote of those who presented themselves to be ordained as clergymen, "They can give no account, or at least a very imperfect one, of the contents of the Gospels, or of the Catechism itself." The truth is that Puritanism in England had lost a great part of its vigor and its influence, and the Established Church had not prepared itself to take its place in leading the English people to a higher religious life.[1]

It was time for a Great Awakening. He to whom the church is dearer than the apple of His eye was preparing a group of men with remarkable gifts to serve as His agents in a work that was to give a new direction to modern thought, as well as to modern Christianity. Some of these great evangelists were trained in Great Britain, as Whitefield and the Wesleys. Others had been trained in this country, such as Edwards, the Tenants, Parsons, and Wheelock. The Church of England needed the Awakening quite as much as the Dissenters, or the Puritan Churches of New England.

[1] See Prof. Fisher's History of Doctrine, 389–391. Greene's Short History of the English People, 736. Bibliotheca Sacra, 1897, pp. 69–80.

II

JONATHAN EDWARDS was the son of Timothy Edwards, the pastor for sixty years at East Windsor, Connecticut. His mother was the daughter of Solomon Stoddard, Early Life of Edwards. whose pastorate at Northampton lasted from 1672 to 1729. He was born October 5, 1703. He was a precocious boy. He has been compared to Pascal in respect to the early manifestation of intellectual power. His early writings, and the books that he read even before he entered college, show a decided bent towards the study of nature and of mind. He entered Yale College at the age of thirteen, and was graduated at seventeen. Afterwards he spent two years in the study of theology in connection with the College. He was licensed to preach at the age of nineteen. His first preaching was in New York, where he was very much liked. After eight months in New York he declined to remain longer, and went back to the College, where he served for two years as tutor, continuing his studies in divinity and in psychology. He was ordained at Northampton, February 15, 1727, in his twenty-third year, as colleague pastor with his grandfather, then in his eighty-fourth year.

Eight years later, the Great Awakening began

in that parish, in connection with the preaching of that remarkable man. He is spoken of most frequently as a hard logician, a metaphysician, a Calvinistic theologian. If that had been all, the revival would not have begun in his parish. He was undoubtedly a man of the highest order of intellect. He was a brilliant scholar. He was a man of deep piety. He was accustomed, while yet a child, to go by himself to secret places in the woods for the purpose of prayer. He passed through very deep religious experiences during his college life. A little later he wrote, "I made seeking my salvation the main business of my life." The Diary which he kept in his early years shows how deep his religious experiences were, and how entire his consecration. He recorded his solemn engagement always "to do whatever he thought to be most for the glory of God and his own good, without consideration of the time, whether now or never so many myriads of ages hence; no matter how great or how many the difficulties he might meet; to do his duty, and what is most for the good of mankind in general." He resolved never to lose a moment of time, to live while he lived with all his might. An instructive parallel might be drawn between the early religious exercises of John and Charles Wesley and those of Jonathan Edwards. The revival on both sides of the sea had its spring in the deep searchings of heart, and in the complete consecration of these men.

Jonathan Edwards was a man of tender feelings, and of very strong affections. He had the imagination of a poet. "He had a Qualities of rare combination," says a recent his Mind. writer, "of fervor of feeling, of almost oriental richness of imagination, with intellectual acumen which clothed all that he said with glowing force, while beneath his words flowed the stream of a most carefully elaborated theological system."

Let us select two or three specimens from the writings of this representative Puritan pastor. On a certain day, in his early youth, he walked in his father's pasture. He says: "As I was walking there, and looking up in the sky and clouds, there came into my mind so sweet a sense of the glorious majesty and grace of God, as I knew not how to express. I seemed to see them both in a sweet conjunction, majesty and meekness joined together; it was a sweet and gentle and holy majesty, and also a majestic sweetness, an awful sweetness, a high and great and holy gentleness."

"I spent the most of my time," he says, "in thinking of divine things, year after year; often walking alone in the woods and solitary places for meditation, soliloquy, and prayer, and converse with God; and it was always my manner at such times to sing forth my contemplations."

In one of his private papers, written in middle life, he says, " The soul of a true Christian appeared like such a little white flower as we see in the spring of the year, low and humble on the ground, opening its bosom to receive the pleasant beams of the sun's glory, rejoicing as it were in a calm rapture, diffusing around a sweet fragrancy, standing peacefully and lovingly in the midst of other flowers round about; all in like manner opening their bosoms to drink in the light of the sun."[1]

Here is a passage from his Journal, in which he describes Sarah Pierrepont, who became his wife a few years later: " They say there is a young lady in . . . who is beloved of that Great Being who made and rules the world, and that there are certain seasons in which this Great Being, in some way or other, invisibly comes to her, and fills her mind with exceeding great delight, and that she hardly cares for any thing except to meditate on Him; that she expects after awhile to be received up where He is; to be raised up out of the world, and caught up into Heaven, being assured that there she is to dwell with Him, and to be ravished with His love and delight forever. She will sometimes go about from place to place singing sweetly, and seems

[1] Life of Edwards. New York reprint of the Worcester Edition, i. 18.

to be always full of joy and pleasure, and no one knows for what. She loves to be alone, walking in the fields and groves, and seems to have some one invisible always conversing with her."

He describes an experience which he had while in middle life, in which he had "a view of the glory of the Son of God, as Mediator between God and man, and His wonderful, great, full, pure, and sweet grace and love, and meek and gentle condescension. The person of Christ appeared ineffably excellent, with an excellency great enough to swallow up all thought and conception, — which continued, as near as I can judge, about an hour, which kept me the greater part of the time in tears, and weeping aloud. I felt an ardency of soul to be, — what I know not otherwise how to express, — emptied and annihilated; to lie in the dust, and to be full of Christ alone; to love Him with a pure and holy love; to trust in Him; to live upon Him; to serve and follow Him; and to be perfectly sanctified and made pure with a divine and heavenly purity."

In his personal appearance Mr. Edwards is said to have been a tall, slender man, upwards of six feet in height. His face was of His Personal the feminine type, like that of the Appearance. Apostle John, rather than that of the Apostles Peter or Paul. There was about him the air of a seer, of one inspired. His appearance in the pulpit was graceful, his delivery natural, easy, and very solemn. His voice was not loud or strong, but he spoke with such distinctness, clearness, and precision, his sentences were so full of ideas, set in a plain and striking light, that he commanded the attention of the audience. His sermons were written, but he was not closely confined to his notes. He was accustomed to lean on one arm, fastening his eyes upon some distant part of the meeting-house.[1] He used very little action in the pulpit, but he spoke with such fervor and earnestness that his words had great power. He was one of the great preachers of the age, — Prof. A. V. G. Allen speaks of him as the greatest of them.

III

It was the mission of this man of great intellectual power and profound spiritual insight to apply the truths of the Gospel to a people in a very low religious condition. He had to meet what was then called Arminianism; a system that differed radically from the evangelical Arminianism which Wesley preached, and which has been a leading factor in the revivals of religion of the last century and a half. This so

[1] Edwards's Works, Life, i. 29. Life of Jonathan Edwards, by Prof. A. V. G. Allen.

called Arminianism was combined with Arian and Socinian opinions. It had grown up in New England, as a reaction from the extreme Calvinism of the early New England fathers. Its progress had been helped by the working of the Half Way Covenant. Inasmuch as the change at conversion was supposed to be altogether beyond human power, men inquired whether there were not some religious acts which they could perform which would lead on towards conversion. The Arminians of that day taught that the use of "the means of grace," such as the State of the reading of the Scriptures, prayer, at- Churches. tendance on public worship, and especially the use of the sacraments, would prepare them for the kingdom of Heaven. Men were not taught that it was their duty to repent of their sins, and begin at once to serve and obey God, trusting to His promised help and grace, but only that it was their duty to use the means of grace. This relieved them from a sense of responsibility for their continued impenitence. They persuaded themselves that they were doing their part of the work, and that there was nothing more for them to do until they should receive the Divine Spirit, who had power to change their evil nature, and give them the new heart and the new spirit. The preaching of the time was mainly didactic. It was addressed to the understanding, rather

19

than to the heart. Its tone was ethical, rather than spiritual. It dwelt mainly on the duties of men to each other and to God. Multitudes were lingering among the so called preliminaries to regeneration, waiting for the Divine work in their hearts. So that in many of the Puritan churches the people were trusting in forms and outward observances, while spiritual religion was losing its power.

The long and very able ministry of Mr. Stoddard at Northampton had moulded the opinions and habits of the people of that town. He had taught them that the Lord's Supper was a converting ordinance. The Half Way Covenant had brought into that church a large number who were not, even in their own opinion, regenerated persons. Mr. Edwards tells us, in his Narrative, that the town had at that time about two hundred families. He believed that the religious condition of the people was at least as good as that of the people in other parts of New England. But, he tells us, it was a time of extraordinary dulness in religion; that for some years licentiousness had prevailed among the young people of the town; that many of them were very much addicted to night walking, and frequenting the tavern, and to lewd practices; that they would frequently get together for what they called frolics, and would spend the greater part of the night in them, without any regard to order in the families they belonged to; and that indeed family government did much fail in the town. He found also that many of the young people were indecent in their conduct in meeting.[1]

Two or three years after the beginning of the ministry of Mr. Edwards, there began to be a marked improvement in the habits of the young people of his congregation. They became more decorous in their behavior during the religious services, and more disposed to keep the Lord's day, and to listen to religious instruction. Late in the year 1734, the young pastor determined to meet the errors which prevailed among his people by a series of sermons on Justification by Faith alone, the doctrine with which, **The Great** as Luther declared, a church stands **Awakening.** or falls. He tells us that, "although great fault was found with meddling with the controversy in the pulpit at that time, by such a person" (as the young and inexperienced pastor), "and though it was ridiculed by many, yet it proved a word spoken in season, and was most evidently attended with a very remarkable blessing of Heaven to the souls of the people."

In these sermons he attempted to sweep away the hopes which men had built upon their moral-

[1] Edwards's Works, i. 29. Narrative of Surprising Conversions, Works, iii. 233. The Great Awakening, by Dr. Joseph Tracy, 213. Allen's Life of Edwards, 40 and 126.

ity, their "owning the covenant," partaking of the Lord's Supper, and using the other means of grace. He taught that the first thing, and the only thing for them to do, was to come to Christ, with penitence for their sins, relying only upon the free promises of the Gospel. " This way of the Gospel was made evident," to use the words of Edwards, " as the true and only way. Then it was, in the latter part of December (1734) that the Spirit of God began to work wonderfully amongst us, and there were, very suddenly, five or six persons, to all appearances, savingly converted, and some were wrought upon in a very remarkable manner." [1]

The revival was connected very closely with the preaching of Mr. Edwards. He set forth with great power the Calvinistic system of doctrine, but in the stress and pressure of the religious work he was led into those modifications of the older Calvinism, out of which the New England theology has grown. His system was a modified Calvinism. The urgent motive with the great evangelist was to present the truth in such a way as *to deepen the sense of personal responsibility.* He made much of the difference between natural and moral ability. He taught that the sinner has a natural ability to repent, and is therefore under obligation to repent. His

---

[1] Works, iii. 234.

inability is moral, and consists in an unwillingness to do his duty. For this unwillingness he is responsible. To continue in the use of means, without repentance, is only to add to the sins of the past. The promises of God are addressed only to those who repent. He insisted, therefore, upon immediate repentance. Means were nothing without repentance; strivings and resolutions were nothing. He exhorted his people to cast themselves just as they were upon the mercy of God, and trust Him to save them in His infinite love and grace.

The revival spread rapidly into all parts of the town, and reached persons of all ages and conditions in life. Religion became the great subject of thought and conversation. " There was scarcely a person in the town," says Mr. Edwards, " unconcerned about the great things of the eternal world. In the spring and summer following, the town seemed to be full of the presence of God. Our assemblies were then beautiful. Our public praises were greatly enlivened. Our young people when they met were wont to spend the time in talking of the love of Jesus Christ, the wonderful, free, and sovereign grace of God, — His glorious work in the conversion of souls, — and the truth and certainty of the great things of God's word."[1] Mr. Edwards believed that more than

[1] Narrative, 235.

three hundred were brought to Christ, in that town, within six months, and that almost everybody in the town at that time, above sixteen years of age, was a true Christian. He mentions that some thirty children, of from ten to fourteen years, were among the subjects of this work. He gives an interesting account of the conversion of a child about four years of age.[1] It appears from his statements that religious meetings for children were very common during the revival.

The work extended from Northampton into the adjoining towns. In March, the revival was general in South Hadley and in Suffield. It soon appeared in Sutherland, Deerfield, Hatfield, West Springfield, Longmeadow, and Northfield. There were revivals of great power in ten or twelve of the leading towns of Connecticut. It continued in the Connecticut Valley for about six months. It reached towns as far apart as Stratford, New Haven, Groton, Lebanon, and Coventry. The next year, Mr. Edwards wrote his "Narrative of Surprising Conversions," which was published first in Great Britain, and, two years later, was republished in Boston, with several of the sermons that had been most useful in promoting the work.

It will not be necessary to follow at great length the history of the Great Awakening in the ten

[1] Works, iii. 265, also 348.

years that followed 1735. Mr. Edwards had a very important part in the work through all those years. He was, in a sense, the moving spirit of the revival. By his preaching, and his personal labors, and his counsels to the pastors who were constantly consulting him, and by his publications, he helped on the work, and gave it steadiness and permanent influence. In 1740 and 1741, there was a work of grace in Northampton even more extended than the one seven years before. There was another revival two years later, and a third two years afterward.[1] During these years, the religious work extended into all parts of New England, and into the middle and southern Colonies. The period of religious inertia had been effectually broken up. A rift had been made in the old fatalism, which had paralyzed so many of the churches. The revivals gave them a new sense of the spiritual power that was within their reach. A considerable number of pastors began to labor as evangelists in parishes near their own. There was an interchange of such labors at that time that was very profitable. There was also a class of itinerant evangelists who were employed in many of the churches.

We have accounts of the preaching of Mr. Edwards in Westborough, Leicester, Sutton, En-

---

[1] Christian History, i. 367.

field, Boston, and various other places.[1] In some instances he spent several weeks in a place.

Of the effect of his famous sermon at Enfield, we have an account written by an intelligent minister who was present. He says : " While the people of the neighboring towns were in great distress for their souls, the inhabitants of Enfield were very secure, loose, and vain. A lecture had been appointed there, and the neighboring people, the night before, were so affected at the thoughtlessness of the inhabitants that they spent a considerable part of the night praying for them. When the time for the lecture came, a number of the neighboring ministers attended, and some from a distance. The appearance of the assembly in the meeting-house was thoughtless and vain. The people hardly conducted themselves with common decency. Mr. Edwards preached from a passage in Deut. xxxii. 35, ' Their foot shall slide in due time.' As he advanced in unfolding the meaning of the text, the most rigid logic brought him and his hearers to conclusions which the most tremendous imagery could but inadequately express." The effect was such as might have been expected. " Before the sermon was ended the assembly appeared deeply impressed, and bowed down with an awful convic-

[1] Journal of Rev. E. Parkmore of Westborough, in the library of the Antiquarian Society, Worcester.

tion of their sin and danger. There was such a breathing of distress and weeping that the preacher was obliged to speak to the people and desire silence that he might be heard. This was the beginning of the same great and prevailing concern in that place, with which the Colony in general was visited." [1]

This sermon is often quoted as though it were a fair specimen of the preaching of Mr. Edwards. One has only to read the titles of his published sermons to learn how great a variety of topics he presented in the pulpit. "The Excellency of Christ," "Ruth's Resolution," "The Peace which Christ gives His true Followers," "A Divine and Supernatural Light imparted to the Soul," "A God who heareth Prayer," "God the best Portion of the Christian," — these suggest a style of thought and discourse much more in accordance with the other works of the great preacher. He believed and taught that love is the chief of the Christian graces, and that from love of God all other graces flow. He felt that the state of opinion and practice at that time made it necessary to preach the terrors of the Lord, and he knew how to uncover the hypocrisy and unbelief of men in a convincing way; but the dominant tone of his preaching was argumentative and per-

[1] Rev. Mr. Wheelock of Lebanon, quoted in Trumbull's History of Connecticut, ii. 145.

suasive. If he was ever a son of thunder, it was in the same sense with the Apostles James and John.

IV

ABOUT the time when the Great Awakening was in progress in New England, the Great Methodist Revival in the Mother Country was beginning, in connection with the ministry of John and Charles Wesley and George Whitefield. These three remarkable men had been together at Oxford University, and they had been prepared for their mission as leaders in the religious work of their time by profound religious experiences. They were all members of the Church of England, and in the beginning do not seem to have disagreed in theological opinion. Later, the Wesleys adopted the Arminian system of doctrine, while Whitefield announced himself a Calvinist. Their work was essentially the same work, though carried on by different methods, and as the result of it the old indifference was broken up, and the churches in the various English speaking countries on both sides of the sea received a powerful religious impulse which has continued to this day.[1]

The Great Awakening in England.

The visit of Whitefield to New England was in 1740. His work in the South, and in the

[1] Centenary of American Methodism, Stevens, 11–78.

middle Colonies, and in England was already so well known that he was very cordially welcomed by the ministers and churches here. He was then twenty-six years of age, with a fine physical form, and a gift of extemporaneous speech such as few have ever possessed, and with a voice of marvellous power and flexibility. A Connecticut farmer who heard him preach in Hartford said of him: "He looked almost angelical, a young, slim, slender youth before some thousands of people, and with a bold undaunted countenance. It solemnized my mind and put me in a trembling fear before he began to preach, for he looked as if he was clothed with authority from God."[1] His style was natural and clear, animated and pathetic, and sometimes truly sublime. He had a voice of wonderful flexibility, compass, and power; and his action was graceful, impressive, and appropriate. As an orator, the world perhaps never saw his superior.

He preached first in Newport, then in Bristol, and then in Boston. No church in the town was large enough to contain the crowds that came to hear him. It is said that he preached to twenty thousand people on Boston Common. From Boston he went to all the principal towns in Massachusetts and Connecticut. It was a novel

[1] Dr. Walker's Religious Life in New England, 91.

experience to New Englanders to listen to such a preacher, and wherever he went multitudes came to hear him. He visited Northampton, and preached with great eloquence in Mr. Edwards's pulpit. Mr. Edwards himself was deeply affected, and wept during almost the whole service. The people were equally moved.[1]

The preaching of Mr. Whitefield extended the religious work very widely among people who were not likely to be reached by the regular ministers. He also interrupted the harmony of the churches by the methods which he followed. He was still a young man, and was apt to be opinionated and censorious. He made too much of certain physical manifestations which were connected with the great excitement that accompanied his impassioned addresses. Mr. Edwards himself suggested to him that he was giving too much importance to things of that sort.

But after all that may be said of his indiscretions, Mr. Whitefield did more than any other man excepting Mr. Edwards to extend the work of grace through all the English Colonies in America, and to give the churches here new power to mould the masses of the people for good.

[1] Tracy's Great Awakening.

V

THE most careful students of this critical period in our religious history agree that this religious work has never been equalled in this country for its intensity and permanent results. The estimates of the *Extent of the Great Awakening.* number of people who were brought into the churches, which were made by the older writers, vary from twenty-five thousand to fifty thousand. We have no reliable statistics of the number of churches and communicants in New England at that time. So far as we are able to *Additions to the Churches.* learn, it would seem that the number of Congregational churches was about three hundred and eighty. President Styles states that a hundred and fifty new churches were formed in the new towns and parishes in the twenty years following 1740. This does not include the large number of Baptist churches that were gathered in those years, nor the number of the Separatist churches.

More important than the increase in numbers was the change in the methods of administration in the Congregational churches. The great revival led them to correct the practical mistakes they had made in the earlier years. The prominent part which Mr. Edwards had as the leader in the Great Awakening enabled him to guide the churches into a better way.

One of the most useful of his works is his "Humble Inquiry into the Rules of the Word of God concerning the Qualifications for Full Communion." He stated the question at the outset, "whether any persons except such as are in profession and appearance endued with Christian grace or piety ought to be admitted to the Christian sacraments." It is a clear and convincing argument in favor of the Puritan practice of admitting "only those who give evidence that they are the children of God." His views on this matter probably cost him his pastorate at Northampton, but his arguments, taken in connection with the evil results of the Half Way Covenant led the people back to the earlier and better practice. After that time the methods of the Half Way Covenant were gradually abandoned by the more spiritual and evangelical churches.

The union of Church and State was not at once given up. It required the separation from Great Britain, and the adoption of a free republican government to prepare the way for the voluntary system. But the Great Awakening gave an impulse to the religious life of the churches which prepared them in the course of time to dispense with the aid of the state.

Still more important was the modification of the theological views and methods of preaching among Congregationalists. The cold and formal Arminianism, with its Arian and Socinian elements, was no longer dominant in the Congregational churches. Under the influence of the quickened religious experiences of the revival, men learned how to preach the sovereignty of God in such a way as to deepen the sense of freedom and responsibility. The Edwardean theology, as it has been developed by the younger Edwards, and Bellamy, and President Dwight, and Professor Park, and their associates and successors, has changed the style of preaching in the Puritan pulpits, and has led the ministers to lay hold in a new way upon the truths of the New Testament. There have been, it is true, periods of religious declension since that time, and yet, on the whole, the century and a half since the Great Awakening has been characterized by revivals of religion, and by great movements for the conversion of the world. From the time of the Great Awakening there have been " two wings in the Congregational body." On the one side were the Old Calvinists and the followers of Edwards with his modified Calvinism. These were the friends of the revival, and they were confirmed in their evangelical views by the results of that work of grace. On the other side were the so called Arminians, who found themselves out of sympathy with the spirit and methods of the revival. In the course of about two generations, these two divergent tendencies led to the separation of the Puritan churches into two bodies, which we designate as Orthodox and Unitarian Congregationalists.

The rise and growth of the Methodist Episcopal Church in this country has had much to do in moulding the methods of preaching in the Puritan churches. It has given to the pulpit an added intensity and directness, and a wiser adaptation to its purpose of arousing men to their religious duties, by following more closely the methods of the New Testament.

During this period the Home and Foreign Missionary Societies have come into existence, while the English settlements have been pushed out into the valley of the Mississippi, and on to the Pacific coast. Most of the new churches have been Missionary churches. The new colleges have been planted by Home Missionaries. The Puritan churches have certainly done their part in educating and evangelizing all parts of our country.

So it has come to pass that in these later periods the churches of the Puritan fathers have come much nearer the ideals of their founders than they did in the earlier years. They have

become freer, and more spiritual. They have
learned a better theology. They have a larger
charity, and a sweeter spirit, and they are ful-
filling a more important mission to the world;
and, as a result of these changes, they have come
into a closer relation to the other branches of
the Church of our Lord. They are prepared to
unite very heartily with all the true followers of
Christ in united efforts for the conversion of the
world.

20

V

Shakespeare and the Puritans

Shakespeare and the Puritans

OUR New England ancestors were very intelligent men and women. They brought their books with them when they planted their settlements on this side of the sea. One could hardly be a Puritan who was not able to read the Geneva Bible. Their ministers were graduates of Cambridge or Oxford, and their libraries contained volumes of history, and poetry, and philosophy, as well as of theology.[1] Myles Standish left a library which contained volumes on military tactics, and science, and history, a copy of Homer's Iliad, and an English Dictionary, besides a large number of religious books. William Blackstone, who first gained a title to land in Boston, and who lived there almost alone with his servants, had a library of a hundred and eighty-six volumes, many of them in Latin. William Pynchon, the first settler of Springfield, a business man, was able to quote Greek and Latin and Hebrew, and he wrote in a clear and vigorous English style. Governor Winthrop of Massachusetts had a good library, comprising not only

[1] The Puritan in England and New England, 124.

English books, but also French and Latin books. The younger Winthrop is said to have had a library of a thousand volumes. These are instances which might be multiplied of the books that were to be found in Puritan homes. The Puritans founded Harvard College while their settlements were in their infancy, and established a public school in every township of fifty families for "all such children" (boys and girls) "as shall resort to it."

The Protestant Reformation in England had brought the great middle class of the English people to a higher grade of intelligence and a closer relation with the real life of the nation. The Puritans were in large part from this great middle class. Most of those who were distinguished as scholars and authors, and leaders of the people in England at that time, were of humble origin. The Puritans of England shared very fully the new desire for education. A few grammar schools had been founded in different parts of the kingdom for the education of the children of the people, and these schools had much to do in preparing the English people to secure their freedom at home, and to plant free Colonies on this side of the sea.

I

IT is well known that the age of Queen Elizabeth was the great age of English literature. It
was the later period of the Renaissance,— that
awakening of Europe from the sleep of centuries, out of which has come our civil and religious liberty, with its searching intellectual spirit,
— its insistence upon the rights of the thinker,
the citizen, and the Christian. For a century
and a half after the death of Chaucer, England
had produced very few authors whose works are
worthy to be classed as literature; but in the
time of Elizabeth, it produced a large number
of historians, and poets, and dramatists, whose
works are read to this day. The singers flooded
the land with their songs, and England became,
as one old writer has told us, "a nest of singing
birds." The Puritan party included a fair proportion of the men of genius and of learning in
England. The literature which the Puritan
divines have left us is certainly profound and
scholarly.

Edmund Spenser, our earliest great poet since
the time of Chaucer, was born in 1553, eleven
years earlier than Shakespeare. He **Edmund**
took his Bachelor's degree at Pem- **Spenser.**
broke, Cambridge, in 1573, and his Master's degree in 1576. He was the friend of Sir Philip

Sidney and of the Earl of Leicester. Mr. Lowell tells us that he was "fortunate in the friendship of the best men and women of his time. All that we know of him is amiable and of good report. He was faithful to the friendships of his youth, pure in his loves, unspotted in his life." In 1579, he published his "Shepherd's Calendar," which showed him to be in hearty sympathy with the Puritans. About the year 1590, he published a part of the "Faery Queen," which he dedicated to Queen Elizabeth. It was received with enthusiasm by all classes of the English people. One of the old writers has said, "It became the delight of every accomplished gentleman, the model of every poet, the solace of every soldier. It expressed the earnest spirit of the time." The poem is Protestant and Puritan in its whole spirit and tendency. It celebrates the contest of the English Queen with the Papacy. "The worst foe of the Red Cross Knight," said John Richard Green, "is the false, and scarlet clad Duessa of Rome."[1] King James wished to have the poet prosecuted for the references which he recognized to his mother, Mary Queen of Scots, as the Duessa of the poem. Spenser was the most learned of our poets excepting Milton. He was well read in natural and moral philosophy, and was an admirable Greek scholar.

[1] Green's History of the English People, ii. 463–465.

He was familiar with the Divine Comedy of Dante, and with the writings of many other Italian authors.

The other great Puritan poet who was read by our Puritan ancestors was John Milton, who was born in 1608, fifty-five years later than **John Milton.** Spenser. He was the highest and most complete type of Puritanism. Spenser was his model as a poet. He admired Shakespeare also : —

> "Sweetest Shakespeare, Fancy's child,
> Warble his native wood notes wild." [1]

He was a student at Christ College, Cambridge, and took his first degree in 1628, and his second in 1632. All his earlier years were given to literature, and he became one of the most accomplished scholars of his time. He began to publish poetry while yet a youth. He travelled in Italy, and was about to cross to Sicily and Greece when he learned of the civil war in England. "I considered it disgraceful," he said, "that, while my fellow countrymen were fighting at home for liberty, I should be travelling abroad for intellectual purposes." He returned to England to take his part in the struggle, to which he devoted his life from 1640 to 1660. He became the literary leader of the Puritans, as Cromwell was their political leader. He was the Latin Secretary to the Council, and his state papers were

[1] L'Allegro, line 128.

of the greatest service. His sight was impaired by his devotion to his duties, but when he was warned of the danger of total blindness if he continued to use his eyes, he said that his duty was pressing, and that he should shut his ears to Æsculapius himself, speaking in his temple, so long as the work needed to be done. He went on with his work, but he lost his sight, and his best years were passed in total darkness. His greatest poems, which "the world will not willingly let die," were written during those years.

A still more notable poet of the Puritan age, greater in some respects than Spenser or Milton,
William Shake- was William Shakespeare. He lived
speare. in the earlier half of the Puritan age, as Milton lived in the later half of that age. His public career was comprised between the years 1586 and 1616, a period of thirty years. This was a very important period in English history, in some respects the most important. It included the later seventeen years of the great reign of Elizabeth, and thirteen years of the reign, not so great, of James the First. It covered the best part of the Elizabethan period of our literature. It was the time of Lord Bacon and Sir Philip Sidney and Sir Walter Raleigh, of Ben Jonson and the rest of the early dramatists. The plans for the settlement of this country were forming during those years. The first Colony in

Virginia was planted nine years before Shakespeare died; and the Mayflower landed at Plymouth only four years after his death. The line between the Cavaliers and the Puritans was drawn during his lifetime. Virginia was settled by representatives of the one party, and Massachusetts by representatives of the other party.

II

WILLIAM SHAKESPEARE, "the sweet bard of Avon," was born three hundred and thirty-five years ago, in Stratford on Avon, a small village in Middle England, of Shakespeare's Early Life. fourteen or fifteen hundred people. It is a pleasant country, of green meadows, leafy hedges, and shade trees. The road from London to Liverpool crosses the River Avon at this place by an old bridge of fourteen arches. There were two handsome public buildings in Stratford in Shakespeare's time, — the Guildhall, with its chapel and Grammar School, its chime of bells, and its fine frescos, — and the Church of the Holy Trinity, in which Shakespeare was baptized, April 26, 1564, and in which he was buried fifty-two years later. We do not know the day of his birth, for family records were not kept in those days among the plain people, like the Shakespeare family of that generation. It is probable

that it was three or four days before the date of
his baptism. That was not an age of general
education, as we may infer from the fact that,
although the father of the poet was a man of
business, and also the Bailiff, and a Justice of
the Peace, he was unable to write his name in
the baptismal register. He made his mark, as
did also his wife, Mary Arden, who was of an
ancient English family, which traced its history
back to the time of William the Conqueror. It
is very likely that the poetic genius of Shakespeare would have been lost to the world but for
the fact that a Grammar School had been established in Stratford a few years before. This was
one of the small number of such schools at that
time in England. To this school the son of the
Bailiff of Stratford was sent when he was about
seven years old. We do not know very much of
his childhood, but it is probable that he remained
in this school six or seven years. The school
hours occupied the whole day, with intermissions
for meals and for recreation. In the fourth
act of "The Merry Wives of Windsor" there is
a reminiscence of these school days, where the
schoolmaster, Sir Hugh Evans, a Welsh parson,
hears William repeat his *hic*, *hæc*, *hoc*, and reminds him that *lapis* means a stone, and *pulcher*
means fair.[1]   In this school the young poet

[1] Act iv. Scene 1.

gleaned the rudiments of his education; — including the "small Latin and less Greek" which Ben Jonson tells us he possessed. The school course was generally over when a boy was fourteen. It is said that when William was of about that age he was removed from school as his father had need of him in his business. Visitors to Stratford are still shown the room in the Grammar School in which he is said to have been taught, and the desk at which he is said to have studied.

It is commonly stated that William assisted his father in his business as a glover, and a small farmer, for some years after he left school. Some tell us that he was a clerk in the office of an attorney for a part of the time, and that his remarkable knowledge of legal terms and legal proceedings was gained during those years.

When he was eighteen, he married Anne Hathaway of Shottery, a hamlet in the same parish, a woman eight years older than himself; and he seems to have made his plans to settle down in Stratford, and to follow the same way of life that his father was following. So little did the youthful poet and dramatist forecast his future. But his father was in serious financial difficulties about that time. He lost the larger part of his property, and the business was too small for the support of two families. William

Shakespeare had three children born to him within less than three years after his marriage, and there was a probability that both the families would fall into poverty. There is also a tradition that the young man fell into evil company, and that he was led by his companions to encroach upon the park of Sir Thomas Lucy, the great landowner of that region, and to shoot rabbits and deer. It is even said that Sir Thomas had him " oft whipt and imprisoned."

So that, in consequence of his poverty, and perhaps also his misdeeds, Shakespeare left his native town at about the age of twenty-one, and went to London to begin the illustrious career which he would very likely have missed but for his misfortunes. His wife and children remained in Stratford, and he saw them only at long intervals. But he never lost sight of Stratford, and as soon as he was able he began to purchase land and other property there, for the benefit of his family, and that of his father.

Arrived in London, he connected himself at once with the theatre. The tradition is that he earned his first money by holding the horses of the gentlemen who had ridden to the play, and that he won so much favor that he had to engage boys as his assistants, who were called " Shakespeare's boys." His first business in the theatre itself was that of a prompter's attendant, whose duty it was to give notice to the players of the time for their entrance. He soon rose above these menial positions, and became an actor. At first he played the minor parts, and, as he gained experience, those that were more important. There is no evidence, however, that he was especially successful as an actor. The most important part which we know that he played was that of the ghost in his own " Hamlet." After a time he began to write. At first he was content to revise and improve such plays as were already in use in the theatre. He came by degrees to do more important work, and work that was more original. Within about three years after he left his native village, he became connected with a company of actors, known as the Lord Chamberlain's Company. In the course of time, he was a shareholder in this company, and he continued to be a member until he left London.

Some of his earliest tragedies were the historical plays, which are so excellent that Lord Chatham used to say that he had gained his knowledge of history from the plays of Shakespeare. In these plays, he follows the older English chronicles, especially those of Holinshed, so that the genius of the dramatist appears not so much in the story as in the filling out of the plot. The more original plays of Shakespeare were written between 1592 and

1612. These twenty years of greatest literary activity cover the period from his twenty-ninth to his forty-ninth year. His income during those years must have been considerable. In 1597, when he was thirty-three, he bought the New Place, or Great House, in Stratford, for sixty pounds sterling, a sum equal to $1,500 of our present money. It had been built by Sir Hugh Clypton. It was at that time the largest and finest house in Stratford. The possession of this place enabled Shakespeare to gather his family, and perhaps the family of his father, into a comfortable home, and it also added to his own importance, and gave him a better social position. About this time the elder Shakespeare applied at the Herald's College for a coat of arms. The conferring of a coat of arms implied formal admittance into the ranks of the gentry. The application was granted in 1599, so that John Shakespeare had a right from that time to write his name John Shakespeare, Gentleman. In later years, Shakespeare bought other property in Stratford. A few years later, he purchased a house in London. A little before he was fifty, Shakespeare left the theatre, and retired to his home in Stratford, where he died at the age of fifty-two.

III

THIS sketch of the life of William Shakespeare will help us understand *his relation to the English Puritans*. The defeat of the Spanish Armada in 1588 gave the English people a new sense of security and of power. When Elizabeth began to reign, England was hardly recognized as one of the great powers of Europe. The victory over Spain, three centuries ago, made England the mistress of the seas, and at the same time it placed her at the head of the Protestant powers of Europe. The Puritans were the advanced Christians of their time, as the Methodists were two hundred years later. The name Puritan was given in derision, as the name Methodist was given. The Puritans were rising into greater prominence all through the time of Shakespeare. They stood for freedom in the Church and in the State, against arbitrary government. They were not at first hostile to the Established Church of England. The leading Puritans were members of that church, and they were seeking its growth, and its purity.

In 1603 Elizabeth died, and James the First became King. In the first year of his reign a large number of clergymen of the English Church presented an earnest petition, asking for certain reforms in the services of the church. The peti-

21

tion expressed the wishes of a decided majority of the Protestants of the kingdom. But it was rejected, with the threat that force would be used to compel them to conform to the usages and ceremonies to which they had declared their conscientious opposition. In 1604, while Shakespeare was still in London, the House of Commons, which contained a majority of Puritans, began the great contest for the rights of the people, which continued, with some interruptions, until the Revolution in 1688, which secured the freedom of England for all time. The most prominent English historians of later times have given emphatic testimony to the earnestness and the success of the efforts of the Puritans in behalf of English liberty. Hume, for example, states that they "kindled the precious spark of liberty," and that "England owes the whole freedom of its constitution to the Puritans alone."

It is a question of very great interest, why we have no adequate reference to these greatest events of the time in the dramatic works of Shakespeare. We find constant references to them by other great writers of that splendid period of our literary history. Why should not Shakespeare have made such references? We naturally expect to find the spirit of an age reflected in its literature. That is one of the highest functions of a national literature. Our

American poets — Bryant, Longfellow, Whittier,
Lowell, Mrs. Howe, and the rest — have entered
very heartily into the great events of the time
in this country, such as the Antislavery movement, and the War for the Union. They have
written our patriotic odes, and our war songs,
such as the Battle Hymn of the Republic. It
is very true there has been a variety of opinions
among American authors in respect to some of
the questions involved, as there has been among
the other people of the country, but as a class
they have entered into the great questions of the
age. They have been men of convictions, and
have expressed their convictions in their works.
Why should not our greatest English dramatist
have reflected in his dramas the highest aspirations of his time?

It adds a little to the force of these inquiries
to call to mind the fact that Stratford, the early
home of Shakespeare, was one of the The Puritans
strongholds of Puritanism. Richard in Stratford.
Byfield, a Puritan minister, was vicar of the
church of the Holy Trinity in Stratford in 1596.
William Whately and Dr. Robert Harris, both
eminent Puritans, were among the "lecturers"
at Stratford. Sir Thomas Lucy, the aristocratic
gentleman of the region, and its representative
in Parliament, was a leader among the Puritans.
John Fox, author of the Book of Martyrs, found

refuge from persecution in his hospitable mansion. Warwickshire was at that time one of the Puritan districts of England. Thomas Cartwright, the great Puritan preacher, was in Warwick for many years. The Martin-mar-prelate press was at one time concealed in the same county.[1]

The eldest daughter of Shakespeare was also a Puritan. Her husband, a skilful physician, is said to have been "a zealous Protestant," which meant in those days a Puritan. We are told that, "so eminent was he, that even those who hated him for his religion made use of him." We learn from the epitaph of his wife that she was

> "Witty above her sex, but that's not all,
>   Wise to salvation, was good Mistress Hall.
>   Something of Shakespeare was in that: but this
>   Wholly of Him with whom she's now in bliss."

It is plain from the dramas that Shakespeare knew all about the Puritans, and that he did not like them. He makes use of the name Puritan a few times, but it never has any special significance. Thus, we read in Twelfth Night: —

"*Maria.* Marry, sir, sometimes he is a kind of Puritan.
"*Sir Andrew.* O, if I thought that, I'd beat him like a dog.
"*Sir Toby.* What! for being a Puritan? thy exquisite reason, dear knight?

[1] Prof. John W. Hales, in Contemporary Review, January, 1895. Shakespeare and Puritanism.

" *Sir Andrew.* I have no exquisite reason for 't, but I have reason good enough.

" *Maria.* The devil a Puritan that he is or anything constantly, but a time pleaser." [1]

In Winter's Tale, the Clown says: —

"But one Puritan amongst them, and he sings psalms to hornpipes." [2]

In Pericles: —

"She would make a Puritan of the devil if he should cheapen a kiss of her." [3]

In All's Well That Ends Well, the Clown says: —

"Though honesty be no Puritan, yet it will do no hurt." [4]

But although Shakespeare does not make much account of the Puritans, he never reviles them, as the other writers of plays in his time were continually doing. There was too much fairness and kindness about "the gentle Shakespeare" to permit him to indulge in the pastime of Puritan baiting. He may have been restrained by regard for his favorite daughter, and for his old neighbors at Stratford. It is said, on the authority of an ancient record, that after his return to Stratford, Shakespeare entertained a Puritan preacher at the New Place.

[1] Act ii. Scene 3.
[2] Act iv. Sc. 2.
[3] Act iv. Sc. 5.
[4] Act i. Sc. 3.

It has been common to speak of Shakespeare as remarkable for comprehensiveness. We have called him the "myriad-minded Shakespeare." A recent writer has said: "His universality is the secret and measure of his power. He was a man of universal sympathy, and universal observation. His reading was extensive for his day. He read nothing that he did not remember, and make real to himself. He saw nothing in the present which was not to him prophetic of the future."[1] Statements quite as strong as these could be quoted from some of the latest discussions of the dramas of Shakespeare. But did not our great dramatist find anything prophetic of the future in English Puritanism?

IV

ONE thing that is plain from his writings is this: The sympathies of Shakespeare do not

The Common People.

seem to have been broad enough to include the common people, such as the larger number of the Puritans were. He was himself a country boy, accustomed to the habits of a rural town. He seems to have gone to London in poverty, and to have lived a frugal and industrious life in the metropolis, so as to

[1] Prof. William S. Tyler of Amherst, Bibliotheca Sacra, 1855, p. 494.

better his fortunes, and provide for his family.
His wonderful genius enabled him to succeed
as a dramatic poet, and to acquire a fortune that
was ample for those times.

It would have been natural for Shakespeare,
whose early life placed him so near the common
people, to enter with all his heart into the movement in behalf of the rights of the people. But
his sympathies seem to have been the other way.
In the historical plays he never introduces the
people who are struggling against tyranny, except
to show that they are fools who deserve their
chains. He represents every uprising against
oppression as an outbreak of

> " Moody beggars, starving for a time
> Of pell-mell havoc and confusion."

In Julius Cæsar, for example, Flavius says to
the laborers : —

> " Hence ! home, you idle creatures, get you home." [1]

And Marcellus says to them : —

> " You blocks, you stones, you worse than senseless things ! " [2]

In the next scene Casca says : —

> " The rabblement shouted, and clapped their chapp'd
> hands, and threw up their sweaty night-caps, and uttered
> such a deal of stinking breath, because Cæsar refused the
> crown."

[1] Julius Cæsar, Act i. Sc. i.   [2] Ibid.

And further on : —

" If the tag-rag people did not clap him, and hiss him, according as he pleased and displeased them, as they use to do the players in the theatre, I am no true man." [1]

In Coriolanus, Agrippa says to the people : —

" Rome and her rats are at the point of battle." [2]

But this was in old Rome. How does he speak of the people in the English historical plays? In the Second Part of King Henry VI. he represents the famous Jack Cade and his followers as a crowd of ignorant and unreasonable rebels.[3] But that is not as they are represented by the historical writers whom Shakespeare usually followed. There was great and general discontent in certain counties of England in 1450. An insurrection broke out, and an army of twenty thousand men was gathered. It included a considerable number of men of intelligence and of wealth. Some great landowners were there, and some ecclesiastics. Jack Cade was a soldier of experience and courage. The complaints that they set forth were reasonable. They called for reforms in the administration, and a more careful expenditure of the revenues. Even a writer so favorable to Shakespeare as Richard Grant White says: "Shakespeare did

[1] Act i. Sc. 2.   [2] Act i. Sc. 1.   [3] Act iv. Sc. 2 and 6.

not conform strictly to history in this scene." [1] In fact, for some reason, he departed from the statements of Holinshed, and put the speeches of Wat Tyler and his companions, of seventy years before, into the mouth of Jack Cade. So unwilling was Shakespeare to give any credit to the complaints of the people, that he perverted the facts of history in this instance, although in most instances he has reproduced historic facts with wonderful accuracy.

Another instance of the same kind is found in the play of King John, which covers the period of Magna Charta, that earliest and greatest charter of the rights and liberties of the English people. King John was claiming autocratic power, just as the Stuarts did at a later day. How great an addition to this drama would have been the scene at Runnymede, where the King was compelled by his armed barons to give his assent to the parchment which secured to all his subjects a government of law, meting out equal justice to the commons and to the nobles.

The truth is, the sympathies of Shakespeare, country bred as he was, seem to have been with the nobility, and not with the rising middle classes, who were contending for their rights as

[1] Notes to the Second Part of Henry VI. Also Greene's History of the English People, i. 565. Brandes' Shakespeare, i. 132.

men and as Englishmen. He was the poet of gay and merry England, not of thoughtful and serious England. His associates were young English noblemen, who frequented the theatres, such as Essex and Leicester. " His heroes," says a recent Danish writer, " were princes and noblemen, the kings and barons of England. It is always they, in his eyes, who make history, of which he shows throughout a naïvely heroic conception. In the wars which he presents, it is always an individual leader and hero on whom everything depends. It is Henry V. who wins the day at Agincourt; just as in Homer it is Achilles who conquers before Troy. Yet in fact the whole issue of these wars depended upon the foot soldiers. It was the English archers who at Agincourt defeated the French army. Shakespeare certainly did not divine that it was the rise of the middle classes, and their spirit of enterprise that constituted the strength of England under Elizabeth. He regarded his age from the point of view of the man who was accustomed to see, in richly endowed and princely young noblemen, the very crown of humanity, the patrons of all lofty efforts, and the originators of all great achievements."[1]

The fact is, there were two Englands in the time of Elizabeth and of James the First: — the

[1] A Critical Study of Shakespeare by George Brandes, i. 131.

England of the Court, the nobility, the clergy of the Established Church, all those who were clinging to the traditions of the past; — and the England of the common people, who were rising into a condition of intelligence, and who were seeking to secure their freedom in the state, and to build up a truly Protestant Church. These people had some democratic ideas. They were represented in those times by the leaders in the House of Commons. A great many of this class of Englishmen were Puritans. Shakespeare, with his limited historic culture, failed to recognize the tokens of a new life for his native land.

It was not so with Milton, or with Spenser. Milton showed a prophetic insight in his political pamphlets entitled "A Defence of the People of England," and "The Tenure of Kings and Magistrates," and "A Speech for the Liberty of Unlicensed Printing." Spenser saw very clearly how much the Protestant Reformation meant for England, and his sympathies and influence were with the party of progress.

On the other hand, Shakespeare was a man of large and generous sympathies. His personality was especially attractive. He is oftenest spoken of by his contemporaries as the "gentle Shakespeare." He was perhaps in sympathy with those in the aristocratic classes, because in his London life he knew them better than he knew the

common people.   They were the patrons of the
Generous Nature   theatre, while the Puritans, as a class,
of Shakespeare.   were unfriendly to theatrical exhibitions.   They passed laws which restricted such
exhibitions, and in some localities they prohib-
ited them.   In Shakespeare's time, the most of
them were not the patrons of art.   There was a
natural reason why the great dramatist was especially friendly to those who patronized the
drama most generously.   The common people
were, in the opinion of men of his class, unable
to appreciate it.   He could not have foreseen
that three centuries after he had ceased to write,
his dramas would be published in great popular
editions, and read and appreciated by multitudes
of people who did not belong to the classes which,
in his time, had so high a social position.

In the drama of Henry the Eighth, which
covers the time of the beginning of the English
Henry the   Reformation, there is hardly a sug-
Eighth.   gestion of the great changes in the
English Church that were in progress.   We learn
in the fifth act, quite incidentally, that Archbishop
Cranmer was something of a heretic, who by his
teaching and his chaplains was filling the realm

> " With new opinions,
> Divers and dangerous, which are heresies,
> And, not reformed, may prove pernicious." [1]

[1] Act v. Sc. 2.

It is also mentioned that Anne Bullen, the Queen, is

> "A spleeny Lutheran, and not wholesome to
> Our cause." [1]

But that is about all that we learn from that play of the profound changes among the people of England which placed them on the Protestant side. Shakespeare quotes very often from Fox's "Book of Martyrs," from which it is reasonable to infer that he was acquainted with the outward facts in Puritan history. But it was not given to him to enter into the meaning of the great political and religious movements from which so much of what is best and most distinctive in our modern life has come.

V

THERE are other facts which point to some of the limitations of Shakespeare. He seems to have had little interest in the future *His Estimate of* of the dramatic works on which so *his Plays.* much of his fame rests. Some of his poems, as The Venus and Adonis, he gave to the press himself. His Sonnets also were perhaps edited by himself. We have no reason to think that he intended to publish his dramas. Such of them as were given to the press in his lifetime were published without his consent, perhaps without

[1] Act iii. Sc. 2.

his knowledge. The first edition of his collected dramas was published some years after his death. It contained nineteen plays that had been printed in his lifetime, and eighteen that had not been printed before. But for the care of the editors of the first folio, it is very likely that all these would have been lost to the world

These facts give us an insight into the spirit and methods of Shakespeare. He was an artist, intent upon the work he was doing. He found his gratification in bringing out the thoughts and visions that came to him. He must have written rapidly, with a full mind, a glowing imagination, and profound sensibility. But he had little thought of his literary reputation. He was also interested in the pecuniary profits of his dramatic works. He was a very thrifty man for a great poet. But he does not seem to have been a man of large interest in the events of his time, or of a generous public spirit. There is no evidence that he calculated the influence of his plays upon the world, or that he anticipated that he would stand at the head of modern dramatists.

Mr. White, who is one of the best and most appreciative of the recent biographers of the poet, states that "Shakespeare has left no trace upon the political or the social life of his time." He adds: " There is no evidence whatever that he was personally known to the eminent men who were his contemporaries, Sidney, Bacon, Hooker, Spenser, Raleigh, Drake, Hampden, Coke, Pym, and Selden."[1]   We know who the intimate friends of Shakespeare were, — the young men who frequented the theatres, and the actors and writers of plays.   His acquaintance in London does not seem to have gone much beyond these classes of men.

On the other hand, Shakespeare was a man of tender sensibilities. Few men have been so loved by their friends as he was. He was also intensely patriotic. There are no finer passages in his dramas than those which breathe the spirit of that noble English patriotism, which had so strong a hold upon the nation in the sixteenth century: He loved his native land: —

> "This scepter'd isle,
> This earth of majesty, this seat of Mars,
> This other Eden, demi-paradise,
> This fortress, built by nature for herself,
> Against infection and the hand of war ;
> This happy breed of men, this little world,
> This precious stone set in the silver sea, . . .
> This blessed plot, this earth, this realm, this England,
> This nurse, this teeming womb of royal kings, . . .
> Renowned for their deeds. . . .
> This land of such dear souls, this dear, dear land,
> Dear for her reputation through the world."[2]

[1] White's Shakespeare, vol. i. p. cxi.
[2] King Richard II., Act ii. Sc. 1.

Shakespeare appears to have been depressed by the low estimate of his profession. In one of his Sonnets he chides Fortune, —

> "That did not better for my life provide
> Than public means which public manners breeds.
> Thence comes it that my name receives a brand
> And almost thence my nature is subdued
> To what it works in, like the dyer's hand." [1]

It is doubtless true that the popular estimate of the theatre in his time was very low. The corporation of London compelled the players to erect their theatres outside the limits of the city. So they were built on the south of the Thames, near the Bear Garden. The theatre brought in its train a loose, frivolous, and rowdy population. The position of the actors was much below what it is at present. No woman appeared on the stage. There was very little scenery, and all the arrangements upon the stage were very much simpler and ruder than they are at present. The most fashionable seats were on the stage itself, as they are now in the Chinese theatres. "There," says a recent writer, " sat the amateurs, the noble patrons of the theatre, Essex, Southampton, Pembroke, Rutland. There too sat the author's rivals, the dramatic poets, who had free admissions ; and there too sat the shorthand writers, commissioned by piratical booksellers." [2]

[1] Sonnet cxi.   [2] Brandes, i. 118–120.

It is stated by some writers that dramatic works were hardly ranked as literature in the time of Shakespeare. He wrote his dramas under the inspiration of his matchless genius, but he seems to have estimated them less highly than he did some of his poems.

VI

THE question has been much debated whether Shakespeare *had any conscious moral purpose* in his dramatic works. On the one hand, Mr. White says that "the direct moral influence of Shakespeare is nothing, and we may be sure that he wrote with no moral purpose."[1] Jonson says that Shakespeare "carries his persons indifferently through right and wrong, and at the close dismisses them without further care, and leaves their example to operate by chance." Mr. Lowell tells us that "it is doubtful if Shakespeare had any conscious moral intention in his writings. In this he was purely and primarily a poet. . . . He had no moral intention, for the reason that, as an artist, it was not his to deal with the realities, but only with the shows of things; yet with a temperament so just, an insight so inevitable as his, it was impossible that the moral reality,

The Ethical Element in Shakespeare.

[1] White's Shakespeare, vol. i. p. ccxliv.

which underlies the *mirage* of the poet's vision
should not always be suggested." [1]

On the other hand, inasmuch as the moral
nature of Shakespeare seems to have been re-
markably pure and healthy, it is reasonable to
suppose that he would aim to secure a good
moral influence by his dramas. He had what I
may almost call a Puritan conscience, the conscience which, as he said, "doth make cowards of
us all." He constantly recognizes the distinction
between right and wrong. It is the King in
Hamlet who says that,

> " In the corrupted currents of this world,
>   Offence's gilded hand may shove by justice,
>   And oft 't is seen the wicked prize itself
>   Buys out the law : but 't is not so above :
>   There is no shuffling, there the action lies
>   In his true nature ; and we ourselves compell'd,
>   Even to the teeth and forehead of our faults,
>   To give in evidence." [2]

The Puritans of his time insisted that there
was no moral purpose in his dramas, and they
gave this reason for their opposition to the theatre. But it cannot be denied that the moral
tone of the works of Shakespeare is very much
higher than that of many other English dramatists of his time. If he had no " conscious moral

---

[1] Among My Books, i. 226, 227.
[2] Hamlet, Act iii. Sc. 3.

purpose in his plays," yet unconsciously, as a man of lofty ideals, he would naturally lean to virtue's side in his representations of life. It is quite possible that some men will learn more of truth and duty from the great tragedies of Shakespeare than from direct moral teachings.

It is perhaps impossible to determine from his works, how far he had a distinct moral purpose. There are some passages which indicate that it was his opinion that it is not the proper function of the drama to teach moral lessons. We have, for example, in Hamlet's directions to the players, the statement that it is the purpose of the theatre "to hold the mirror up to nature, to show virtue her own feature, scorn her own image, and the very age and body of the time his form and pressure." [1] But, as Professor Dowden has said, "The mirror has no tendency. We only inquire whether the mirror reflects objects clearly and faithfully." Is it true that a poet, with the highest endowments of genius, is to be only a mirror? Is that the purpose of the highest life?

In his Lectures on Dramatic Art and Literature, Schlegel has said, "We may perceive in Shakespeare himself, notwithstanding his power to excite the most fervent emotions, a certain cool indifference, but still the indifference of a

[1] Hamlet, Act iii. Sc. 2.

superior mind, which has run through the whole sphere of human existence, and survived feeling."[1] Whether we accept this statement or not, it is undoubtedly true that there is a certain lack in Shakespeare of moral earnestness, of enthusiasm for truth and duty. This is what Schlegel calls the "irony" of Shakespeare.

It is not certain that the highest art is without a moral purpose. The paintings of the old masters, for example, are many of them representations of Biblical scenes. It is well known that these paintings were intended to teach moral and religious truth to the people. Raphael painted his finest works for the churches. Who will deny that a large part of the works of art that are set up in our public libraries, and legislative halls, and churches are intended to teach lessons of justice, and patriotism, and religion? Art is the handmaid of religion.

VII

THIS brings us to the inquiry, *whether there is a religious element* in the plays of Shakespeare. The Puritans, with their intense convictions, insisted that religion should pervade and color all literature, and their opposition to the drama was based upon the opinion that its influence was not

[1] Schlegel's Dramatic Literature, 369.

religious. This question is having a fresh discussion in our time, and it is likely to attract more attention in the future.

The question has been much debated whether Shakespeare was a Roman Catholic or a Protestant. It is certainly surprising that there should be room for such a question in regard to one of the greatest of Englishmen, who lived through the time of the Spanish Armada. No such question could be asked in respect to the other great men of his time, with whom we are accustomed to compare him.

Very different statements have been made by Shakespearian scholars in respect to the religion of the great dramatist. An article has recently been published in Boston, in "The New World," on "The Absence of Religion in Shakespeare."[1] On the other hand, Richard Grant White tells us, with a singular confusion of terms, that "Shakespeare, although he seems to have been a man of sincere piety, appears to have been without religious convictions."[2]

We find many references in the historical dramas to the church and its services, and to clergymen. But Shakespeare's clergymen are decidedly worldly, and some of them unscrupulous. He does not give us any pictures of sin-

[1] The New World, December, 1896.
[2] White's Shakespeare, vol. i. p. cxiii.

cere and self-denying pastors, like Chaucer's
Clerke : —

> "That was a poure persone of a towne,
> But rich he was of holy thought and work.
> Criste's lore and his apostles twelve,
> He taught, but first he folwed it himselve."

Or like George Herbert's saintly " Priest to the
temple," or like Longfellow's faithful monk,

> "Who saw the blessed vision
> Of our Lord with light Elysian,
> Like a vesture wrapped about him,
> Like a garment round him thrown."

One of the words frequently used in the dramas
is music.   Shakespeare had a poet's sense of the
charm of music : —

> "Look how the floor of heaven
> Is thick inlaid with patines of bright gold ;
> There's not the smallest orb which thou behold'st
> But in his motion like an angel sings,
> Still quiring to the young ey'd cherubins :
> Such harmony is in immortal souls." [1]

> "The man that hath no music in himself,
> Nor is not moved with concord of sweet sounds,
> Is fit for treasons, stratagems, and spoils ;
> The motions of his spirit are dull as night,
> And his affections dark as Erebus :
> Let no such man be trusted.   Mark the music." [2]

[1] Merchant of Venice, Act v. Sc. 1.
[2] Ibid.

It is very significant, however, that, with all these eloquent references to music, Shakespeare never refers to sacred music. Perhaps he did not often hear it.

Shakespeare frequently refers to the Bible, but never in any way of special significance, as Spenser, and Milton, and Wordsworth, and **The Bible in** Longfellow, and Tennyson do. There **Shakespeare.** were a number of English translations of the Bible in his day. A large proportion of the people had become very familiar with it. Its language entered into their common speech. It was quite as natural for writers and speakers to quote it, as it is to-day. The version of King James was hardly in common use while Shakespeare was writing his plays, so he quotes the Bishops' Bible, or the Genevan version. Thus we read, in The Merchant of Venice: —

> "The quality of mercy is not strain'd :
> It droppeth as the gentle rain from heaven
> Upon the place beneath. It is twice bless'd ;
> It blesseth him that gives, and him that takes." [1]

In Love's Labor's Lost we find: —

> "For charity itself fulfils the law,
> And who can sever love from charity." [2]

And in Richard III.: —

> "Charity that renders good for bad, blessings for curses." [3]

[1] Act iv. Sc. 1.   [2] Act iv. Sc. 3.   [3] Act i. Sc. 2.

In the same tragedy: —

> " Rail on the Lord's Anointed." [1]

In another play: —

> " The New Heaven, and new earth." [2]

Richard II. inquires: —

> " Did they not sometimes cry, All hail to me?
> So Judas did to Christ." [3]

In Henry VI.: —

> " So Judas kissed his Master,
> And cried, ' All hail!' when he meant all harm." [4]

In another part we read: —

> " Now by the death of Him that died for all." [5]

These are specimens of the references to the words of the Bible, which one finds not infrequently in the works of Shakespeare, as in the other English literature of that age. It is not necessary to quote them all. Bishop Wordsworth, in his well known book, entitled " Shakespeare's Knowledge and Use of the Bible," has brought out a large number of such references. They are not very significant. They do not show any special familiarity with religious truth,

[1] Act iv. Sc. 2.   [2] Antony and Cleopatra, Act i. Sc. 1.
[3] Act iv. Sc. 1.
[4] Third Part of King Henry VI., Act v. Sc. 7.
[5] Second Part of King Henry VI., Act i. Sc. 1.

or any lively sympathy with it. They do show that, under the religious teachings of the Puritan age, perhaps in his early home, — perhaps in that venerable Trinity Church in Stratford, — perhaps by reading, — he had become familiar with the more striking facts of sacred history, and with the general teachings of the Bible, and he quoted it as literature.

Shakespeare was not an Agnostic. He seems to have believed in God, and in some of the other truths of religion. He always speaks with reverence of our Saviour. In the First Part of King Henry IV. the king says : —

> "Therefore, friends,
> As far as to the sepulchre of Christ,
> Whose soldier now, under whose blessed cross
> We are impressed and engaged to fight,
> Forthwith a power of English shall we levy
> To chase these pagans in those holy fields
> Over whose acres walk'd those blessed feet
> Which fourteen hundred years ago were nailed,
> For our advantage, on the bitter cross." [1]

This is a part of the history of the Crusade. The dramatist could hardly avoid this reference to the purpose of the holy war. But we cannot conclude that we have in this speech by the King an expression of the religious sentiments of the author of the play.

[1] First Part of King Henry IV., Act i. Sc. i.

There is a suggestion of immortality in Hamlet, not indeed as the assured hope of man, but rather as a terror, which holds one back from self-destruction : —

> " To be, or not to be ; that is the question : —
> Whether 't is nobler in the mind to suffer
> The slings and arrows of outrageous fortune ;
> Or to take arms against a sea of troubles,
> And by opposing end them ?   To die : to sleep, —
> No more : and, by a sleep to say we end
> The heartache, and the thousand natural shocks
> That flesh is heir to, — 't is a consummation
> Devoutly to be wish'd.   To die, to sleep :
> To sleep ! perchance to dream : ay, there 's the rub :
> For in that sleep of death what dreams may come
> When we have shuffled off this mortal coil,
> Must give us pause.   There 's the respect
> That makes calamity of so long life :
> For who would bear the whips and scorns of time,
> The oppressor's wrong, the proud man's contumely,
> The pangs of despised love, the law's delay,
> The insolence of office and the spurns
> That patient merit of the unworthy takes
> When he himself might his quietus make
> With a bare bodkin ?   Who would these fardels bear
> To grunt and sweat under a weary life,
> But that the dread of something after death, —
> The undiscovered country, from whose bourne
> No traveller returns, — puzzles the will,
> And makes us rather bear those ills we have,
> Than fly to others that we know not of." [1]

[1] Act iii. Scene i.

This is one among a number of passages in which suicide, — the cowardly crime, — is dealt with in such a way as to indicate that for the poet himself it was a subject of frequent thought.

In the comedy called "As You Like It," one of the characters says,

> " All the world 's a stage,
> And all the men and women merely players;
> They have their exits and their entrances;
> And one man in his time plays many parts, —
> His acts being seven ages. . . . . . .
> . . . . Last scene of all,
> That ends this strange eventful history,
> Is second childishness and mere oblivion." [1]

It is said by some recent critics that the " Tempest " was the latest of the plays of Shakespeare, and that Prospero, the magician, stands for the great dramatist himself. It is Prospero who says: —

> " These our actors,
> As I foretold you, were all spirits, and
> Are melted into air, into thin air:
> And, like the baseless fabric of this vision,
> The cloud-capped towers, the gorgeous palaces,
> The solemn temples, the great globe itself,
> Yea, all which it inherit, shall dissolve,
> And like this insubstantial pageant faded,
> Leave not a rack behind.   *We are such stuff*
> *As dreams are made on : and our little life*
> *Is rounded with a sleep.*" [2]

[1] Act ii. Scene 7.   [2] Act iv. Scene 1.

The truth is Shakespeare never rises into the region of Christian faith. He gives no pictures of sublime, self-sacrificing goodness, for the love of Christ. He seems to have no confident expectation of human improvement. He never expresses a longing for spiritual progress. He never rises from ethics into religion. He depicts the life of man with a marvellous insight into human motives and purposes, but he does not seem to know whence we have come, or whither we are going. The impression one gets, especially from the later dramas, is that the meaning of life in this world was still an enigma to him.

Macbeth says, when his wife is dead, and conscience is stinging him, and troubles are closing about him : —

> " To-morrow, and to-morrow, and to-morrow,
> Creeps in this petty pace from day to day,
> To the last syllable of recorded time :
> And all our yesterdays have lighted fools
> The way to dusty death.   Out, out brief candle !
> Life 's but a walking shadow : a poor player,
> That struts and frets his hour upon the stage,
> And then is heard no more : it is a tale
> Told by an idiot, full of sound and fury,
> Signifying nothing."

> " I 'gin to be a' weary of the sun,
> And wish th' estate o' th' world were now undone.
> Ring the alarm ; blow wind ! come wrack !
> At least we 'll die with harness on our back." [1]

                        [1] Act v. Scene 5.

There is sometimes in Shakespeare a recognition of God's providence in the world. Hamlet says : —

> "There's a divinity that shapes our ends,
> Rough-hew them how we will." [1]

Edgar in King Lear says: —

> "The gods are just, and of our pleasant vices
> Make instruments to plague us." [2]

Macbeth says : —

> "Even handed justice
> Commends the ingredients of our poisoned chalice
> To our own lips." [3]

There is an impressive passage in King Henry Fifth, in relation to his bearing after the victory of Agincourt. He exclaims : —

> "O God, thy arm was here :
> And not to us, but to thy arm alone,
> Ascribe we all ! "
>   "Take it, God,
> For it is none but thine ! "
> " Come, go we in procession to the village :
> And be it death proclaimed through our host
> To boast of this, or take that praise from God
> Which is his only."
>   " Do we all holy rites :
> Let there be sung Non Nobis, and Te Deum." [4]

[1] Act v. Scene 2.   [3] Act i. Scene 7.
[2] Act v. Scene 3.   [4] Act iv. Scene 8.

This recognition of Divine aid is very proper
for the King: and yet no part of this is original
with Shakespeare.   He has simply copied the
narrative, as he often does, from the chronicles
of Holinshed, where we may still read it almost
word for word.

Another passage is in King Richard Second.
The Bishop of Carlisle says : —

> " Many a time hath banished Norfolk fought
> For Jesu Christ in glorious Christian field,
> Streaming the ensign of the Christian cross
> Against black pagans, Turks, and Saracens;
> And, toil'd with works of war, retir'd himself
> To Italy: and there at Venice gave
> His body to that pleasant country's earth,
> And his pure soul unto his Captain Christ,
> Under whose colors he had fought so long." [1]

This also is a part of English history.   It is
quite in keeping with the character of a Christian bishop in that century.   It expresses the
spirit of war, and that of religion also.   It
cannot be quoted as an indication of religious
faith.

Perhaps the most impressive passage bearing
upon the religious ideas of Shakespeare is contained in one of his sonnets.   It is the more significant because it is in a poem so personal as a
sonnet : —

[1] Act iv. Scene 1.

" Poor soul, the centre of my sinful earth,
  Fool'd by these rebel powers that thee array,
  Why dost thou pine within, and suffer death,
  Painting thy outward walls so costly gay?
  Why so large cost, having so short a lease,
  Dost thou upon thy fading mansion spend?
  Shall worms, inheritors of this excess,
  Eat up thy charge?   Is this thy body's end?
  Then, soul, live thou upon thy servant's loss,
  And let that pine to aggravate thy store ;
  Buy terms divine, in selling hours of dross ;
  Within be fed, without be rich no more :
  So shalt thou feed on death, that feeds on man,
  And, death once dead, there 's no more dying then." [1]

This sonnet should be interpreted by the other sonnets, and by the general tenor of the dramatic works.   One swallow does not make a summer, and a few passages, such as these and a few others that might be quoted, have failed to change the general impression that one gets from the works of Shakespeare, that he fails to lead those who read him into the realm of the spiritual and the eternal.

The earlier dramas of Shakespeare are full of the youthful, hopeful spirit.   But those written after his fortieth year show a very perceptible change.   We know too little of his life during those years to be quite sure of the cause.   In respect to his business and his reputation those

[1] Sonnet cxlvi.

were very prosperous years. Some have thought that the death of his only son and heir cast a dark shadow on his life. The misfortunes of his friends and patrons, Essex, Southampton, and Pembroke changed very much his social life in London. The sonnets are full of suggestions of some mysterious shadow that darkened his life. Some of the most intelligent critics believe that many of the sonnets are autobiographical. Professor Dowden says, "The friend in whose personality Shakespeare found a source of measureless delight — high-born, beautiful, young, accomplished, ardent — wronged him. The woman from whom Shakespeare for a time received a joyous quickening of his life, — a woman of stained character, and the reverse of beautiful, but a strong character, — a lover of art, and possessed of curious magnetic attraction, — with her dark eyes which illuminated a pale face, — wronged him also."[1] It is of this dark lady, from whom perhaps he drew the character of Cleopatra, that Shakespeare says : —

> "When my love swears that she is made of truth,
>   I do believe her, tho' I know she lies."[2]

The cloud passed by after a time, and Shakespeare regained his full power, with a profounder view of life and its responsibilities. One observes

[1] Professor Dowden, 354.   [2] Sonnet cxxxviii.

in his later dramas a new sense of the mysterious power of evil, which sometimes holds the will in helpless bondage. Thus the King in Hamlet says : —

> "What form of prayer
> Can serve my turn?   Forgive me my foul murder?
> That cannot be, since I am still possess'd
> Of those effects for which I did the murder,
> My crown, mine own ambition, and my queen.
> May one be pardon'd and retain the offence?"
>   "What then?   What rests?
> Try what repentance can : what can it not?
> Yet what can it, when one cannot repent?
> O wretched state!   O bosom black as death!
> O limed soul, that, struggling to be free,
> Art more engaged!"[1]

Shakespeare did not have the key to unlock these profound mysteries. Wonderful as his powers were, he deals only with this present life. Here is the limitation of his universality. As Scherer has said, "It is on the boundaries of the invisible world that Shakespeare's vision fails." The greatest poets of the world have certainly been full of the religious spirit. Homer was full of it. So were the Greek dramatists. So have been the great poets of the modern world, — Dante, Spenser, Milton, Wordsworth, and Tennyson. But Shakespeare is the poet of the secular, and not of the religious, of the temporal, and not of the eternal.

[1] Hamlet, Act iii. Sc. 3.

23

It is not surprising, therefore, that in that age of conflict there was a lack of sympathy between the Puritans and Shakespeare. They represented an intensely religious life. They lived, as Milton said, "as ever in the great Taskmaster's eye." The spiritual was far more than the temporal to them. The reform of the Church seemed to them the greatest work of the age. Next to that, they were seeking to establish the rights of the people on a secure basis. They did not find Shakespeare in sympathy with the ideas which they were seeking to realize.

On the other hand, the Puritans seemed, to men like Shakespeare, to be narrow and bigoted. They were ready to fight for the inheritance of the privileged classes against the rising democracy. A large part of England at that time was with Shakespeare. A larger part was with the Puritans. It was not until the questions which were then at issue had been adjusted, partly by mutual compromises, and partly by the mellowing influence of many years, that the English speaking race of all parties was prepared to enjoy and appreciate that wonderful body of literature that is our common inheritance from Sidney and Spenser, from Bacon and Shakespeare, from John Milton and John Bunyan.

Index

Index

ELIOT, JOHN, 209; birthplace, his father, 210; baptism, 211; childhood, 211; graduation at Jesus College, 212; scholarship, 212; usher at Little Baddow, 212; influence of Thomas Hooker, 213; goes to New England, 213; preaches in Boston; settles in Roxbury, 215; marriage, his ministry in Roxbury; political principles, 215; his Christian Commonwealth, 216; retracts parts of the book; a devoted minister, 216; his theology, 217; fondness for Hebrew, 217; facetiousness, 217; wit, 218; interest in schools, 218; Cotton Mather's statement, 218; learns the Indian language, 218; motive of his missionary work, 218; his teachers; Cockenöe, Job Nesutan, 220; methods of study, 219, 221; Indian languages, 220; preaches at Nonantum, 222, 223; his companions, 223; narrative of the services, 223; the second meeting, 227; preaching in other places, 228; results of the work, 230; civilization, 231; an Indian town, 232; secures contributions from England, 234; his salary, 234; plea for help to his missions, 235; his foot-bridge, 239, 242; translation of the Bible, 250, 252; ride to Brookfield, 256; exposure, 257; success of this excursion, 258; missionary journals, 258; numbers in Churches, 258; effect of King Philip's War, 262; resumes his missionary work after the war, 266; reasons why it was not of larger success; fidelity of the missionary, 267; his old age, 268; publishes books, 268; his last words, death, his burial place, 269; his children; list of his publications, 269; inscription on his tomb, 270.

ELIOT, SIR JOHN, 68, 210.

ELLIOT, ELLSWORTH, DR., 210 (note).

EMIGRATION TO NEW ENGLAND ON A GREAT SCALE, 87; character of the emigrants, 88; number, 90.

ENDICOTT, JOHN, 70; letters to, 74; proposal for an independent church, 79, 83; present at Natick, 242.

ENFIELD SERMON, 296; not a specimen of the ordinary preaching of Edwards; the condition of that congregation; the subject of the sermon; effect of the discourse, 297.

ENGLISH BLOOD OF THE COLONISTS, 192.

ENTERPRISE OF THE PILGRIMS, 56.

EXPEDITIONS TO BOSTON HARBOR, 22, 23.

EXPEDITIONS TO MASSASOIT, 21.

FAITH IN THE SPIRITUAL, NOT IN SHAKESPEARE, 348.

FAMINE AT PLYMOUTH, 36.

24

Boston, 299; Northampton, 300; results of his preaching; his indiscretions, 300.

WHITMAN, SAMUEL, ELECTION SERMON, 275.

WIDFORD, ENGLAND, 210.

WILDE, THOMAS, 109.

WILLARD, PRESIDENT, QUOTED, 279.

WILLIAM AND MARY, 190; Provincial charter for Massachusetts, 190.

WILLIAMS, ROGER, ARRIVAL IN BOSTON, 126; his education and early life, 126; a rigid Separatist; opposition to Sunday laws, 127; preaches in Salem, in Plymouth, again in Salem, 127; his banishment, 128; plants Providence, 128; his banishment a mistake, 129; refuses to persecute the Quakers, 174.

WILSON, JOHN, 91; salary of, 94; pastor, 96; returns to the colony, 109; at Nonantum, 223.

WINDSOR SETTLED BY THE PILGRIMS, 132; purchased by the Puritan colonists, 132.

WINSLOW, GOV. EDWARD, MARRIES SUSANNA WHITE, 21; gives an account of the colony, 24; visits Massasoit, 30, 31; one of the capitalists, 41; sent to England by Massachusetts, 121, 164; agent of the colonies in England, 235; letter from Eliot, 238.

WINSLOW, JOHN, ARRIVES, 26.

WINTHROP, GOV. JOHN, 86; elected Governor, 87; history of, 88; sails, 89; arrives in Salem, sends for provisions, 92; re-elected Governor, 103; his library, 309.

WINTHROP, JOHN, JR., his library, 310.

WITCHCRAFT A COMMON SUPERSTITION, 176; Sir Matthew Hale, Governor Winthrop, trials for witchcraft in England; Connecticut; Massachusetts, 176; Salem witchcraft, 177; epidemic of folly and cruelty, 177; causes; numbers in jail, 178; trial by jury; twenty executed, 178.

WORD OF GOD TO BE THE LAW IN ABSENCE OF OTHER LAWS IN CONNECTICUT, 134; in Quinnipiac, 136; rules for courts, 150.

WORDSWORTH'S REGARD FOR THE BIBLE, 344.

WORSHIP, SERVICES OF PUBLIC; PLYMOUTH, 48. Puritan churches, 150.

YARMOUTH, 49, 53; Eliot at, 229.